THE WILDERNESS
(YÜAN-YEH)

原
野

CHINESE LITERATURE IN TRANSLATION

Editors

Irving Yucheng Lo
Joseph S. M. Lau
Leo Ou-fan Lee

THE WILDERNESS

(YÜAN-YEH)

by

TS'AO YÜ

Translated

by

CHRISTOPHER C. RAND

and

JOSEPH S. M. LAU

HONG KONG UNIVERSITY PRESS, Hong Kong

&

INDIANA UNIVERSITY PRESS, Bloomington and London

Manufactured in Hong Kong

Library of Congress Cataloging in Publication Data

Ts'ao, Yü.
 The wilderness = (Yüan-yeh)

 (Chinese literature in translation)
 Translation of *Yüan-yeh*.
 I. Title.   II. Title: Yüan yeh.   III. Series.
PZ3.T7835Wi 1979 [PL2815.A8]   895.1'2'5   78-65981
ISBN 0-253-17297-7   1 2 3 4 5 84 83 82 81 80

(HONG KONG UNIVERSITY PRESS
ISBNs   962-209-017-6   Hard cover
       962-209-018-4   Paper back)

CONTENTS

INTRODUCTION

Modern Chinese spoken drama (*hua-chü* 話劇) is little known in the West. To be sure, there have been opportunities in recent years to view the most prized theatricals of Communist revolutionary romanticism. But a large part of the inventive and sensitive dramatic writing of pre-1950s China that sacrificed little to mere political harangue has not been available to the general Western reader. Undoubtedly, this lack of exposure in Europe and America is due to a paucity of translation work in a field that heretofore has received less study than other literary experiments, and also to the fact that contemporary drama in China has yielded fewer obvious popular and critical successes than the novel or short story. The former explanation is, of course, the result of academic preference on the part of relatively few researchers, but the latter has much more complicated origins. Even for urbane Chinese audiences long inured to Peking opera's stylization of movement, voice, and costume, the adoption of an alien dramatic form from the West, lacking sophisticated singing roles and highly conventionalized dramaturgy, and requiring a new attitude toward theater as communication as well as entertainment, demanded a difficult adjustment. And similarly for the playwright, to shift from a standard repertoire of song tunes, character types, and storylines to pure dialogue, unique *dramatis personae,* and original plots was a clumsy process, necessitating several years of theoretical reorientation in the purposes of drama, not to speak of technical training and an education in Western traditions.[1]

By the late 1930s, however, after only three decades of erratic development spoken drama had become a respectable and popular literary genre, which, in the hands of a few exceptional writers, was exemplified in plays of impressive craftsmanship and growing maturity. The most noted of these writers, Ts'ao Yü 曹禺 (pen name of Wan Chia-pao 萬家寶; sobriquet, Hsiao-shih 小石), represents the best of this brief period of burgeoning excellence in the spoken drama before the onslaughts of war and Maoist orthodoxy prevented untrammeled artistic growth. What I wish to examine here is the author's view of the Chinese world as it is manifested in his trilogy of initial plays— *Thunderstorm* (*Lei-yü* 雷雨, 1934), *Sunrise*, (*Jih-ch'u* 日出, 1936) and *The Wilderness* (*Yüan-yeh* 原野, 1937), focusing mainly on the inner workings of *The Wilderness*.

I

As with most twentieth-century Chinese writers, little is known of Ts'ao Yü's early life. Though his ancestral home was Ch'ien-chiang 潛江, Hupei province, he himself was probably born in Tientsin in either 1909 or 1910.[2] His

---

[1] For background on Peking opera, see Colin Mackerras, *The Chinese theatre in modern times, from 1840 to the present day*. Amherst, Mass., University of Massachusetts Press, 1975.

[2] The two fullest and most accurate synopses of early biographical details on Ts'ao Yü are Yen Chen-fen 顏振奮, "Ts'ao Yü ch'uang-tso sheng-huo p'ien-tuan" 曹禺創作生活片斷 ["A piece from Ts'ao Yü's creative life"], *Chü-pen* 劇本 7(1957) 52–55 and Liang Meng-hui (Ryō Mukai) 梁夢迴 "Sōgū" 曹禺 ['Ts'ao Yü'], *Shingeki* 新劇 6 (May 1959) 71–77. Also see Howard L. Boorman (ed.), *Biographical dictionary of Republican China*, III. New York, Columbia University Press, 1970, pp. 356–57; *Who's who in Communist China*, II. Taipei, Institute of International Relations, 1971, pp. 236–37. Additional information was obtained from Professor Chi Wen-shun during an interview held at Stanford University in August 1969. The birthdate has been in doubt until recently, and the references have claimed 1905, 1909 and 1910. But the date was settled during an interview conducted by Nieh Hua-ling 聶華苓 with Ts'ao Yü in 1978 when the playwright said he was 68,

father, being the commander (major-general) of an army
unit in the port city, and head of an elite household
(situated opposite the offices of the daily newspaper *I-shih
pao* 益世報) in the foreign concessions, could afford to give
his sons a superior education. But, according to a 1963
interview, Ts'ao Yü did not feel these growing years were
entirely happy ones. His parents and elder brother led, in
the words of the interviewer, Yang Yü, "indolent lives
seldom arising before noon", while Ts'ao Yü remained
under the care of a private tutor. "That was a grim existence and I hated it from the bottom of my heart. . .
Those surroundings made me rather a gloomy boy. My
home and the world outside seemed so grey and hopeless
that I detested them."[3]

Still, his childhood memories included happy episodes
of lasting influence. He recalls his first visit to a local
playhouse at the age of three to see the opera virtuoso
T'an Hsin-p'ei 譚鑫培,[4] and reminisces with pleasure how
in the following years his mother took him often to
performances of Peking and local drama, as well as the
newly fashioned *wen-ming hsi* 文明戲 (civilized drama)—a
mixture of classical acting conventions and spoken dialogue,
usually with farcical content—that had become popular
during the second decade of the century.[5] Soon he was
also introduced to the standards of Chinese vernacular
fiction, such as *Dream of the red chamber* and *Water margin*,

---

that is, he was born in 1910. See Nieh Hua-ling, "I-tuan-man-chang
man-chang-ti sui-yüeh: Ts'ao Yü ho Yang Mo" 一段漫長，漫長的歲月—曹
禺和楊沫 ["A long, long period of time—Ts'ao Yu and Yang Mo: an
interview"], *The Seventies Monthly* 七十年代 27 (October 1979) 42–48.

[3] Yang Yü, "The playwright Tsao Yü", *Chinese Literature* 11 (1963)
97–103.

[4] For information of T'an Hsin-p'ei and other Peking opera actors whom
Ts'ao Yü remembers seeing, such as Ch'en Te-lin 陳德霖, Yang Hsiao-lou
楊小樓, Yü Shu-yen 余叔巖, see Mackerras, op. cit., pp. 43–47, 52–59.

[5] For information on the early years of spoken drama in China, see the
following: Hung Shen 洪深, "Ts'ung Chung-kuo-ti hsin-chü shuo tao
hua-chü" 從中國的新劇說到話劇 ["From Chinese 'New Drama' to spoken

as well as the satirical novels of late Ch'ing, and Lin Shu's translations of Western literature. Furthermore, we hear from Ts'ao Yü's preface to *Thunderstorm* of his peculiar delight in the macabre and diabolical, which resurfaces during his first creative period:

> Viewed from one angle, *Thunderstorm* is an emotive vision, a sign of nameless horror. The attraction of such a vision resembles precisely that of my listening, when a child, to some elderly man, whose face was engraved with wrinkles of experience, telling enthusiastically on a bleak night the stories of will-o'-the-wisps on grave tops and walking corpses in desolate temples. My skin was studded with cold drops of fear, and the shadows of ghosts seemed to be flickering in wall corners. But strange to say, the very fear was itself a temptation. I huddled my body closer to the aged story-teller, swallowed the saliva of interest while my heart throbbed with fear, yet I grappled his wizened hand and implored, "Tell one more! tell one more!"[6]

---

drama"], in Chu Chao-le 朱肇洛 (ed.), *Hsi-chü lun-ts'ung* 戲劇論叢. Peiping, Wen-hua hsüeh-she, 1932, pp. 156–80; T'ien Ch'in 田禽, *Chung-kuo hsi-chü yün-tung* 中國戲劇運動. Shanghai, Commercial Press, 1944; Wan Chia-pao, "The modern Chinese theatre", *National Reconstruction Journal* 7 (July 1946) 33–48; Chang Keng 張庚, "Chung-kuo hua-chü yün-tung shih ch'u-kao" 中國話劇運動史初稿 ["First draft history of the Chinese spoken drama movement"], *Hsi-chü pao* 戲劇報 1 (February 1954) 34–36; 1 (March 1954) 31–34; 1 (April 1954) 21–25; 1 (May 1954) 33–36; 1 (July 1954) 30–34; and 1 (September 1954) 40–46; T'ien Han 田漢, *et al.*, *Hsi-chü lun-ts'ung* 戲劇論叢, 4 vols. Peking, Chung-kuo hsi-chü ch'u-pan she, 1957; T'ien Han, *et al.*, *Chung-kuo hua-chü yün-tung wu-shih nien shih-liao chi* 中國話劇運動五十年史料集. Peking, Chung-kuo hsi-chü ch'u-pan she, 1958; A. C. Scott, *Literature and the arts in twentieth century China*. London, Allen and Unwin, 1965, pp. 35–41; A. R. Davis, "Out of 'Uncle Tom's Cabin', Tokyo, 1907: a preliminary look at the beginnings of spoken drama in China", *Journal of the Oriental Society of Australia* 6 (1 & 2) (1968–69) 33–39.

[6] *Lei-yü*. Shanghai, Wen-hua sheng-kuo ch'u-pan she, 1936, p. vii. Trans. by Yao Hsin-nung in *T'ien Hsia Monthly* 3 (1946) 274.

Because of his father's élite status, these otherwise ephemeral juvenile interests in theater and fiction were fortified by his attendance at the socially exclusive Nankai Middle School in Tientsin, which had shown precocious progress in Western-style theatricals. Since 1909, just two years after the first production of *hua-chü* (occurring in Japan),[7] Nankai had already established an unusual tradition of annual spoken drama presentations, which, during the late 1920s, Ts'ao Yü probably helped to continue and expand.[8] Through the encouragement and direction of Chang P'ing-ch'ün 張平羣 (younger brother to the school's principal, Chang Po-ling 張伯苓), Ts'ao Yü was introduced to and played in works by Ting Hsi-lin 丁西林, Ibsen, Galsworthy, and Molière, and he may even have collaborated with Chang P'ing-ch'ün in a no longer extant translation of Galsworthy's *Strife*.[9] Thus, by the time he left Nankai in 1930 to attend Tsinghua University near Peking, Ts'ao Yü had not only developed his early affection for the theater, but was already initiated into the newest trends of modern drama, both technically and literarily.

At Tsinghua his pursuit of dramatic arts continued with a concentration in foreign languages and literatures (especially English literature) and an avid participation in the college dramatic club, both as a player of male

[7] These productions were by an organization of overseas students, the Ch'un-liu she 春柳舍 (Spring Willow Society), whose members later returned to China with the intention of developing *hua-chü* as a medium for social change. See, for enample, Ou-yang Yu-ch'ien 歐陽予倩, "Hui-i Ch'un-liu" 回憶春柳 ["Recalling the Spring Willow (Society)"], in T'ien Han, *et al., Hsi-chü lun-ts'ung*, III, 43–68.

[8] Chang Keng points out, however, that Nankai's attempts were not radical, but followed the trends of the new drama movement at large in a cautious though enthusiastic manner. See "Chung-kuo hua-chü yün-tung shih ch'u-kao", *Hsi-chü pao* 1 (September 1954) 40.

[9] See Hu, op. cit., p. 21. We are also told by Yen Chen-fen that he translated "a few stories by Maupassant" ("Ts'ao Yü ch'uang-tso sheng-huo p'ien-tuan", p. 52).

characters and as a female impersonator.[10] The tradition of classical theater to use men for both male and
female roles was still not entirely eradicated from Chinese
versions of Western drama—particularly in an all-male
school. Thus, Ts'ao Yü with his slight physique, high
voice, handsome complexion, and sense for feminine grace,
became rather popular for roles such as Nora in Ibsen's
Doll's house (in which he had first played at Nankai). Moreover, with the benefit of his high school experience, he was
invited, while still an undergraduate, to become a tutor
for younger dramatic art students at Tsinghua.

Aside from the fact that he translated Shakespeare's
Romeo and Juliet during his first three years at college, we
have no record that he attempted any original drama.
However, he engrossed himself in the plays of, among
others, Gorky, Chekhov, G. B. Shaw, O'Neill, Euripides,
and Aeschylus, and by 1934 had launched his career as a
dramatist with the publication of his first and most
celebrated play, *Thunderstorm.*[11]

II

We have no space here to analyze this or his second play,
Sunrise, in any great detail.[12] However, it is important for
understanding *The Wilderness* to point out the possible
philosophical-cum-psychological well-springs of these two
plays. It appears from the author's confessions to Yang Yü

[10] See *Kuo-li Ch'ing-hua ta-hsüeh nien-k'an* 國立清華大學年刊 1934;
Ch'ing-hua t'ung-hsüeh lu 清華同學錄 1935.

[11] For background on the first productions of *Thunderstorm,* see Yen Chen-
fen, op. cit., p. 53 and Liang Meng-hui, op. cit., pp. 73–74. Two translations
of the play are available: one by Yao Hsin-nung, *Thunder and rain,* in *T'ien
Hsia Monthly* 3 (1936) 270–95, 363–411, 486–530; 4 (1937) 61–95, 176–221
and another (incomplete) by Wang Tso-liang and A. C. Barnes, *Thunderstorm.* Peking, Foreign Languages Press, 1964.

[12] Two translations of *Sunrise* are available: one by H. Yonge, *The Sunrise.*
Changsha, Commercial Press, 1940; and another by A. C. Barnes, *Sunrise.*
Peking, Foreign Languages Press, 1978. See synopses of both *Thunderstorm*
and *Sunrise* on page xli.

that Ts'ao Yü's initial motives for playwrighting lay in expressing in imagined actions what he felt himself incapable of enacting in real life. The bold rhetoric and furtive rebellions of his college friends, who, unlike Ts'ao Yü, were willing to risk their careers and reputations for what they considered vital ideals, spawned certain passionate conflicts in Ts'ao Yü that fueled his literary efforts. Sensitive to contradictions and uncertainties in himself and his milieu, he opted for the vicarious world of theater, where he could dramatize these social-moral dilemmas, and yet demonstrate real political commitment.

> Shakespeare wrote in *Julius Caesar*: "Men at some time are masters of their fates: The fault, dear Brutus, is not in our stars,/But in ourselves, that we are underlings." At that time [ca. 1934] I was sincerely convinced that those who dared to revolt were masters of their fate, while I had the desire to do so but not the strength. I felt frustrated, hostile to all around me, borne off on a swirling torrent of emotion. The need to express my bottled-up indignation was probably what impelled me to write *Thunderstorm*.[13]

But even in choosing dramatic writing as ersatz political involvement, he harbored doubts about the outcome of his toil. *Thunderstorm* is indelibly marked by the form and spirit of ancient Greek tragedy. Not only are the Aristotelian principles of drama adhered to, the omnipresent force of Hellenic Fate permeates the play, silently manipulating unprescient human characters toward their inevitable demises. Tied though it is to the themes of oppression and hypocrisy in antiquated Chinese society, *Thunderstorm* is, in essence, an adaptation of a Western dramatic and intellectual tradition, with the intent of illuminating China's infirmities and resolving personal anxieties. Ts'ao Yü seemed to be searching beyond immediate debilities for

[13] See Yang Yü, op. cit., p. 100.

dark, universal energies affecting human behavior, while yet highlighting the concrete circumstances of China's present.

Thunderstorm is to me a temptation. The sentiment that came to me with it culminated in a sort of inexplicable vision which I saw in numerous mystic things in the cosmos. *Thunderstorm* may be said to be "the remnant of savage nature" in me. Like our primeval ancestors, I open my eyes wide with astonishment *vis-à-vis* those phenomena that cannot be explained in terms of reason. I cannot make certain whether *Thunderstorm* was motivated by "deities and spirits", fatalism, or what other apparent powers. In feeling, what it symbolizes for me is a kind of mystic magnetism, a devil that holds my psyche in its grip. What *Thunderstorm* reveals is not the law of *karma* [cause and effect], nor that of *pao-ying* 報應 [retribution for something done or given], but the cosmic cruelty (*T'ien-ti-chien-ti ts'an-jen* 天地間的殘忍) that I have sensed. . . . If the reader is willing to appreciate delicately this idea of mine, this play will continuously but flickeringly betray, in spite of his attention being distracted at times by a few tenser scenes or one or two characters, this bit of mystery—the cruelty and inhumanity of all the struggles in the universe. Behind them all, perhaps, there is a ruler exercising His jurisdiction. The Hebrew prophets hailed this ruler "God"; the Greek dramatists named Him "Fate"; modern men, dismissing these mystifying conceptions, straightforwardly call Him "The Law of Nature". But I can never give Him an appropriate name, nor do I possess the ability to depict His real character. For He is too great, too complex. What my emotion has forced me to give expression to is merely my vision of the cosmos.[14]

14 *Lei-yü*, pp. iv–v (trans. Yao Hsin-nung, p. 273).

Not surprisingly, leftist critics have failed to empathize with Ts'ao Yü's subjective musings about the cosmic meaning of human actions, preferring to praise only his revelations of feudalistic inequities.

Aside from the good points noted above [realistic dialogue, refined dramaturgy, etc.], a few faults still exist. Expressed in the work here are shades of fatalism and mysticism. . . .[15]

This [reliance on mysticism] is a fault of the work, because in doing this he has only reduced the work's high degree of congruence with reality, diluting any social meaning.[16]

If the author had concentrated his entire effort to illuminate the tragic encounters of Lu Ma 魯媽, the deaths of Chou Ch'ung 周冲 and Ssu-feng 四鳳, and the roots of Fan-i's 蘩漪 abnormal psyche in order to induce in people a clenched hate of the feudal system, this theme and technique would obviously have been very strong and fresh. But the author, unable to do this, only uses misapprehensions of true blood relationships, deaths of characters, and insanity, thus vitiating the tragedy's effect; this cannot but emasculate its social significance. As for perceptions of the future, the play is very confused; even though the author molds the figure of Lu Ta-hai 魯大海, a mine laborer, with some success, and writes of struggle between workers and capitalists, there still seems to be a weakness, a feebleness; the work is lackluster. Even after the author has whipped the black façade of society, he is unable to provide man a clear exit [from his difficulties].[17]

[15] Foreword to Shih Ch'iao 石橋 (ed.), *Chung-kuo hsin wen-hsüeh ta-hsi hsü-pien* 中國新文學大系續編. Hong Kong, Wen-hsüeh yen-chiu she, 1964, I, 34.

[16] Lin Mang 林莽 (ed.), *Chung-kuo hsin wen-hsüeh nien nien* 中國新文學廿年. Hong Kong, Shih-chieh ch'u-pan she, 1957, p. 124.

[17] Department of Chinese, Futan University, *Chung-kuo hsien-tai wen-hsüeh shih* 中國現代文學史, 1919–1942. Shanghai, Fu-tan ta-hsüeh, n.d., p. 442.

These observers failed to acknowledge the validity of Ts'ao Yü's search for the suprarational, the "objective imperative" that moves him and the characters he creates irreversably to their unseen, irrational ends. Anchored, as he assures us, in his actual experience, Ts'ao Yü seems to have been groping for some invisible, metaphysical matrix which would explain contemporary Chinese injustices and dispel his philosophical misgivings. The contradictions and ambivalences which resulted provided the energy for his early playwrighting; they are, one might say, the source of Ts'ao Yü's initial artistic successes. For, by elucidating the ambivalences in the lives of his characters, he could hope to discern and demonstrate the patterns of man's triumphs and defeats—the competing forces, the unremitting strivings, and the ineluctable deaths. "Extremes and contradictions are the two basic modes of nature in the humidly hot atmosphere of *Thunderstorm*."[18]

III

As we mentioned earlier, these dramatic tensions in *Thunderstorm*, though existentially based, are almost purely derivations from an ancient Greek prototype. Only fleetingly in his preface do we sense the probable appropriation of more modern elements, namely, nihilism and moral relativism, which may also suggest the classical Taoistic notion of a Godless dynamic in the universe.

> Idealism is like bubbles that float before his eyes, broken into nothingness one after another by reality's steel needle at a mere touch. When idealism is destroyed, life dwindles as a matter of course into an empty shadow. Chou Ch'ung is thus only a rosy dream in a trying summer. In the sultry atmosphere of *Thunderstorm* he is a note out of harmony, yet it is with him that the light and shade in *Thunderstorm* come out

[18] *Lei-yü*, p. ix (trans. Yao Hsin-nung, p. 275).

in distinct contrast. His untimely death, with Chou P'u-yüan 周樸園 still going strong, makes us feel that there is no wise God ruling the universe. And the fact that Chou Ch'ung should have come and gone so evanescently and such a lovely life must need be so ephemeral and vanish in agony, moves us to ejaculate, "This truly is too cruel!"[19]

In *Sunrise*, however, this somber awareness of disinterested, authorless violence is made more apparent by Ts'ao Yü's attempt to treat his dramatic characters in an equally disinterested, Chekhovian manner.[20] He was clearly unsuccessful in duplicating the detached vividness of *Three sisters;* his intractable introspection militated against it. Still, amid the naturalistic brutalities perpetrated on and by the harlots, servants, creditors, gigolos, lovers, and unseen proletarians of this play we find a wisp of the Russian master's penchant for inconclusiveness and irony, which serves to intensify the clash of expectation and sadness. On the one hand, *Sunrise* broaches the possibility of man creating a new, more favorable world for himself in spite of the fortunes that canalize him. The cries of the toiling construction workers at dawn's light seem to portend a brilliant beginning, when the chaotic cannibalism of a benighted China will yield to the red glow of social equality. And yet, the suicides of the once innocent Ch'en Pai-lu 陳白露 and Hsiao-tung-hsi 小東西, the family tragedy of Li Shih-ch'ing 李石清, the fatuous gamboling of Mrs. Ku 顧八奶奶 cast doubt on all optimism. Repeatedly we are made aware of the tragi-comic incon-

---

[19] *Lei-yü,* p. xiv (trans. Yao Hsin-nung, p. 279). For a comparison of female protagonists in *Thunderstorm* and O'Neill's *Desire under the elms,* see Joseph S. M. Lau, "Two emancipated Phaedras: Chou Fan-yi and Abbie Putnam as social rebels", *Journal of Asian Studies* 25 (1966) 699–711.

[20] See *Jih-ch'u.* Shanghai, Wen-hua sheng-kuo ch'u-pan she, 1936, "Pa" 跋 [Postscript], pp. xiv–xv. Also see Joseph Lau, "Ts'ao Yü, the reluctant disciple of Chekhov: a comparative study of *Sunrise* and *The Cherry Orchard*", *Modern Drama* 9 (1967) 358–72.

gruities of resilient hope, naked despair, impotent defiance, and unqualified resignation, which are reflective of the playwright's own mental dissonances. Lacking Chekhov's stoic acceptance of an indifferent but viable world, Ts'ao Yü is plunged into existential questioning about the validity of socio-cosmic order. His long, quizzical postscript to *Sunrise* begins:

> I must confess that I am still young, and have a young man's irrepressible instincts, for as questions arise in me I cannot but immediately search out their answers. When my mind is troubled, I am confused and disquiet; I sweat, and it thrashes angrily in me like a deadly medicine swallowed by mistake. Wandering idly in this topsy-turvy society, I see so many nightmarish, frightening acts of man, which I shall not forget until I die; they turn into so many urgent problems that strike mortally upon me, that singe my emotions, that aggravate my disquiet. As though suffering from a fever, all day I sense beside me a demon of death making low persuasions in my ear, grinding at me, allowing me no peace. I envy those penetrating and perceptive people who quietly comprehend the central meaning of things, and I love those rude farm men with wide, childlike, undepraved eyes, healthy as mother cows, leading without deep reflection their simple, upright lives. I can imitate neither of these admirable people, and yet I will not continue living in ambiguity; hence, I sink like a stupid drunk into the frying firepit. This kind of distress, day after day, pierces the mark; I am locked in a room. When by accident I arrive at something, I have a spell of mad delight; I think that I have found a great Way. But after a while, I quiet down and realize that such a great problem cannot be so dubiously solved by avoiding the difficult and relying on the easy; unconsciously I am involved in an iron

web of despair, which I cannot disentangle myself from, nor rid myself of.[21]

Ts'ao Yü, however, seems to have suggested a provisional resolution for his crisis of belief in a series of quotations which prefaces *Sunrise*. First comes *Lao Tzu*:

Is not the way of heaven like the stretching of a bow?
　　The high it presses down,
　　The low it lifts up;
　　The excessive it takes from,
　　The deficient it gives to.
It is the way of heaven to take from what has in excess in order to make good what is deficient. The way of man is otherwise. It takes from those who are in want in order to offer this to those who already have more than enough.[22]

Second, he draws upon biblical scripture, beginning with Romans:

. . . God . . . has given them up to their own depraved reason. This leads them to break all rules of conduct. They are filled with every kind of injustice, mischief, rapacity, and malice; they are one mass of envy, murder, rivalry, treachery, and malevolence. . . . Those who behave like this deserve to die, and yet they do it; not only so, they actually applaud such practices.[23]

Then, Jeremiah:

Oh, the writhing of my bowels
　　and the throbbing of my heart!
　　I cannot keep silence.
I hear the sound of the trumpet,
　　the sound of the battle-cry.

---

[21] "Pa", pp. i–ii.

[22] *Lao Tzu* 77 (trans. by D. C. Lau, *Lao Tzu, Tao Te Ching*. Harmondsworth, Penguin, 1963, p. 139).

[23] Romans 1.28–30, 32 *(New English Bible* version).

> Crash upon crash,
> the land goes down in ruin. . . .
> I saw the earth, and it was without form and void;
> the heavens, and their light was gone.
> I saw the mountains, and they reeled;
> all the hills rocked to and fro.
> I saw, and there was no man,
> and the very birds had taken flight.
> I saw, and the farm-land was wilderness,
> and the towns all razed to the ground. . . .[24]

He returns to the letters of Paul:

> . . . Brothers, . . . hold aloof from every . . . brother who falls into idle habits, and does not follow the tradition you received from us. . . . We were no idlers among you; we did not accept board and lodging from anyone without paying for it; we toiled and drudged, we worked for a living night and day. . . . For even during our stay with you we laid down the rule: the man who will not work shall not eat.[25]

> I appeal to you, my brothers, . . . agree among yourselves, and avoid divisions; be firmly joined in unity of mind and thought.[26]

Two pronouncements of Christ:

> . . . "I am the light of the world. No follower of mine shall wander in the dark; he shall have the light of life."[27]

> . . . "I am the resurrection and I am life. If a man has faith in me, even though he dies, he shall come to life. . . ."[28]

[24] Jeremiah 4.19–20, 23–26 *(New English Bible version)*.

[25] 2 Thessalonians 3.6–10 *(New English Bible version)*.

[26] 1 Corinthians 1.10 *(New English Bible version)*.

[27] John 8.12 *(New English Bible version)*.

[28] John 11.25 *(New English Bible version)*.

And finally, an epiphany from the Revelation of John:

> Then I saw a new heaven and a new earth, for the
> first heaven and the first earth had vanished. . . .[29]

Connoting no religious commitments to Judeo-Christian
dogma, Ts'ao Yü's biblical citations, when linked with
Lao Tzu, adumbrate a more structured view of man-cosmos
relations. The anomalies of human experience arise when
man willfully fails, as he must, to perceive the arbitrary
and "heartless" movements of Heaven; conversely, justice
appertains only to those who move in harmony with the
balancings and unbalancings of Nature and his own
human society. Since few men so resonate, however, it can
be said that man is doomed to rebel against the Way of
Heaven, taking from those who are in want in order to
provide for those who already have more than enough;
so he is condemned to suffer the wrath, the "cosmic
cruelties" of Nature. But still there is a new, better world
coming if one will only strive in unity with one's brothers,
faithful to a glorious, beatific vision of harmony, to elimi-
nate those hateful but pitiable men, obnoxiously recalcitrant in their arrogant ignorance of human limitations.
Ts'ao Yü's postscript substantiates this eclectic thesis,
while yet passionately renewing his frustrated commitment
to rebel against human injustices.

> . . . And so I read *Lao Tzu*, Buddhist sutras, the Bible,
> and so many writings thought to be fearfully calami-
> tous. I weep, and praise these great, lonely spirits
> who have harbored the tragic and oppressive bitter-
> ness of human existence, opening the way for their
> unfilial progeny. And yet, those I hate more are the
> stupid, insensitive animals that call themselves "men".
> For they insist on blocking their ears, unwilling to
> heed the great and grievous call of the wilderness
> (k'uang-yeh 曠野). They close their eyes, wishing to

---

[29] Revelation 21.1 *(New English Bible* version).

become like moles in their pits, to flee the light by
sticking their heads into ignorance like ostriches. I
cannot bear this; I thirst to see a ray of light. I think
I will not see the greater part of the sun; but during
my lifetime I yearn to see a crack of great thunder
[lightning?] come to earth and strike these squirming
goblins to a pulp, though I fear the earth would sink
into the sea. I am still young, yet deathless memories
that make one's hair stand straight attack me from
all quarters; I can think of no wise way to go, though
I ponder every tack. Rushing upon my mind are the
times in the study when, rolling my head in a blur,
I mumbled the *Classic of documents;* the phrase of
determined oaths that horrifies most a child—"When
will this sun expire? We will all perish with thee!"
(see *Shang shu* 尙書, "T'ang shih" 湯誓)—winds
around my mind, with a feeling like approaching
tempest. Viciously I curse injustice wherever it lies,
but unless these putrid men are rid of, I cannot see
much light ahead. Truly it is like what Jeremiah, in
passion, declared in the Old Testament: "I saw the
earth, and it was without form and void; the heavens,
and their light was gone." I sense the "vexing anxiety"
preceding the Great Quake; I see landslides, "the
farm-land was wilderness, and the towns all razed to
the ground." Feeling so, "I hear the sound of the
trumpet, the sound of the battle-cry." I want to write
something to relieve my angry breast; I want to
shout, "Your last day has arrived!" to the perverse,
shameless people who have cast out the sun.

"But, must you start your work in such bewilder-
ment?" I quiz myself. I know it is all a joke; to do no
more than raise my hands and stamp my feet, yelling
on a pedestal, is insane. What I look for is a little
hope, a ray of light. For in the end people want to
live, and what's more, they should live in happiness.
Rotten flesh is scooped out so that new cells may

grow. We want new blood, new life. The winter has just now passed, and as golden rays shoot down on every sprout of the field, shaken by the wind, the dead will be reborn! We want the sun, the spring sun, and a good life, full of happiness, whatever the chaos of the present. So it is I decided to write *Sunrise*.[30]

The panoply of characters Ts'ao Yü introduces in his second play are, thus, not products of Chekhovian disinterest, but are examples of imperfect humanity in which Ts'ao Yü invests both scorn and dismay.[31] What results is, again, a work of moral ambiguity, *engagée* but at the same time uncertain of any extrinsic program for improvement.

IV

As already suggested, though *Thunderstorm* and *Sunrise* were generally popular among reviewers and masses alike for their stirring depictions of societal ills, there have been critics then and since who reviled the playwright's obvious reliance on European techniques, or rued his manipulation of characters to meet predetermined objectives, or winced at the touch of Fate which tainted the "proper" social-political message they thought drama must communicate in a time of crisis.

Ts'ao Yü's third play, *The Wilderness*, was ignored or, in later years, denigrated for similar reasons, with especial

---

[30] "Pa", pp. iv–v.

[31] Chang Keng likewise has recognized—but with disapproval—the combination of hate and pity Ts'ao Yü shows for his *Sunrise* characters: "These angry and confused feelings of the author [shown in the postscript] obstruct his power of sharp investigation; they cause him to have two rather distinct attitudes towards the characters in *Sunrise*, namely, revilement and sympathy. If one must speak of exceptions, there is only Ch'en Pai-lu. According to his "rule", her way of life should be decidedly cursed by the author, but instead, the author gives her a great amount of sympathy." "Tu *Jih-ch'u*" 讀日出 ["Reading *Sunrise*"] *Hsi-chü shih-tai* 戲劇時代 (Shanghai) 1 (May 1937) 241.

emphasis on the "untoward" mystical, unreal aura encompassing the storyline. Ting I, for example, said of the work:

> After *Sunrise* came *The Wilderness*. In this play he turned his attention from the city to the countryside. *The Wilderness* is the story of a peasant's revenge on a despotic landlord. The theme is good, but unfortunately the author was unfamiliar with the life of the peasants, the chief class contradictions, and class struggle in the countryside. Moreover, his ideas were dominated by a belief in fatalism, and as a result, the play, which could have been treated in a most realistic way, became full of mysterious, abstract, and even strange conceptions. Mysticism, symbolism, and psychological analysis combine to arouse a sense of terror and give the play its atmosphere of dismay. The play gives the impression of being detached from reality. It does not seem like a real story. . . .[32]

Lin Mang had a similar opinion:

> Among the three plays, the realism of *The Wilderness*, even if it is not the same as that of *Thunderstorm* or *Sunrise*, is a failure. The reason is that the author did not carve out the protagonist, Ch'ou Hu 仇虎, in the form of a real peasant, but only sculpted him as a manifestation of an abstract idea. He does not represent the character of a social man, but the illusionary form of a man of the wilderness.[33]

[32] Ting I, *A short history of modern Chinese literature*. Peking, Foreign Languages Press, 1959, p. 182. For an almost identical opinion, see *Chung-kuo hsien-tai wen-hsüeh shih, 1919–1942*, p. 445. Yang Hui 楊晦 is also critical of Ts'ao Yü's lack of emphasis on concrete social issues in *The Wilderness* and most of the other pre-1949 works; he theorizes that the playwright's isolation from "real life" during his years in Tientsin and Peking caused him to over-intellectualize the state of Chinese society. See *Wen-i yü she-hui* 文藝與社會. Shanghai, Chung-hsing ch'u-pan she, 1949, pp. 81–155.

[33] Lin Mang, op. cit., p. 127. Another Communist writer, Liu Shou-sung 劉綬松, had a similar view of *The Wilderness*: "This kind of story, set in a hamlet of old China, should be well known; in tracing it [Ts'ao Yü] certainly reveals the contradictions and struggles of the old Chinese village. But this

Lü Ying, in a much more receptive attitude, also interpreted *The Wilderness*, not as a realistic social play *manqué*, but as an abstract rendering of the conflict between Fate and man in society. For Lü, "Ch'ou Hu, who in the [state] primeval rebels against Fate, is not depicted as a peasant (a man in society)." Rather, he is a symbol of primeval man in general. "In *The Wilderness* the author daringly rebels against destiny, but still he does not escape the realm of conceptual thinking; in this realm the author's understanding of society's future can only take the form of pure idea: a yearning for the primeval—the reappearance of the Way of Heaven." Thus, he contends, there is a kind of primitivism in the play—a revolt against modern civilization and a wish for the moral simplicity of antiquity —which is portrayed in abstract form.[34]

Joseph Lau has also observed a kind of "primitivism" in *The Wilderness* which, though directed against Fate, is posed as the source of regeneration for an effete nation. "Primitivism", however, is not intended here as an atavistic

---

was not the author's original intention. He wanted to permeate [the work] with the fear and coarseness of primitive character; he wanted to demonstrate the opposition of man and abstract destiny—a non-scientific and purely conceptual theme. The play's protagonist, Ch'ou Hu, is not drawn as a true peasant figure. He is only a transformation of a purely abstract idea. What is manifested in a concentrated way in his person is not the character of a man of society, but the illusory likeness of a man of the wilderness (a man of the wilderness with primitive feelings and primeval power)." *Chung-kuo hsin wen-hsüeh shih ch'u-kao* 中國新文學史初稿. Peking, Tso-chia ch'u-pan she, 1956, I, 397. Wang Yao's 王瑤 review, though generally favorable, also points out the lack of "reality" in the characters of the play; they have lost their complex social natures and instead are given abstract, simplistic forms. See *Chung-kuo hsin wen-hsüeh shih kao* 中國新文學史稿, *1919–1950*. Peking, K'ai-ming shu-tien, 1951, I, 275.

[34] Lü Ying 呂熒, "Ts'ao Yü ti tao-lu (shang)" 曹禺的道路(上) ["Ts'ao Yu's road (1)"], *K'ang-chan wen-i hsüan-k'an* 抗戰文藝選刊 (Shanghai) 1 (1946) 7–16. For a rebuttal to Lü Ying's position which claims that Ch'ou Hu is a true representative of social rebellion, not a "psychological figure", and accuses Lü of being a reactionary follower of Hu Feng 胡風, see Ch'u Pai-ch'un 楚白純, "Lü Ying tsai 'Ts'ao Yü ti tao-lu' i wen chung ti fan-tung lun-tien" 呂熒在曹禺的道路一文中的反動論點 ["The reactionary position of Lü Ying in 'Ts'ao Yu's Road' "], *Chü-pen*, 12 (1955) 66–79, esp. p. 73.

desire for the culture of the primordial past. Rather, it appears to Lau to be the glorification of strength, simplicity, physical endurance, etc.—the qualities of a persecuted "noble savage", such as Ch'ou Hu (and in some measure, Chin-tzu 金子), and thus of the "new man" in modern Chinese society. By this interpretation, Ts'ao Yü equated "primitivism" with "nobility", "beauty", "virtue", and "strength", and thence conjured up an image of Ch'ou Hu that was "a romantic conglomeration of Ts'ao Yü's wishful thinking, invented by a mind long obsessed with the problem of China's rejuvenation".[35]

All of these analyses offer certain valid criticisms and perceptions. Ts'ao Yü may indeed have been so unacquainted with real village life that he was not capable of handling such material except in a mystical, abstract way. But the play must be examined in the light of the *Weltanschauung* outlined in the previous two works in order to capture the full significance of *The Wilderness*'s conflicts and meanings.

If this were *Thunderstorm* or *Sunrise*, one could turn, as we have, to the playwright's own commentary to fathom the roots of *The Wilderness*. But in this case, all that remains is a short self-critique concerning a few isolated items in the play, some advice about staging, and a typical but uninformative apology for shortcomings. It is "only an uncertain rough draft," he says, "which in places still has possibilities of improvement". Revealingly, he acknowledges a debt to O'Neill for some technical borrowings, which confirms the generally held intuition about the impact of *Emperor Jones's* expressionistic structure on the play:

[35] Joseph S. M. Lau, *Ts'ao Yü—a study in literary influence*. Hong Kong, Hong Kong University Press, 1970, pp. 48, 50. P'ei Hsien 佩絃 likewise recognizes the "primeval power" in Ch'ou Hu's violent hate and love. See *"Yüan-yeh yü Hei-tzu erh-shih-pa* ti yen-ch'u" 原野與黑字二十八的演出 ["Performances of *The Wilderness* and *Black characters twenty-eight*"], *Chin-jih p'ing-lun* 今日評論 2 (1939) 189–191.

Writing the third act was comparatively troublesome; in it there are two devices, one the sound of a drum, and the other gunfire at the ends of two of the scenes, which I took from O'Neill's *Emperor Jones*. At first I had not realized it, but after finishing the play and reading it over a couple times, I suddenly discovered that unconsciously I had been influenced by him; these two devices are actually O'Neill's, and if I have aptly utilized them, I should make it clear here that they are [due to] O'Neill's talent and are not my creations.[36]

But these notes offer no clues to the key conceptual mechanisms operating in the work The impression one forms of *The Wilderness* is that, like its predecessors, it is a montage of various influences, technical, literary, and philosophical. It was not intended primarily as a social-political drama, though applications to Chinese society are surely one of its aims. Nor is it principally concerned with "a yearning for the primeval", or with "primitivism", though Lau's interpretation is to the point here. Instead, *The Wilderness* is a mythic, "Taoistic" work which recasts the socio-cosmological thoughts of his first two plays in language both profane and poetic, rife with symbol and metaphor.

Firstly, it is mythic because, aside from the seemingly unconscious borrowing of an expressionistic format from O'Neill in the third act, there is an unequivocal return (with probably greater consciousness) to the themes of Greek tragic theater. In particular, we see a number of significant conceptual extracts from Attic lore (i.e., the story of Prometheus and Io as retold in Aeschylus' *Prometheus bound*), which imbue *The Wilderness* with the vengeance, Fate, and sympathy for human depravity that

---

[36] Fu-chi" 附記 ["Addendum"], *Wen-ts'ung* 文叢 1 (1937) 958. For a detailed comparison of *Emperor Jones* and *The Wilderness*, see David Y. Ch'en, "The Chinese adaptation of Eugene O'Neill's *The Emperor Jones*", *Modern Drama* 9 (1967) 431–39.

were present in *Thunderstorm*. Secondly, it is a "Taoistic" work because it reveals a cognizance of the non-benevolent, *tzu-jan* (i.e., self-so, causeless) actions of Nature upon man, and the moral relativism and nihilism that results therefrom. It will be shown here that these two complexes of elements are drawn upon by Ts'ao Yü to create in *The Wilderness* a remarkable blending of philosophy and sensuous, emotive energy.

Let us begin with a comparison of the Aeschylus play and its Chinese counterpart. In Ts'ao Yü's evocative stage direction to the Prologue we read: "The giant tree with its enormous trunk, scratched with old and cracked grains, stands upright in the blue indefinite atmosphere of the plain, commanding dignity, malice, enmity, and a dark, lonely anxiety, like a chained Prometheus tied upon his precipice" (p. 1). Ch'ou Hu appears, and "with one hand on his hip, leans against the giant tree, gazing at the sunset, panting but making no sound" (p. 2). This association leads us to a recognition of certain similarities between the Greek god and the "Vengeful Tiger", of which there are reminders throughout the play. Like the Aeschylus hero, Ch'ou Hu is a rebel against the injustices of a brutish, godlike force (Chiao Yen-wang 焦閻王 [King of Hell] — Zeus), who has caused him to seek revenge. He, too, wishes a just, enlightened life for mortal humanity, and knows that, in time, there will be a Heracles to right the wrongs against him. Similarly, Chin-tzu, daughter-in-law of Chiao Yen-wang, has certain resemblances to Io, daughter of the King of Argos and priestess in the temple of Zeus's spouse, Hera; both are victims of jealous wives, tormented by them for stealing the affection of loved ones (in one case, a son; in the other, a husband); both must journey long to reach peace from their oppressors (Io finds respite in Egypt, while Chin-tzu presumably finds her "road to life").

Of course, the non-parallels are also important. Ch'ou Hu is not an Olympian god, but, as we increasingly find, an imperfect mortal; indeed, with his apish physique, he seems something even less than human. Marred by an obsession for revenge, he does not merit the name Prometheus in its literal sense of "foresight", but embodies only the titan's behemoth will to fight back in the name of human honor. As distinct from the suffering Prometheus, Ch'ou Hu is panged by moral incertitude in taking his revenge, for his oppressor, unlike Zeus, is in hell; Ch'ou Hu must quench his hate with the murder of an innocent son-surrogate and the regretted destruction of a grandson as well.

Neither is Chin-tzu an identical twin of Io. In contrast to the beleaguered maiden, Chiao Hua 焦花 is a cunning lass with "fox-fairy"-like ambitions—a gypsy eager to seize the best from life. Encountering Ch'ou Hu, to whom she was once unknowingly engaged, she, unlike Io, immediately responds to her male counterpart's sexual and spiritual strength, and sees in him a long-awaited opportunity to escape her impotent mate, Ta-hsing 大星, and her vicious mother-in-law, Chiao Ta-ma 焦大媽, to find a land of perpetual joy. This departure from the Aeschylus model also means that Chin-tzu is bound in desperate love with a pseudo-Prometheus—a being possessing human imperfections as well as titanic prowess.

It is evident, then, that the principal characters of the ancient Greek tragedy are not retraced precisely in the chief protagonists of Ts'ao Yü's work. But the themes of one have clear impact on those of the other: injustices suffered are compounded by the folly of the avenging victims; Fate may reign over all, but, pitiably, it is its subjects who, by their own rebellions, create ill for themselves. Hermes' words are as true for Ch'ou Hu, the primeval mortal, as for Prometheus, the maverick god:

> Like an unbroken colt, you try your strength, and take
> The bit between your teeth, and fight against the reins.
> Yet all your violence springs from feeble reckoning;
> For obstinacy in a fool has by itself

No strength at all. . . .
And when you are caught by calamity
Don't lay the blame on Fortune, or say that Zeus
Plunged you in suffering unforeseen;
Not Zeus but yourselves will be to blame.
You know what is coming; it is neither sudden nor
    secret.
Only your own folly will entangle you
In the inextricable net of destruction.[37]

Still, the Promethean urge is not purely negative; by it
there is hope for new greatness, providing one's fore-
knowledge is sufficient to avoid the obstacles of Fate.

Fate fulfills all in time, but it is not ordained
That these events shall yet reach such an end. My lot
Is to win freedom only after countless pains.
Cunning is feebleness beside Necessity.[38]

Typically, the issue in *Prometheus Bound* results in ambivalence, in contingency, and so also, we shall see, do the
issues of *The Wilderness*.[39]

As for the "Taoistic" strain of moral relativism and
nihilism in the work, additional ideas from the first two
dramas return. The notion of a non-teleological, but often
"cruel", Way of Nature was mentioned in regard to

[37] Aeschylus, *Prometheus bound, The Suppliants, Seven against Thebes, The Persians,* trans. by Philip Vellacott. Harmondsworth, Penguin, 1961, p. 52.

[38] Ibid., p. 35.

[39] In view of the popularity during the beginning decades of the present century of Yen Fu's 嚴復 translations of Spencer, Darwin, J. S. Mill, *et al.,* in which Yen glorified the idea of the Promethean-Faustian energies of man being released in a common effort to regenerate Chinese culture (see Benjamin I. Schwartz, *In search of wealth and power: Yen Fu and the West.* Cambridge, Mass., Harvard University Press, 1964), it might be questioned whether Ts'ao Yü could have been influenced in some degree by these translations. We have no evidence that the playwright did or did not read these restatements in classical Chinese of Western ideals. However, since we are informed of Ts'ao Yü's study of Aeschylus it would seem more likely that the impetus for creating a "Promethean" image in *The Wilderness* came directly from *Prometheus bound*.

Thunderstorm and *Sunrise*. In *The Wilderness* this idea merges with those of Fate and human revenge to heighten the mystical tone of the play and create a vision of man *vis-à-vis* the cosmos that incorporates both traditional Chinese and Western constructs. That is to say, the wilderness, this non-human, non-theomorphic force which looms threateningly in multifarious forms around the characters, has become assimilated with the spirit of oppression in the play. And yet, it remains *tzu-jan*, unheedful of human arrogance, immeasurable, and so, amoral. David Ch'en, discussing the term "cosmic cruelty" in the *Thunderstorm* preface, has discerned the "Taoistic" propensity in the trilogy as a whole.

> He [Ts'ao Yü] seems to be Taoist leaning (which might have sinister precedent) and the nihilism or arbitrariness that connotes seems to explain this preface statement and the bemoanings of his characters in all these plays.
>
> Let us be warned at this point that Ts'ao Yü does not follow the principles of science in the last analysis of life; for science, built upon physical laws, is incapable of explaining the unpredictable human destiny. The mysticism of the Taoistic philosophy reaches above and beyond all disciplines, all knowledge and understanding of man. Not the individual, nor society, nor even the weakness of human nature is the villain in Ts'ao Yü's tragedies. It is the mystic, the unknown. Morality, therefore, is only relative, and often ironical, as life is no more than a throw of dice. . . . On the other hand, he is no genuine Taoist either, because he adopts exclusively the materialistic doctrine of Taoism and ignores the Taoistic transcendental identification of man with nature and the peace and joy man is capable of attaining in nature.[40]

[40] David Y. Ch'en, "The trilogy of Ts'ao Yü and Western drama", in Horst Frenz (ed.), *Asia and the humanities*. Bloomington, Indiana, Indiana University, 1959, pp. 36–37.

Indeed, this "horrification" of Nature occurs in *The Wilderness* because Ts'ao Yü has reconciled the themes of *Prometheus bound,* the Old Testament conception of a vengeful God, and the *Lao Tzu* principle of *tzu-jan.* In the course of the third act, as natural terrors combine with Ch'ou Hu's hallucinations, these Heaven-man perspectives interfuse into a single mesh of obsessive vengeance and angry nihilism. Ch'ou Hu, having convinced himself that killing Ta-hsing is justified in the name of retribution, contrives also for Chiao Ta-ma to inadvertently slay her own grandson (in the hope of murdering Ch'ou Hu). Having thus oversated his thirst for revenge, he takes his lover-comrade, Chin-tzu, into the wilderness in search of that utopia so wished for. But Ch'ou Hu gradually perceives the enormity of his act, and his growing fatigue and hopelessness exacerbates the moral pain he feels for his unprincipled rebellion. Slowly his hallucinations become more intensely real, their movement through the forest more random; Ch'ou Hu grows desperate in his vain contravention of the Way of the wilderness. He even decries Chin-tzu's suppliant call to God for mercy:

> HUA *(mumbling)*:   How can we go on? *(Suddenly walking beneath the white poplar and kneeling down)* Oh, God, have pity on us, give us a little light, spare us just a little bit of light! *(Beseechingly)* Oh, just a little while, a little while; God, have pity on us, we've nowhere to go—

> CH'OU *(exploding)*:   Chin-tzu, who are you begging to, who are you begging to? God, God, God, what God? *(Waving his hands in exasperation)* There isn't any, there isn't any, there isn't any! I hate this God, I hate this God. Don't beg to Him, don't beg to Him!   (pp. 183–84)

Consumed by an ironic sense of justice, Ch'ou Hu must fight on, not with the help of God, but with a Fateful momentum that wreaks destruction. As the posse sent by Chiao Ta-ma closes in, he refuses to surrender. The chains which he strove to disengage in the Prologue reappear to him, but with his last burst of energy he casts them away, confident that his brethren (i.e., the "persecuted masses", and perhaps even his owns on by Chin-tzu) will continue the struggle for human dignity. What is crucial to our understanding of the play, however, is that in the end he is also somehow aware that, whatever the outcome, the impassive, eternal wilderness will survive everything. In other words, Ch'ou Hu's rebellion is both humanly admirable and cosmically trivial; and it is precisely the ambivalence of this combination of "Promethean" heroism and "Taoistic" nihilism that gives the play its philosophical complexity and artistic merit.

Having recognized this skillful blending of foreign and native conceptions into a single "cosmic cruelty", we cannot say that Ts'ao Yü offered his compatriots a clear ideological basis, to say nothing of a political formula, for confronting the pressures of violent change to come. The serious seekers of "new blood, new life" found little comfort in this pessimistic synthesis of Fate and amoralism. C. T. Hsia was perhaps most scathing when, in evaluating the first three plays, he said:

> They capitalize on the stock bourgeois responses to certain decadent and corrupt aspects of Chinese society and vaunt a superficial leftist point of view, of which only the most rigorous Marxist critic could disapprove. A serious artist in his own conceit, Ts'ao Yü complained in his postscript to *Sunrise* that, much as he was attracted to Chekhov, in the absence of a more mature audience he could not experiment in the Chekhovian manner. His plays supply contrary evidence, however: that bad taste is inherent in his manifest inability to represent life in mature and unpretentious terms. Ts'ao Yü solemnly invokes fate,

heredity, jungle law, and the class struggle to illuminate and ennoble the melodramatic action of his plays, but syncretism only underscores his lack of a personal tragic vision.[41]

This is probably too severe a condemnation of Ts'ao Yü's failures. The playwright may indeed have been, at times, melodramatic and immature in his initial writings. But understood as the product of a frustrated and occasionally overwrought artist working out the disturbing contradictions of his world, this trilogy, and particularly *The Wilderness*, which combines the thematic ingredients of the first two plays, demonstrates a true tragic vision, wherein man, though he exhausts his will, cannot escape his fecklessness to resolve universal ambiguities.

V

I have not touched on, nor will I have space to describe in full, other worthwhile facets of *The Wilderness*: the masterful use of dialogue, the deft manipulation of characters moving on and off stage in order to present a connected and organized plot, and the symbolic resonances between the various components of the wilderness "character" and the human cast of the play. But to complete our discussion of Ch'ou Hu, Chin-tzu, and the philosophical elements of *The Wilderness*, it is necessary to provide some brief synopses of the subordinate figures in the drama.

Chiao Ta-ma, like many of Ts'ao Yü's characters, is given multiple meanings in the play. She appears first to us as a virago, a witchly woman, fiercely critical and yet protective of her passive son (who represents her only source of security), and searingly belligerent toward her daughter-in-law. She thus can be identified as a remnant

---

[41] C. T. Hsia, *A history of modern Chinese fiction, 1917–1957*. New Haven, Yale University Press, 1961, p. 318.

of the cultural past and present, an exemplar of Chinese superstition and backwardness. We see this not only in her practice of voodoo magic and "spirit-calling" throughout the work, but particularly in her metaphorical contraposition at the end of the Prologue to the "Promethean" giant tree and to the symbol of a new, Westernized future, Chin-tzu's carriage to utopia—the train. And yet, as the play progresses, and especially so in Act III as her haunting voice mingles with the forest gloom, Chiao Ta-ma's primitive and fearsome ways begin to take on also the unpredictability, violence, and timelessness of the wilderness with which Ch'ou Hu and Chin-tzu must contend. In Act I, for example, when she discovers Chin-tzu wearing a flower given to her by Ch'ou Hu, Chiao Ta-ma demands that it be tossed at her feet.

CHIAO *(rising suddenly and trampling upon the red flower fiercely)*: Now, wear it! Wear it! *(Bending and picking up the flower)* Take it and wear it! *(Taking the crushed flower and tossing it at Hua, hitting Hua right in the face)* You shameless bitch, go ahead, wear it! Bring it along with you to marry the King of Hell.

HUA *(being so angry her face has turned blue; cowering to one side, gritting her teeth, and in a mumble)*: If I ever become the King of Hell's wife, the first thing I'd do is send big-headed demons after you, you old hag!

CHIAO *(not hearing clearly)*: You're muttering something again?

HUA: I was muttering how good my mother-in-law is, that for as long as you live the King of Hell will never invite you to a feast.

CHIAO *(guessing the meaning)*: Oh, I'll not die, my witch. You just wait, I shall live as long as Heaven lives. Your curses will not make me die. I'll take all of you into your coffins.   (pp. 58–59)

On the other hand, Chiao Ta-ma arouses pity from us as a human being subject to the same "cruelties" visited on Ch'ou Hu and Chin-tzu. She has a true motherly concern for her son and grandson, for whom she will fight to the end; she will even allow Chin-tzu and Ch'ou Hu to go away together, if only to preserve her family line. Ch'ou Hu, however, in his blind revenge, insists on isolating her in her obscurantism, a pawn to the unfeeling wilderness, "alive and alone".

Ta-hsing is superficially the most disappointing of the characters in *The Wilderness*. His lack of will and intelligence in the face of Ch'ou Hu's provocations, and his ridiculous self-effacement before Chin-tzu, make him an unsatisfying creature. Yet Ta-hsing serves a very important purpose for Ts'ao Yü. By making him a naive, unresponsive foil to Ch'ou Hu's dire designs, Ts'ao Yü again reveals the recurrent quandary over the validity of Promethean power when Fate and the amoral *tzu-jan* of the Way are transgressed. It is the unnatural irony of a cowardly childhood friend, son to a ruthless landlord, becoming the token of bloody recompense, which sends Ch'ou Hu into the "heartless" wilderness, there to succumb, though triumphant in will. The dichotomy is made poignant to us as Ch'ou Hu recounts Ta-hsing's dying moments in Act II.

> CH'OU *(lifting up his shaking hands; remorsefully)*: My hands, my hands! I've killed, I've killed many men, but this is the first time my hands have trembled like this. *(Letting out a sighing sound from within his chest)* Living doesn't mean a thing, but when you're dead, then it becomes real. *(Fearfully)* I grabbed him and suddenly he woke up—the way he looked at me. He wasn't afraid, he was drunk, but he looked at me as though he wanted to say something; he stared right at me. *(Nodding slowly; sympathetically)* I know he was sad in his heart, so sad he couldn't tell anybody. *(Suddenly with force)* I raised

the knife, and then he knew he had only a moment left; he was suddenly very afraid. He looked at me, *(lowering his head; slowly)* but he was laughing in his throat, laughing so queer-like; he pointed at his heart, and then he nodded to me—. *(Shaking his head suddenly; harshly)* And then I stabbed him! *(Suddenly his voice is nearly inaudible)* He didn't make any cry; he just closed his eyes. *(Throwing the dagger to the floor)* A man's really just a worthless thing, a handful of dirt, a hunk of meat, a heap of bleeding flesh; you get knocked off sooner or later, and then it's over, it's over. (p. 142)

Ta-hsing has tried earlier to act as his father might have, to resist this friend-turned-wife-stealer. But at the point of death he realizes, laughing, how silly it is and perhaps how foolish Ch'ou Hu is to think this murder is suitable compensation for prior injuries. He accepts his death by the misguided "Promethean" activist as if it were part of Nature. Indeed, like Chiao Ta-ma, Ta-hsing becomes, after his death, assimilated into the wilderness: his specter is the first Ch'ou Hu must conquer if his revenge is to be justified. On the other hand, the manner of Ta-hsing's death lends him an aura of pathos; he, like his fellow characters, is a victim of the wilderness—the haunter as well as the haunted.

In this way, the wilderness seems to absorb the supporting characters into its mass, making them both fearful and pitiable in the process. Along with the ghosts of the past and the mirages of the future, Chiao Ta-ma and Ta-hsing serve to magnify the ambiguity of the fight for justice; they are unwelcome reminders to our Chinese "Prometheus" that noble protests are of dubious merit.

The two remaining figures in the play appear, at first glance, to be less directly related to the pervading theme, having rather more "technical" utility for Ts'ao Yü. The first of these, Ch'ang Wu 常五, is surely of this type. A middle-aged "son of a squire", happily mercenary and comically hypocritical, he serves predominantly as a factotum for Chiao Ta-ma, giving away secrets, arranging posses, and generally injecting humor into what would otherwise be a continuous series of tense confrontations. He was probably the most familiar of the *dramatis personae* to Chinese audiences in the 1930s (resembling as he does the comedian [*ch'ou* 丑] of Peking opera), and his appearance in Act I is certainly one of the most memorable of the play.

Pai Sha-tzu 白傻子, or "Doggie", might also be thought as a dramaturgical device. He is used as an innocuous interlocutor for Ch'ou Hu in the Prologue; as an aide and shepherd for the handicapped Chiao Ta-ma; and, like Ch'ang Wu, as a source of comic relief. Moreover, Pai Sha-tzu is valuable to Ts'ao Yü for regulating the cadence of the action, for diminishing tension where appropriate, in order that its later crescendos are made more effective. Though unconscious of the ongoing conflicts, Doggie contributes measurably to the quality of the work by altering the dramatic pace, diversifying the tone of the play, and generally acting as a catalytic ball-bearing for the movements of the principal characters.

But he is at the same time a subtle admonition. He appears to us first in his adoration for the train, which, as has been pointed out, symbolizes passage to a new future. Perhaps as a penumbra to Chin-tzu's dream of traveling far away on a locomotive to her "gold-covered land", Pai Sha-tzu repeatedly expresses his childlike delight for the motion and clamor of the train engine, both with his vigorous mimicry in the Prologue and his dreamy smiles in the last scene. Such moronic ecstasy lays seeds of doubt in our minds whether this new future which Ch'ou Hu and Chin-tzu struggle towards will be anything more than idiotic delusion. Indeed, one can easily see Pai Sha-tzu as the "fool" in the characters of Ch'ou and Chin-tzu—an impression confirmed by Doggie's recitation in Act III of an ominous opera aria on the King of Hell's court: though once a means for Ch'ou Hu to taunt Chiao Ta-ma, the chant suddenly becomes a mocking refrain directed at Ch'ou Hu, i.e., a sign of imminent downfall.

So we see that the characters as a group are closely linked to the complex of conflicts between the eternal mystery of Heavenly dynamics and what humans perceive to be justice and morality. At every point along the way are enigmatic defeats and victories, unresolved crises. One of the values of *The Wilderness* lies in Ts'ao Yü's ability to set forth thes, abstract issues while creating a moving pageant of distinct individuals.

VI

It may be possible to see from these few words on *The Wilderness* that the play, encompassing as it does both Western and Chinese classical themes, is a meaningful opus in twentieth-century world literature. It was not Ts'ao Yü's last assay of "Promethean" strength in a fetid society. The image of primitive man reappears in *Peking Man* (*Pei-ching jen* 北京人, 1941), the story of the crumbling aristocratic Tseng 曾 family. Here again, an ape-like man is used as a symbol of hope that the vigor of China's earliest ancestors can be reharnessed for future spiritual greatness. As in *The Wilderness*, the Faustian energies of the young and ebullient are guided toward Western science, linking the primeval, innocent power of the ancient past with yearned-for glories to come, in order that the decrepit present may be erased.[42]

But the plays that follow *The Wilderness*, though still concerned with the drastic changes necessary for the

---

[42] For analyses in English of *Peking man*, see: David Y. Ch'en, "*The hairy ape* and *The Peking man*: two types of primitivism in modern society", *Yearbook of comparative and general literature* 15 (1966) 214–20; Joseph Lau, *Ts'ao Yü*, chapters 7 and 8; Hu, op. cit., chapter 7. A partial translation of Act I of the play has been made by Lily Winters in *Renditions* 3 (1974) 66–80.

transition from traditional to modern China, possess less of the diffident, bemused tone of the earlier trilogy. As John Y. H. Hu has commented, whereas the first three plays are rather mystical in pointing to the causes of the nation's failings, the works after *The Wilderness* and before the Communist takeover emphasize more concrete, institutional problems and the need for enlightened men to solve them.[43] To this extent, these later plays represent a new, more mature phase for Ts'ao Yü, in which he seems more perceptive of the real conditions and of man's abilities to cope with them effectively, whatever natural restrictions may still exist. It is unfortunate that under Maoist control Ts'ao Yü was not privileged to develop this world-view yet further; his products since 1949 have only been ideological mouthpieces.[44] Nevertheless, *The Wilderness* proves that even in his initial years of artistic growth Ts'ao Yü was able to imbue an essentially Western literary form with Chinese content and style, and to approach classical and ever cogent human issues in a newly syncretic way.[45]

CHRISTOPHER C. RAND

[43] Hu, op. cit., pp. 144–45. These plays include: *Black characters twenty-eight* (*Hei-tzu erh-shih-pa* 黑字二十八, 1938; written in collaboration with Sung Chih-ti 宋之的); *Metamorphosis* (*Shui-pien* 蛻變, 1940); *Family* (*Chia* 家, 1941; a dramatization of Pa Chin's 巴金 famous novel); *Just thinking* (*Cheng tsai hsiang* 正在想, 1946); and *Bridge* (*Ch'iao* 橋, 1947). There is also the as yet unstudied movie script, *Sunny day* (*Yen-yang t'ien* 艷陽天, 1948).

[44] These are *Bright skies* (*Ming-lang-ti t'ien* 明朗的天, 1954), *The gall and the sword* (*Tan chien p'ien* 胆劍篇, 1962; written in collaboration with Yü Shih-chih 于是之 and Mei Ch'ien 梅阡) and *Wang Chao-chün* 王昭君 (1979). A translation of *Ming-lang-ti t'ien* is available by Chang Pei-chi (*Bright skies*. Peking, Foreign Languages Press, 1960).

[45] The text of *The Wilderness* (*Yüan-yeh*) used for translation is that of the Wen-hua sheng-huo ch'u-pan she, 1937.

SYNOPSES OF *Thunderstorm* AND *Sunrise*

Thunderstorm

(Synopsis by Joseph S. M. Lau)

(Reprinted with permission, and with minor orthographical changes, from Joseph S. M. Lau, "Two emancipated Phaedras: Chou Fan-yi and Abbie Putnam as social rebels", *Journal of Asian Studies* 25 (1966) 710–711.)

Chou P'u-yüan 周樸園, head of a well-to-do family and director of a prosperous coal mine, had, in his undisciplined youth, an affair with one of his house maids. Out of this clandestine relationship a child was born and was named Chou P'ing 周萍. The affair between the young master and the maid was, however, interrupted when a second child, Chou Ta-hai 周大海, was born. The Chous, for fear that the secret goings-on between a master and a servant would blemish the family reputation, discharged the maid—with the tacit consent of Chou P'u-yüan. The first-born, Chou P'ing, was kept by the family, whereas Ta-hai, the second son, was placed under his mother's care since he was seriously ill and showed no sign of recovery. To vindicate her honor, the hapless maid had tried to drown herself in the river but was rescued by some passers-by.

After some years of study in Germany, Chou P'u-yüan returns to China, marries Fan-i 蘩漪, has a child (Chou Ch'ung 周沖) by her, and is established as a "pillar of society". Now Chou P'ing has grown into a melancholic young man of twenty-eight—sensitive and little understood by his money-grabbing father. Not happy with his father's exploitation of the mine workers to begin with, the loneliness of his stepmother (twenty years her husband's junior) as a neglected wife is for him another cause for moral indignation. So in no time they become lovers.

But this incestuous relationship has not been carried on very far before Chou P'ing, either disturbed by his conscience or simply tired of his partner, finds himself drawn to an eighteen-year-old girl working in his household. Chou Fan-i is, of course, furious. But her situation is desperate: she can no longer put up with Chou P'u-yüan's cold-blooded mental persecution (in forcing her to admit that she is mad) and wants to leave the family. She doesn't even mind sharing P'ing with Ssu-feng 四鳳 (the maid) as long as he agrees to take her along. This P'ing refuses; and, like his father, he also charges her with madness.

It happens that Ssu-feng's mother, Lu Ma 魯媽, who is no other than the former maid of the House of Chou, has decided to pay her daughter a visit. (Ever since she was saved from her attempted suicide, she has been working as a janitress in a school some distance away from the Chous. She is married to Lu Kuei 魯貴 who is in the same employ as his daughter, Ssu-feng.) Accompanying her on her way is Ta-hai, Ssu-feng's half-brother, who has come as the miners' representative to negotiate with Chou P'u-yüan for better compensation.

Once ushered into the sitting room, she notices, to her horror, that not only the furniture but the decorative arrangements are recognizably the same as those she used to see in her former paramour's house. Sensing forebodings of imminent disaster, she makes haste to go home, intent on taking Ssu-feng with her. But just before she is ready to leave, Chou appears. In an honest attempt to atone for his sins, he offers, in the manner of a successful entrepreneur, a handsome amount of money to solicit Lu Ma's forgiveness. Lu Ma turns down the money and reveals to him that Ta-hai, the miners' representative, is no one if not his own son whom his family rejected. This, for Chou, is already a sure sign of retribution, for nothing can be more unbearable for a father than having his own son stand in opposition to his interest in time of crisis. But retribution has in store for him an appearance far more sinister.

When Fan-i is convinced that Chou P'ing would elope with Ssu-feng despite her pleading, her mind is bent on revenge. In a fit of hysteria, she reveals to Lu Ma, Ssu-feng, and Chou Ch'ung that she has been P'ing's mistress. She is ignorant, of course, in her maniac determination for revenge, of the fatal consanguinity of the two lovers and that Ssu-feng is now with child. Recalling how her son Chou Ch'ung is infatuated with the girl, she shamelessly tries to fan jealousy into the hearts of the two brothers by asking Chou Ch'ung to claim Ssu-feng, who is soon to become P'ing's wife. But to her surprise, Ch'ung admits to her that his love for Ssu-feng has not been more than a juvenile fancy, and now that Ssu-feng has found someone to care for her, he is happy for her sake. This generosity of mind, however, has done little to mellow Fan-i's bitterness. Instead, it accentuates her loneliness, deepens her despair, and exacerbates her morbid fear of betrayal. Hence, as a last measure, she triumphantly summons Chou P'u-yüan down from his sleep to stop the elopement. Yet all her calculations come to no avail, for Chou P'u-yüan comes down only to uncover the true identities of all the family on the spot.

Unable to bear the shame, Ssu-feng runs out of the house and is struck by a live wire. Chou Ch'ung, oblivious to the danger, is also electrocuted in an attempt to save her. At the sight of this calamity, Fan-i, who has not until now realized that her vengeful scheme would precipitate a tragedy far grimmer than her own, at last shows signs of remorse and asks Chou P'ing's forgiveness. But things have gone beyond repair. No sooner are his sister's and brother's deaths reported than he shoots himself to death in his room. Of the surviving four, both Lu Ma and Fan-i have gone mad; Ta-hai, upon learning that the company's director is none other than his own father, disappears from the scene and is never to return; the old man, Chou P'u-yüan, left all to himself, will have to pass his remaining years in penitent memory.

Sunrise

(Synopsis by Christopher C. Rand)

Act I opens in a hotel room with the return of Ch'en Pai-lu 陳白露 and Fang Ta-sheng 方達生 from a night's frolic among the clubs of the city. Once a country girl, Ch'en has escaped from her village confinement and has become a high-class courtesan to the richer segment of a large coast metropolis (Tientsin?). Superficially gay with life, actually she is frustrated by the hypocrisy, venality, and pretentiousness of her clients and acquaintances. Still, she is somewhat proud of her relative independence from traditional taboos of womanhood, and she is eager to show off that inflated self-confidence to her former boyfriend. Fang, who has come to visit her rather unexpectedly, is shocked by her change of personality and her forced bravado; he views her existence with a jaundiced eye and decides he must make his plea of marriage to her before she has lost the innocence he knew her to have back home.

> TA-SHENG *(looking into her shining eyes)*: It's horrible, horrible—it seems impossible that you can now have become so unscrupulous, so devoid of any sense of shame. Sure you realize that once one's head is turned by a lust for money, the most precious thing in life—love—will fly away like a bird.

PAI-LU *(with a touch of sorrow)*:   Love? *(Tapping the ash off her cigarette, in a leisurely voice)* What is love? *(She blows the word away into nothingness in a curling wisp of cigarette smoke.)* You're a child! I've nothing more to say to you.

TA-SHENG *(undaunted)*:   Now, Chu-chun, it seems to me that the way you've been living these last few years has killed a part of you. But now that I've come here and seen how you're living I can't bear to see you going on in the same way any longer. I'm determined to convert you, I'm—

(p. 14; this and subsequent excerpts are taken from A. C. Barnes (trans.), *Sunrise*. Peking, Foreign Languages Press, 1978.)

She laughs at him, but deeply she is conscious of how unblemished her teenage years in the country were in comparison to the contorted life she now leads. As if to validate her thoughts, Chang Ch'iao-chih 張喬治 ("Georgy" Chang), a feckless student just returned from America, stumbles in drunkenly from Pai-lu's bedroom where he has flopped out for the night; and Fu-sheng 福升, a conniving servant, enters to recite his litany of demands from bill collectors and egotistical hangers-on. She really does not revel in her genteel prostitution, but she tolerates the myriad displeasures for an ounce of glory and freedom.

As Ta-sheng leaves for bed, Pai-lu is left alone—or so she thinks. From across the darkened room she sees a small figure rush by. She turns on the light and discovers a young girl dressed in an oversized smock. Questioned about her presence, the child, Hsiao-tung-hsi 小東西, explains in hysterical tones that she is an orphan who has been sold to a prostitute ring situated on another floor of the hotel. Having refused to submit to Chin Pa 金八, a financial monopolist and leader of the ring, she has slipped away. Pai-lu, immediately sympathetic with her plight, decides to ensconce her until a suitable home can be located. P'an Yüeh-t'ing 潘月亭, a longtime admirer of Pai-lu, happens on the scene soon afterwards and reluctantly assents to aid in this plan; but when he finds that his creditor, Chin Pa, is the direct cause of Hsiao-tung-hsi's desertion, he cravenly retracts his offer. Just then, a posse of Chin Pa's henchmen who have found a familiar handkerchief outside Pai-lu's door demands admittance to the apartment. Pai-lu tries to prevent a thorough search, but they are not dissuaded. P'an, however, has had a change of heart, and by dissembling as a spokesman for Chin Pa, he manages to turn the henchmen away.

Act II opens in Pai-lu's sitting room as Ta-sheng and Fu-sheng discuss the chanting of construction workers building P'an's new Ta Feng 大豐 Bank next to the hotel: "The sun comes up from the East, / The sky is a great red glow. / If we want rice to eat / We must bend our backs in toil" (p. 39). Fu-sheng hates the noise of the workmen— "bawling", he calls it—but Ta-sheng is somehow intrigued by their singing. They are interrupted by the arrival of Huang Hsing-san 黃省三, a poor old clerk laid off by the bank, who wants to see P'an about retrieving his old job. Fu-sheng rebuffs his plaint and throws him out of the apartment.

During the remainder of the act we see a train of Pai-lu's acquaintances parade before us in all their folly and perverseness. First comes P'an to assure Chin Pa on the telephone that his deposit in P'an's bank is quite safe, and not to worry about making a withdrawal for at least a few more days. P'an is desperately trying to disguise the fact that, because of heavy speculation in risky government bonds, his business is in danger of collapsing. Recklessly he is attempting to dispel doubts about his solvency by constructing a new building and speculating in the bond market with even greater abandon.

Coming next in view is Mrs. Ku 顧八奶奶, waddling out from a sideroom adorned in her gaudy, gold-bordered gown, her whale-sized buttocks pitching side to side. Though lined with wrinkles, she tries to hide her age behind a paint-and-powder façade, unaware of others' mocking smiles, and straining vainly to be young and vivacious. A victim of her wealth and craving for flattery, she is continually attended by her gigolo, Hu Ssu 胡四 a man at once contemptuous, cynically toadyish, and obsessed by desires for fashionable clothing and movie stardom.

Following quickly thereafter is Li Shih-ch'ing 李石清, a bank clerk who, by comparable sycophancy, has gained the favor of Manager P'an and become his personal secretary, thus entering the circles of the rich and prestigious. In the process, however, Li has forsaken the welfare of his family, and though his wife strives to reform him, not until the unnecessary death of his son in Act IV does he realize his arrogance. Here in Act II his haughtiness is most evident in an encounter with Huang Hsing-san, in which he scorns the old man's punctilious honesty and counsels him to commit suicide if he must insist on being so ethically upright.

In Act III the scene changes to a low-class brothel in another part of the city. It is early evening and the inmates of the house are awaiting the chance arrival of pleasure-seekers. Tsui-hsi 翠喜, a pretty but aging harlot, sits by her window yelling at her beggar-friends passing noisily on the street. Soon Hsiao-tung-hsi enters from a side door. Despite Pai-lu's efforts, Chin Pa's henchmen (Black San 黑三 *et al.*) have kidnapped the young orphan and re-inducted her into prostitution. However, Hsiao-tung-hsi's demeanor is now more reproachful than before; defiant of her masters, she refuses to rouge her face for their sordid gain. Tsui-hsi has tried to rationalize with her about their ill-starred lives, but Hsiao-tung-hsi cannot be so easily convinced of her situation; her resentment only brings upon her the blows of Black San's cudgel when he finds that she has attracted no customers to her bed.

On this particular night Hu Ssu and Fu-sheng visit the brothel and choose Tsui-hsi and Hsiao-tung-hsi as their hostesses. Hsiao-tung-hsi, in her querulous state of mind, incurs Hu Ssu's wrath by quarrelling with him and spilling tea upon his prized new suit of clothes. Black San arrives to investigate the trouble and, with apologies to the two patrons, drags the obstinate girl away to bludgeon her once more. Hsiao-tung-hsi, realizing she has no hope for a better future, decides to take her own life; after the others have retired for the night, she takes a length of rope, ties a loop above the doorframe, and hangs herself.

With Act IV we return to the hotel and a more elegant brothel. It is nearly morning, but Pai-lu's gaggle of socialites is still playing mahjong and carousing about her suite. Though she has been drinking along with them, her blasé air is missing now. She asks Fu-sheng if her guests have departed.

FU-SHENG *(looking at the door on the left)*:   They're all eating and drinking and they've got plenty to keep them amused here, so I can't imagine them being ready to go.

PAI-LU *(nodding sadly)*:   So that's all they come here for: to amuse themselves.

FU-SHENG: Well, of course!

PAI-LU: And what will happen when they've had all the amusement they want?

FU-SHENG: Well, they'll go home, of course. They've all got their own homes to go to—can't stay in a hotel all your life, now can you!

PAI-LU *(in the same colourless tone)*:   Then why haven't they had all they want? *(In a low voice to herself)* No, one can't stay all one's life in a hotel. *(Shaking her head)* I've probably had all the amusement I want, *(Sitting down)* Yes, I've had enough of it, *(pensively)* I'd like to go home myself, back to my old home.

FU-SHENG *(astonished)*: But Miss, you mean you've got a home?

PAI-LU: I've had enough, I should go back home.

FU-SHENG: Are you serious about this, Miss?

PAI-LU: Yes.

FU-SHENG *(hurriedly)*: Look, Miss, if you really are thinking of going back to your old home, what about all your unpaid debts here? You'll have to—

PAI-LU: Yes, I know I'm deep in debt. But surely I've paid in full, all the years I've been here?

(p. 128)

Meanwhile, Li Shih-ch'ing, having cleverly become an assistant to P'an Yüeh-t'ing, has misestimated his superior's good intentions toward him. According to the latest indications, P'an's bond speculations will finally be successful, making it possible to repay Chin Pa's loan. Indeed, this potential good fortune reminds P'an of what an influential man he still is; he will not stand for self-important assistants who might blackmail him with inside information about the bank's real assets. He decides to fire Li and rid himself of that threat. Li is enraged, but, to the surprise of both, it is P'an who suffers the final reversal: a newspaper contact reports that the expected rise in the market will not materialize after all and that instead there will be a substantial slump. Chin Pa demands immediate repayment of his loan and P'an is financially ruined.

All this cannibalism has depressed Pai-lu. Finally convinced that her freedom is actually a mirage, she loses all ambition to carry on this loathesome existence, or even a new life with Ta-sheng. She takes an overdose of sleeping tablets and lies down on the sofa; casually she picks up a book she has recently bought called *Sunrise*.

Suddenly, Ta-sheng enters looking for Pai-lu. He is

annoyed by the darkness of the room and goes to the window to open the blinds.

TA-SHENG: . . . I can't understand you not letting the sun in. *(Going to the door of the bedroom on the left)* Listen while I tell you something, Chu-chun. If you go on living like this you'll be digging your own grave. Now listen, why not go with me after all, instead of tying yourself to these people? Now what about it? Look, *(pointing out of the window)* the sun's shining, it's spring.

(The singing of the labourers is now coming nearer. They are singing: "The sun comes up from the east; the sky is a great red glow. . . .")

(p. 167)

THE CHARACTERS AND SETTINGS

(in order of appearance)

CH'OU HU 仇虎 (CH'OU) *(lit., "vengeful tiger"), an escaped convict, sometimes referred to as "Hu-tzu" 虎子 (lit., "tiger")*

PAI SHA-TZU 白傻子 (PAI) *(lit., "nitwit"), nicknamed "Doggie"; a stupid fool who tends sheep in the wilderness*

CHIAO TA-HSING 焦大星 (HSING), *Chiao Yen-wang's son (the surname, Chiao, literally means "sear" or "burning")*

CHIAO HUA 焦花 (HUA), *Chiao Ta-hsing's new wife, sometimes referred to as "Chin-tzu" 金子 (lit., "gold one")*

CHIAO MU 焦母 (CHIAO) *(lit., "Mother Chiao"), Ta-hsing's mother, a blind woman, sometimes referred to as Chiao Shih 焦氏 and Chiao Ta-ma 焦大媽 (lit., "Madame Chiao")*

CH'ANG WU 常五 (CH'ANG), *a guest of the Chiao family*

Various Apparitions:

A MAN CARRYING AN UMBRELLA AND A RED LANTERN

THE FIGURE OF CHIAO MU HOLDING A SMALL BABY

HUNG LAO 洪老

THREE STRONGMEN

CH'OU JUNG 仇榮, *Ch'ou Hu's father*

CH'OU KU-NIANG 仇姑娘 *(lit., "Miss Ch'ou"), fifteen years old; Ch'ou Hu's younger sister*

CHIAO YEN-WANG 焦閻王 *(lit., "Chiao, King of Hell"), a captain; Ta-hsing's father*

PRISONERS CARRYING DIRT: *"Train Engine"* 火車頭, *"Old Pumpkin"* 老窩瓜, *"Pa Pock"* 麻子爹, *"Little Widow"* 小寡婦, *"Chang Fei Rival"* 賽張飛, *"Wild Ass"* 野驢, *and others—ten men in all*

TWO PRISONERS CARRYING WATER

THE WARDEN

THE OX- AND HORSE HEADED-DEMON-MESSENGERS 牛頭馬面

THE JUDGE OF HADES 判官

TWO BLUE-GREEN-FACED GHOSTLINGS 青面小鬼

THE KING OF HELL 閻羅 (地藏王)

TIME: Autumn

PROLOGUE

By a railroad in the wilderness—late in a day after the beginning of fall (立秋)

ACT I

The main room of Chiao Yen-wang's home—ten days after the prologue, at six o'clock in the afternoon

ACT II

The same scene as Act I—the same day, nine in the evening—the same day, eleven in the evening

ACT III
(Time of action immediately following Act II)

Scene I:　The Dark Forest 黑林子, at forked trails
　　　　— after one o'clock at night

Scene II:　The Dark Forest, a swamp in the woods
　　　　— after two o'clock at night

Scene III:　The Dark Forest, beside a pond in the woods
　　　　— after three o'clock at night

Scene IV:　The Dark Forest, near a small broken-down temple in the woods—after four o'clock at night

Scene V:　The same as in the prologue, by a railroad in the wilderness—break of dawn, after six o'clock

PROLOGUE

At twilight in autumn.

The earth is dark and somber; a vital force hides within. The clay disperses a fragrance and the roots of grain covertly mature in the soil. A giant tree stretches its tossed-hair-like branches into the dusk and the autumn cicadas languidly vibrate their wings. The giant tree, with its enormous trunk scratched with old and cracked grains, stands upright in the vast, blue atmosphere of the plain, commanding dignity, malice, defiance, and a dark, lonely anxiety, like a chained Prometheus tied upon his precipice. Beyond lies a wild pond of muddy, oily-green rainwater; several frogs leap about haphazardly on the bank from time to time, splashing in turn into the water, creating bubbles. And in a moment, in the tranquillity of sunset, from somewhere resounds an intermittent croaking, so very lonely.

In front of the giant tree extends a filled roadbed, and iron rails stretching from some unknown place. The rails are cast in what resembles a copper-gold alloy, very black; they gleam in the light of the cloudy dusk as silently they extend to the horizon, bearing with them man's bitter suffering, happiness, and hope. Now and then the grand, dragon-like train blares out an unsettling clamor, belching black smoke scattered with unruly sparks, and speeding by like wind and lightning. And gone with it are the tears and laughter of man.

Accompanying the tracks to one side are telegraph poles connected one to the other, so that when the wind blows, the black wires hanging on the white-porcelain connectors respond with a moan. The railroad bed slants to become a slope, and in front of it there is a tombstone-like distance marker, a shabby guard post, some wild grass, and a pile of rusty rails and ties.

Strange black clouds swirl about, covering the sky and changing into all sorts of hideous and frightening shapes; they weigh heavily upon the earth.

The distant horizon splits open by degrees into a lake of blood, and on the fringes is sprinkled a dark, reddish brown; it is like a dreadful dream, the peaks and boulders of the heaped black clouds washed with a myriad of odd, alluring hues.

The earth continues to darken and a fog bank gradually rises; it is a plain at an autumn sunset. In the distance, one can see a lonesome building reddened by a lantern from within.

The earth is dark and somber.

As the curtain rises, Ch'ou Hu, with one hand on his hip, leans against the giant tree, gazing at the sunset, panting but making no sound. The frogs suddenly call out from the side of the pond. He picks up a stone and hurls it into the water; it falls crisply on the surface of the pool, and the frogs are frightened into silence. Feeling more relaxed, he squats down, only to hear the cicadas raise another din. He lifts his head and looks up with disgust. He rises and is about to pick up another rock, when far away a train whistle sounds. Turning his head, he watches the distant train rush by, moving further and further away; intermittently come a few weak whistle blasts. He throws down the rock, sighs, tightens an incomparably wide belt, and wipes a foot on a grossly muddy leg; the manacles on his ankles respond with a threatening moan, and he is immediately reminded of the nuisances on his feet. He picks up a large stone beside him and batters vigorously against his chains. Again and again he heaves its weight against his tibia, his black eyebrows wrinkling as blood oozes out. But he refuses to give up and, gritting his teeth, he continues to pound on his chains, while cursing and gasping for breath. When beads of sweat gather on his forehead, he wipes them away with his bloody hand. Finally, with a violent yell he pitches the stone into the pond; something is clogging his gullet like a piece of lead. In despair, his dark face looks up at the sky, while, with his two coarse paws, he attempts frenetically to break the fetters on his ankles.

Far away there seems to be a herd of sheep tramping by; someone is calling after them, chasing them into the pens. The sheep scatter and bleat mournfully in breach of the general serenity. Startled, he looks about in the direction of the sound, alarmed but attentive. Suddenly he leaps to his feet, turns around to face the audience, and fixes his gaze on them in silence. His appearance evokes in them an uncanny feeling, for one would wonder how the Creator could have invented such an ugly creature—his hair like hemp in disarray, his face huge and dreadful, his eyebrows drooping, his eyes burning with hatred. His right leg is lame, and he is so humped over it looks as if he had a bundle concealed on his back. His muscles are firm and sturdy; his legs are like two iron posts. He wears a close-weave, blue-cloth jacket with fasteners, which has been rent by barbed wire, revealing the hair on his chest. On his waist is a special kind of wide, black-leather belt with a tile-size buckle shining on its front. His eyes betray ruthlessness, cunning, craftiness and jealousy. He is a man who has just escaped from Hell.

He stands on his toes to take a look and realizes that someone must be approaching, for with all the shouting and the baaing of the sheep there is surely someone close by. He hides behind the slope of the railroad bed near the pond.

Suddenly there is an incomprehensible and yet gleeful sound— "Chi-cha-ka-cha, chi-cha-ka-cha, chi-cha-ka-cha, tu-tu-tu-tu, tu-tu-tu-tu, tu-tu-tu-tu"—each phrase more forceful than the last, followed by what seems to be the sound of foot-stamping or a fast sprint.

His face red from the exertion, Pai Sha-tzu skips playfully down the railroad bed, carrying a basket of branches and holding an axe in his right hand. He is about twenty years of age, has a plump round face, a nose like a Pekingese dog, and a pair of mousy eyes which never cease to gleam. His hair has grown low, almost covering his eyebrows, and when he laughs his eyes disappear to a slit and his mouth hangs agape. If he should espy something pretty or tasty, his lower jaw falls open involuntarily, and at times he will slobber out saliva. A simpleton and an orphan, he has been entrusted to the care of a distant relative, for whom he tends sheep, chops brushwood, and performs other sundry chores.

PAI SHA-TZU *(running in excitedly, acting like a racing railroad engine)*: "Chi-cha-ka-cha, chi-cha-ka-cha, . . ." *(Suddenly as if puffing black smoke)* "Tu-tu-tu-tu, tu-tu-tu-tu, tu-tu-tu-tu, . . ." *(Turning around abruptly, and drawing back, his arms like a pair of wings, he punctuates each flapping motion with an exclamatory "tu-tu". Imitating the engine's backward motion, he steps back vigorously, ejaculating all manner of noise as his "engine" picks up speed. But, heedless, he trips over a railroad tie and crashes to the ground; his "engine" has all at once tumbled upon the roadbed, giving him considerable pain! He grimaces as though about to cry; his branches are scattered over the tracks and the axe has slid down the embankment. He puts his hands to his eyes and howls wantonly, rubbing his buttocks as he looks about him. Finding no one to question, no one to sympathize with him, he turns his head to look at his rear and caresses the sore spot a few times. Standing up, and as though coaxing a child, he blows a whiff of air to his palm to apply magical power, and pats his buttocks lightly.)* It all right, nothing hurt, go way! *(He whimpers as though being comforted, and then again—)* "Chi-cha-ka-cha, chi-cha-ka-cha". *(He stops, puts down the basket simply, and with his arms flailing, his face dancing, he descends the roadbed incline and races along the thoroughfare, winding as he goes, free as a dragon.)* "Chi-cha-ka-cha, tu-tu-tu-tu, tu-tu-tu-tu, tu-tu-tu-tu, . . ." *(More exuberantly he rounds his mouth and mimics a train whistle)* "Wu—wu—wu, chi-cha-ka-cha, tu-tu-tu-tu, wu—wu—wu—". *(Unexpectedly he turns a somersault.)* "Wu—wu—wu—", look! 'Nother one! "Wu—wu—wu—wu— , chi-cha-ka-cha, tu-tu-tu-tu, —wu—wu—". *(He stops short his blowing, as far away comes the low obscure sound of an engine whistle. For a moment he seems to be in a daze, but finally he runs up to the roadbed, straddles the ties and cleaves an ear to the rail. He closes his eyes as though listening discerningly to angelic music, and his face is filled with innocent pleasure.)* H-ha-ha! *(Laughing involuntarily, foolishly. Ch'ou Hu rises up from behind the roadbed, and though at first he seems to be taken by surprise, he moves casually toward Pai Sha-tzu.)*

CH'OU HU: Hey! *(Lightly kicking Pai's head)* Hey! Whatcha doing?

PAI *(listening to the sound of the onrushing train through the rail and with his eyes closed in a state of seeming bliss, he softly beats the cadence of the flywheel with his hands)*: "Chi-cha-ka-cha, chi-cha-ka-cha, . . ." *(Without even bothering to look, he only waves his arm in irritation.)* You . . . none o' your bus'ness.

CH'OU *(kicking his buttocks)*: Hey, whatcha listenin' to?

PAI *(impatiently)*: Don't bother me! *(Waving his hands)* Don't bother me! Listen, the train! *(Pointing at the tracks)* It's in here! The train! "Chi-cha-ka-cha, chi-cha-ka-cha, chi-cha-ka-cha, . . ." *(Elated, he pricks up his ears and lifts his head; as if lost in thought.)* "Tu-tu-tu-tu, tu-tu-tu-tu"! *(Transported with joy, he gazes into the distance, mumbling to himself)* Hm . . . the train get farther and farther away, farther and farther away! "Tu-tu-tu-tu, tu-tu-tu-tu, . . ." *(Once more he sticks his ear against the iron rail.)*

CH'OU: Get up! *(Pai does not listen; again he kicks him.)* Get up! *(Pai still does not listen; harshly)* Damn it, get up! *(He boots Pai down the incline, nearly tripping himself with his own chains.)*

PAI *(at the foot of the slope he instinctively picks up the axe and with the other hand caressing his smitten buttocks, he looks bewilderedly at Ch'ou Hu)*: You . . . you . . . you kick me.

CH'OU *(laughing menacingly; nodding)*: Huh, I kicked you! *(As he scratches his leg with one foot, his chains clank heavily.)* So what are you going to do about it?

PAI *(unable to see the violent apparition clearly, he retreats a step)*: I . . . I'm not doin' nothin'.

CH'OU *(diabolically)*: Can't you see me?

PAI *(apprehensively)*: Not . . . not too good.

CH'OU *(emerging from the shade of the giant tree and facing the horizon)*: Look! *(Pointing to himself)* Can you see me now?

PAI *(scrutinizing Ch'ou Hu fearfully, then exclaiming)*:   Ah!
Ma! *(Dragging the axe as he runs.)*

CH'OU *(thunderously)*:   Halt!
*(Pai is paralyzed on the spot; his mouth is dripping saliva; his
eyes move constantly.)*

CH'OU *(devilishly)*:   Damn it, where you runnin' off to?

PAI *(making an excuse)*:   I . . . I'm not runnin' away!

CH'OU *(pointing at himself; angrily)*:   What do you think
I look like?

PAI *(staring at him, timorously)*:   Like . . . uh . . . like—
(He scratches his head)—sorta—*(he ponders, shakes his head)*
sorta not like a man.

CH'OU *(spitting his words out through his clenched teeth)*:   Not
like a man? *(Thunderingly)* Not like a man?

PAI *(intimidated)*:   No, you're lik'a, you're lik'a, lik'a,
lik'a, . . . man.

CH'OU *(laughing ferociously; then suddenly agreeably)*:   Am I
bad-lookin', am I ugly?

PAI *(with a bit of inexplicable shrewdness; his eyes widening)*:
You . . . you're not bad-lookin', not ugly. But——

CH'OU *(explosively)*:   Who said I wasn't ugly! Who said
I wasn't ugly!

PAI *(nonplussed)*:   Uh, you're ugly! You're . . . ugly lik'a
demon.

CH'OU: So. *(Walking toward Pai, the iron chains at his feet
jangling)* The demon's callin' for you, the ugly demon's
callin' for you.

PAI *(trembling)*:   Don't! I . . . I come to you.

CH'OU: Then move!

PAI *(uneasily; dragging his recalcitrant feet)*:   Where . . .
where you come from?

CH'OU *(pointing toward the distance)*:   The horizon!

PAI *(indicating the roadbed)*: Horizon? From horizon? You ride train, too? *(Slowly)* "Chi-cha-ka-cha, tu-tu-tu-tu"? *(He backs up, turns to one side, and apes the backward motion of the locomotive.)*

CH'OU *(comprehending, he laughs fiercely)*: Uh, "chi-cha-ka-cha, chi-cha-ka-cha". *(Operating his hands, he starts up another railroad engine and moves toward Pai.)* "Tu-tu-tu-tu, tu-tu-tu-tu". *(He approaches rapidly, retreats slowly; "locomotive" bumps "locomotive"; Ch'ou Hu leaps and clutches Pai Sha-tzu's wrist; he pulls him along.)* Come on!

PAI *(calling out in pain as he tries to free himself; bawling rowdily)*: Ah! Ma! I won't go with you, I won't!

CH'OU *(eyeing him obliquely)*: All right, you know how to chi-cha-ka-cha, so I'll *(he hits Pai's chest with his fist; Pai gasps)* tu—tu—tu—tu for you! *(Fiercely)* Give that axe to me!

PAI *(timidly)*: This . . . this aint mine. *(He hands over the axe involuntarily, however.)*

CH'OU *(grabbing the axe)*: Bring it here!

PAI *(explaining)*: I . . . I . . . *(squinting)* I din't say I won't give it to you.

CH'OU *(holding the axe in one hand, and pointing to his leg chains)*: You see these?

PAI *(stretching his neck and nodding repeatedly)*: I see 'em.

CH'OU: Know what they are?

PAI *(taking a look, then wiping away the mucus on his upper lip, and shaking his head)*: No, I dunno.

CH'OU *(indicating the iron chains)*: These're bracelets— gold bracelets!

PAI *(muttering in response)*: Bracelets—gold bracelets!

CH'OU: Yeah! *(Pointing at his feet)* You just pound off this pair of gold bracelets for me. *(Returning the axe to him)* Pound them off and I'll give them to you to wear!

PAI: Me wear? Those? *(Shaking his head)* I don't, I don't want to!

CH'OU *(again grabbing the axe and lifting it up high)*:   Do you want them or not?

PAI *(blinking)*:   I . . . I . . . I want . . . I want!
(Ch'ou squats down on the roadbed as Pai leans against the embankment. Ch'ou is about to sit down and stretch out his legs.)

CH'OU *(suspiciously)*:   Wait a minute! You tell anybody these bracelets are mine and I'll split you open with this axe.

PAI *(puzzled, but . . .)*:   Hm, hm, O.K., O.K. *(Again he takes the axe.)*

CH'OU *(sitting down on the roadbed and propping himself up with two hands on the track ties behind him; supporting the bulk of his weight he stretches out his legs and faces Pai)*:   Pound away!

PAI *(rapping heavily against the chains once, he stops, thinking)*:   But . . . but this axe . . . aint yours neither.

CH'OU *(impatiently)*:   I know, I know!

PAI *(reasoning)*:   Then you can't split me open wi' this axe. *(He stands up.)*

CH'OU *(leaping up, snatching his axe and lifting it up)*:   Damn you dumb bastard, are you going to do it for me or not?
(The herd of sheep in the plain bleat sadly.)

PAI *(apprehensively)*:   I . . . I din't say I won't do it for you. *(Again he takes the axe; Ch'ou sits down; Pai squats at his side and begins to pound away, one blow after another.)*
(The frogs in the pond croak brittlely.)

PAI *(suddenly glancing strangely at Ch'ou Hu)*:   How y'know about . . . my nickname?

CH'OU: What?

PAI: Not 'til people here want me t'work for 'em do they call me Pai Sha-tzu. When I'm done working they'll always be calling me Dumb Bastard. *(Warmly laughing out loud in a very self-satisfied manner)* Hee! Hee! Hee! *(He scratches an itchy place on his back and then he starts pounding again.)*

CH'OU *(incredulous, unable to recognize him)*: What, you're . . . you're Pai Sha-tzu?

PAI: Uh. *(Mumbling)* They don't care 'bout me, they all just call me Dumb Bastard, but sometimes . . . they call me Dog . . . Doggie. Which name d'you like? *(Unable to get an answer, he mutters away to himself.)* Uh, all those names they've been calling me, they're really not so bad, but maybe Dog . . . Doggie's good. When my ma alive, she was always calling me Doggie. She say, you see 'em, this child grow lik' a dog . . . Got a dog head, an' a dog brain, so we'll call him Dog . . . Doggie, he'll grow . . . grow up big. You see, my . . . my nickname's really . . . *(very happily gives his rear a pat)* Doggie! Hee! Hee! Hee! *(He laughs aloud, and again wipes some mucus away.)*

CH'OU *(looking at him directly)*: Doggie? You're called Doggie?

PAI: Uh-huh, Doggie, you couldn't guess it! *(He proudly scratches again.)*

CH'OU *(suddenly)*: Do you still know me?

PAI *(glances and shakes his head)*: No, I don't. *(Putting down the axe)* You . . . you know me?

CH'OU *(hesitating, then coldly)*: No, I don't. *(Hastily)* Hurry up, pound faster, cut out your jabber, come on!

PAI: It's gettin' dark! I can't see yer bracelets too good.

CH'OU: Damn you dumb bastard! Give the axe to me! Get away!

PAI *(standing up)*:   T' you? *(Lifting the axe high)* No, that aint right! This axe's not mine. This axe's Chiao . . . Chiao Ta-ma's.

CH'OU: What'd you say? *(Also standing up.)*

PAI *(tongue-tied)*:   Chiao . . . Chiao Ta-ma. She say, if . . . if I'm late in bringing it back, she'll kill . . . kill me. *(Rubbing his neck; the thought of Chiao Ta-ma gives him courage and he points at Ch'ou's face.)* If . . . if you steal 'er axe, she'll kill . . . kill you too! *(To stress his point and intimidate him he uses a hand on his neck to simulate the slicing through of a blade.)* "Cha . . . cha . . . cha"! Aren't you scared o'that?

CH'OU: Ah, is she a blind old woman?

PAI *(more emphatically)*:   She . . . she's a blind old woman, cruel and poison, very bad!

CH'OU: She's not dead yet?

PAI *(curious)*:   No, you seen her?

CH'OU *(in deep thought)*:   Yeah. *(Suddenly he grabs Pai's arm.)* What about the old man?

PAI *(staring)*:   Ol' man?

CH'OU: Her husband, Yen-wang, Yen-wang.

PAI *(finally comprehending)*:   Ah, you mean Yen-wang, Chiao Yen-wang. *(Casually)* Yen-wang's already . . . already in his coffin.

CH'OU *(dumbfounded)*:   Wha' . . . what? *(He stands upright.)*

PAI: He's dead, buried, gone into the ground.

CH'OU *(bitterly)*:   What? Yen-wang's in his coffin?

PAI *(indifferently)*:   Dead couple years ago.

CH'OU *(sullenly)*:   Dead! So, even Yen-wang has his end!

PAI: Uh, *(not knowing where he heard it)* naked we come, and naked we go, sooner or later we all hafta die.

Ch'ou *(disappointed)*: So, I came for nothing, for nothing.

Pai *(curious)*: You . . . were looking for Yen-wang, wha' . . . wha' for?

Ch'ou *(suddenly turning about; infuriated)*: But how . . . how could he be dead? How could he die without waiting for me to come back? Why didn't he wait for me to come back! *(He stamps his foot, his iron chains clank against each other; ranting wildly.)* Not t'wait for me! *(Clenching his teeth)* Not t'wait for me! You took our land! You ruined our family! You burned our house, and accused us wrongly of being bandits. And then you took me to the yamen and you had people beat me 'til I was lame. I held out in that prison for eight years because of you, while you hid here, all the time thinking up ways to destroy us. Now that I'm back, you're dead, you're dead!

Pai *(uncomprehending, so the only thing to say——)*: Yeah, he's dead!

Ch'ou *(raising his fist and dropping his voice)*: So, you've dropped dead, so quiet-like. *(Excitedly)* But how could I let you die, and let you die so easy. I'm telling you, Yen-wang, I've come back, I've come back, Yen-wang! You killed us, and you all have to pay for it; you destroyed us, and I'm gonna get even with you! You poked out my eyes, and I'm gonna poke out yours, too. You crippled me, and ruined everyone in my family. You think you can run away from it by hiding in the grave? Huh? You think I'm gonna let you lie down in peace? Ah, Yen-wang, there's no such easy deal in this world!

Pai *(amazed)*: What you talking t'yourself about? You still want me to knock off your bracelets?

Ch'ou *(returning to the present)*: Uh, uh, yeah . . . *(Fiery)* Keep pounding!

Pai *(at once)*: Uh, uh! *(He spits, and lifts the axe to strike.)*

CH'OU: So, what about his son?

PAI: Who?

CH'OU: I'm talking about Yen-wang's son, Chiao Ta-hsing.

PAI *(not clear)*: Chiao . . . Chiao Ta-hsing?

CH'OU: I mean Chiao Ta.

PAI *(finally)*: Oh! He just married a new bride, and he's a father now.

CH'OU: So, he's married, is he!

PAI *(gnashing his teeth)*: New wife very pretty, she call'd . . . call'd Chin-tzu.

CH'OU *(surprised)*: Chin-tzu! Chin-tzu?

PAI: Uh, you . . . you know Chiao Ta?

CH'OU: Uh, *(laughing fiercely)* we're old friends. *(Reflecting)* Since we were small, this big, *(indicating with his hand)* we've known each other.

PAI: Then I call him for you. *(Pointing to the lonesome building in the distance)* He live right in that house. *(He runs toward the homestead.)*

CH'OU *(harshly)*: Come back here!

PAI: Wha' . . . wha' for?

CH'OU *(extending his hand)*: Give the axe to me!

PAI: Axe?

CH'OU: I want to beat these bracelets off myself and give them to Chiao Ta-ma.

PAI *(again obstinate)*: But this axe belongs to Chiao . . . Chiao . . . Chiao Ta-ma.

CH'OU *(not waiting for him to finish, he walks ahead and grabs the axe)*: Give it here.

PAI *(cowering, he retreats)*: I! I won't! *(Ch'ou presses on.)*

CH'OU *(grabbing the axe, and pressing down on Pai's neck as if to chop his head off)*:   You . . . you dumb bastard.

(From the right side of the roadbed a woman's voice is heard; beside her is a man consoling her.)

PAI *(his face reddening from the effort to free himself)*:   There . . . there somebody!

CH'OU *(releasing him, listening for a moment; finally)*: Doggie, you can thank your lucky star.

PAI *(as if receiving an amnesty)*:   I can go?

CH'OU *(clutching him again)*:   Move, you're coming with me!

(Ch'ou pulls Pai toward the left edge of the pond; Pai follows helplessly. In a while one can hear a muted clash of axe and iron chains.)

(Two persons—a man and a woman—appear from the left side of the roadbed. The woman is in an angry mood, unwilling to speak even a single word; her eyebrows conceal a touch of wildness, and her gilded earrings jingle as they quiver. She is a bewitching woman—with crowblack hair, thick lips, long eyebrows, a pair of gleaming black eyes filled with seductiveness and stubbornness. Her face is rather heavy, and her darkish complexion has a healthy, brown glow. Her figure is not altogether tall, but elegant and graceful; as she walks she gazes self-confidently, sways continuously. She wears large, red trousers, and her hair is combed in a bun; the gilt bracelets on her wrist duplicate the oscillations of her gait. Her voice is very low, even muffled, but consummately agreeable, beguiling.)

(The man, Chiao Ta-hsing, is about thirty years of age and is dressed in a two-piece Chinese suit. His face is covered by a heavy moustache and beard, and very thick eyebrows; his eyes are sunken. His manner is open and his laugh candid and radiant, but his complexion is sallow and a certain melancholy shows on his brow; the blue veins on his forehead jerk from time to time. From his left ear hangs a brass earring—a kind of talisman given to him by his father to ward off evil spirits. He has a stalwart body,

and in his clear eyes there is so much passion he cannot express. He dreads his mother, but is infatuated with his beautiful wife; the conflict between his mother and wife has been a great cause of his distress, so much so that he is reduced to being a man without a mind of his own. Treading a long steady pace, he presently shoulders a large cloth bundle without difficulty. He wears a pair of dark-grey trousers, from which is suspended a silver watch chain, and he has donned a blue felt hat. In his hand he clutches a stick pared from a small tree; he follows Chiao Hua onstage.)

CHIAO TA-HSING: Chin-tzu!

(Chiao Hua ignores him, and continues to walk ahead.)

HSING *(pulling her)*:   Chin-tzu, stop a minute.

HUA *(pulling away from him)*:   What is it?

HSING *(imploringly)*:   Why don't you speak to me?

HUA *(scornfully)*:   Speak? Am I worthy of speaking to you?

HSING *(accommodatingly)*:   Chin-tzu, what's the matter now? Has someone offended you?

HUA *(standing on the railroad tracks)*:   Offended me? Who'd dare offend me! Hm! I'm Chiao Ta's wife, who'd dare?

HSING *(putting down the cloth bundle)*:   Now don't speak this way; let's talk this out before I go away.

HUA *(glancing at him obliquely)*:   Go away? Why bother? I think you'd better go straight back to your mama.

HSING *(half understanding)*:   What is it between you and Ma again?

HUA: There's nothing between us! *(Mockingly)* Huh, such a filial son you are! The way you acted before leaving her—telling her to eat this, and wear that—blah, blah, blah—as if the moment you're away some tiger would come and eat her up. Humph, why don't you turn your life around a few years, grow small like this *(showing with her hands)* so you can gurgle at your mama's breast!

HSING *(embarrassed; but trying to explain)*:   But Ma . . . Ma's blind!

HUA *(tilting her head to one side, viciously)*:   I know she's blind! *(Jeeringly)* Humph, Chiao Ta sure is an obedient son; Mama's this and Mama's that; bring this to Mama, bring that to Mama. Say, I think I should go to the yamen and ask for an arch in honor of your filial piety. *(Sighing intently)* Ay! If only I had a son. . . .

HSING *(startled)*:   What did you say? A son?

HUA *(casting him a glance)*:   Don't look so frightened. I only mean, if I had a son, now that we're married, a little Chiao Ta, I'd train him to be just as obedient as you are. Uh, a son just like you. *(Looking at Chiao Ta intently)* Exactly like you!

HSING *(thinking of scolding her, but then does not)*:   Chin-tzu, you always talk so crazy. There'll be trouble again if Mama hears about this.

HUA *(imperiously)*:   Huh, you're the one who's afraid of trouble! I'm not! You should be happy I just "talk crazy" now. Someday I might even do the way I talk.

HSING *(concerned)*:   What . . . what did you say you'll do?

HUA *(impulsively)*:   What will I do? I'm a fox-fairy! She says sooner or later I'll steal a man. You just watch, I'll make her words come true. Huh, a fox-fairy!

HSING *(unhappily)*:   What, you mean you'd have me see you're unfaithful, too?

HUA: If that's the way you treat me, I'll sleep. . . .

HSING *(standing up, and grabbing Hua's wrist; fiercely)*:   Sleep with who? With who?

HUA *(suddenly laughing giddily)*:   Now, don't you worry. I'll sleep with you, *(pointing at her husband's chest)* with you, my darling little boy, O.K.?

HSING *(laughing helplessly)*:   Chin-tzu, ay—between Mama and you—I really don't know what to do with the two of you.

HUA *(changing her mood)*:   Mama again, always your mama. How can you open and close your mouth and never talk of anyone but your mama? Your ma is your shadow, everywhere you go, she goes, too.

HSING *(sitting on the cloth bundle; sighing)*:   Funny, why is it women can't get along with one another?
(Frogs croak briefly in the pond; a gust of wind; from far away come the cries of wild birds.)

HUA *(abruptly pulling his hand)*:   Ta-hsing, do you love me?

HSING *(lifting his head)*:   What?

HUA *(sitting beside him)*:   Do you love me?

HSING *(bashfully)*:   I . . . of course I love you.

HUA *(sticking closer to him)*:   Then I'm going to ask you something, and when I'm finished you must tell me. And don't beat around the bush.

HSING: But what . . . what are you going to ask me?

HUA: Now never mind. Don't you really love me? Won't you answer my questions?

HSING *(shaking his head in assent)*:   Yes, yes, I will.

HUA *(pointing at his face)*:   Now promise me, I'll say it and then you answer right away. Don't stall!

HSING *(anxious to know)*:   All right, say it, quickly!

HUA: If I fell into the river——

HSING: Hm.

HUA: ——and your Mama also fell into the river——

HSING *(understanding gradually)*:   Uh.

HUA: ——and you were on the bank, which one would you rescue first?

HSING *(distressed)*: Which . . . which one would I rescue first?

HUA *(looking at him directly)*: Hm, which one would you rescue first, your Mama or me?

HSING: I . . . I—*(he lifts his head and looks at her)*.

HUA *(pressing him)*: Huh? Quick now, your mother, or me?

HSING *(anxious)*: But . . . but how could this be?

HUA: I know it couldn't be. *(Persistently)* But if it were, if it were, what would you do?

HSING *(smiling helplessly)*: This . . . this can't be.

HUA: Now don't muddle. I asked you, what if this were true?

HSING: If this were true, *(looking at her)* then . . . then . . .

HUA: Then, what?

HSING *(rapidly)*: Then I'd rescue both of you. *(Smiling)* I'd *(gesturing)* pull Mama in with my left hand, and pull you in with my right hand.

HUA: No, no good. I said you could only rescue one. So who would you rescue? *(Siren-like)* Me or your mama?

HSING *(exasperated)*: I . . . I . . .

HUA *(enraged)*: Of course you'd rescue your mother, not me.

HSING *(honestly)*: It's not that I wouldn't rescue you, but Ma's . . .

HUA *(disappointed)*: Blind! Right?

HSING *(looking at her pitiably)*: Uh. She's blind, she has to be rescued first.

HUA *(sticking up her mouth)*: All right, good, go ahead! *(Spitefully)* You want to see me drown, you wouldn't rescue me at all, not at all! O.K.! O.K.!

HSING *(trying to explain)*: But you *haven't* fallen into the river——

HUA *(starting her plaint)*: So, you want me dead. *(Angrily)* You're just like your mother. You both hope I die quick so you can marry another woman; that's what both of you want. You would rather see me drown.

HSING *(explaining)*: But I didn't say I wouldn't rescue you.

HUA *(inquiring urgently)*: Then, who would you rescue first?

HSING *(the same problem again)*: I'd . . . I'd first . . . I'd first . . .

HUA *(threatening)*: If you stall again, then it's all over for us.

HSING *(spurting out)*: I . . . I'd rescue you.

HUA *(amending him)*: You'd rescue me first.

HSING *(mechanically)*: I'd rescue you first.

HUA *(with her eyes flashing a ray of victory)*: You'd rescue me first! *(Pursuing his statement and changing her tone)* Me alone?

HSING *(dumbly)*: Uh.

HUA *(speaking a little more precisely)*: You'd *only* rescue me . . .

HSING *(unthinking)*: Uh.

HUA: Only me, not her.

HSING: But, Chin-tzu, that . . . that . . .

HUA *(compelling)*: You said it; you'd only rescue me and not her.

HSING *(standing up angrily)*: Why do you want to drown my mother?

HUA: Who wants to drown her? Isn't she still in one piece?

HSING *(unable to endure anymore)*: Why do you keep making me say these unbearable things?

HUA *(defiantly)*: Uh, I like to hear them, I like it. Go ahead, say it again.

HSING: But, say what?

HUA: Say "drown her"!

HSING *(deliberately backing off)*: Who?

HUA: Say "drown my mama"!

HSING *(looking at her frightened)*: What, drown . . .?

HUA *(urgently anticipating)*: Say it, and then I'll love you, I'll love you. *(Enticingly)* Say it, and whatever you want me to do, I'll do it. Look, I'll give you a kiss now. *(She hugs Hsing's face and warmly kisses him.)* Sweet?

HSING *(looking at her stupidly)*: You . . . uh!

HUA: Will you say it or not! Out with it! *(Pulling Hsing)* Sit down! *(Pushing him onto the cloth bundle)* Say it! Say you'd drown her! Drown mama!

HSING *(foolishly)*: I said, I won't say it!

HUA *(surprised)*: What! *(About to explode, but suddenly changing to a smile)* All right, all right, if you won't say it, then don't! *(Suddenly in a childish tone of voice)* Ta-hsing, do you love me? *(She sits on Hsing's lap, embraces his neck closely, puts her face against his, and cuddles and caresses him.)* Do you ache for me, do you love me?

HSING *(wanting to draw away from her, but is embraced snugly by her)*: Don't . . . don't be this way, people will see. *(He looks all about.)*

HUA: I don't care. I can do whatever I want with my husband. Who'd dare bother us? Ta-hsing, am I elegant? Am I beautiful?

HSING *(unconsciously staring at her)*: Yes, elegant! . . . beautiful!

HUA *(her serpent-like hand brushing his face, head, and hair)*: When you're away, do you think of me? Do you want me?

HSING *(involuntarily clutching her hand tightly)*: I do!

HUA *(more bewitchingly)*: Can you bear to part from me?

HSING *(licking his lips; hoarsely)*: I . . . can't . . . be . . . without you. *(Suddenly he turns about and embraces Hua; he wants to take hold of her, panting)* I . . .

HUA *(quickly forcing him away; smiling and raising her eyebrows slowly)*: If you can't be without me, then why don't you say it?

HSING *(confused)*: Say . . . say what?

HUA *(venting her malice)*: Say you would drown her, drown Mama.

(A gust of wind blows the telegraph lines so they whistle.)

HUA: Say it and I'll let you have me.

HSING *(sighing)*: All right, so—I'd drown her *(nearly sobbing)* and then I'd drown my—

(From behind the roadbed to the left appears a rugged, old woman, about sixty years of age. Most of her hair is streaked white, and on one temple is a purple scar; her facial features are notably precipitous and stern. She holds a heavy cudgel. Her eyes are wide open, but they are vacant, as there are no pupils; the fronts of her eyes appear to be covered with a white gauze, and she stares forward. No one can fathom what secrets are hidden in those pupilless eyes, but she has the suspicions of a sightless person, and a volatile temper. Her sharp ears are carefully attuned to sounds coming from any direction, and her voice is shrill and decisive. She still wears mourning clothes in respect for her husband—a grey outer garment covered by a black sleeveless blouse, grey trousers—and is remarkably neat from head to toe.)

(She walks onto the roadbed and, without a word, pounds heavily on the tracks.)

CHIAO SHIH *(coldly)*: Humph!

HUA *(startled)*:   Mother! *(She pushes Ta-hsing away instinctively and stands up.)*

HSING *(his erstwhile emotions instantly dissipated; unsteadily)*: Ah, Mama!

CHIAO *(sternly)*:   Hm, you fox-fairy! I knew you were here! What were you two talking about?

HUA *(falteringly)*:   No . . . nothing, Mother!

CHIAO: Ta-hsing, you tell me!

HSING *(indistinctly)*:   We . . . we didn't say anything.

CHIAO *(turns her head; spurting the words out through her teeth)*: You witch! Haven't you done enough with him at home? Why, you even drag him outside to bedevil him! Where's Ta-hsing? Why don't you speak up?

HSING *(alarmed)*:   Mama, I'm here,

CHIAO *(pointing her staff at him)*:   You stiff! What're you waiting for? Run, go to the station and start earning your keep. *(Brutally)* Do you mean to tell me you still want to die in the arms of this witch! You stiff! Haven't you seen enough what a woman is like? Why don't you just have your wife swallow you up like a rice ball? Old as I am, I've never seen a man the likes of you. You aren't worth the upbringing your dead father gave you!

HSING *(timidly)*:   Mama, *(glancing at Hua)* I'm going. *(Hua mutters something.)*

CHIAO: Go on! Go on! Beat it! Don't get me riled!— *(Suddenly)* Chin-tzu, what are you cussing about?

HUA *(hushing up)*:   Nothing! It's the wind blowing the telegraph lines, don't be so suspicious.

CHIAO: Huh! *(Pointing her stick at her, nearly spearing her eye)* Don't think that I'm blind; I'm as sharp as If I could see. Ta-hsing—

HSING: Mama, I'm here. I'm going now. *(He shoulders the large cloth bundle.)*

HUA: Ta-hsing, you go on!

CHIAO *(turning her head)*:   Never you mind! You want to cast another spell on him? *(To her own son)* Remember now, while you're away don't fool around with strangers. Eat and drink as much as you want, and think nothing about the cost. But, listen, don't gamble. Send whatever money you save to me and I'll keep it for your first-wife's son. Now let me tell you once more. Don't you ever let yourself be fooled by women. If a woman really wants to be with you, you don't need money to buy her. But if she doesn't want to be with you, you can't win her heart, even if you die for her. Do you understand me?

HSING: I understand.

CHIAO: Go on, then. *(Suddenly she throws out a bag of money, which falls at Hsing's feet.)* This here's my money, take it.

HSING: Ma, I still have some money.

CHIAO: Pick it up and take it with you, don't play games with me. I know what little money you've got you've used buying Chin-tzu bracelets and earrings. *(To Hua)* You witch!

HSING: All right, Ma, I'm going. Take good care of yourself. The train goes by the dooryard there, so don't go walking on the tracks anymore than you need to.

CHIAO *(hastily)*:   I know, I know, stop your jabbering. Go on.

HUA: Ha! Ma doesn't care about anything you say; so why don't you go on?

CHIAO: Who says so? Who says I don't care? He's my son, not yours. If he's got something good to say, I want to listen to him. D'you have to poke yourself into this? Ta-hsing, go on, go, go; stop flustering at my ears. Go on, quickly.

HSING: I'm going! *(In a low voice)* Chin-tzu, I'm going.
(Ta-hsing walks off to the right four or five steps.)

CHIAO *(suddenly)*:   Come back here!

HSING: What for?

CHIAO *(loudly)*:   You come back here! *(Hsing walks back dispiritedly.)* Where's the money I just gave you?

HSING *(holding it out)*:   It's here.

CHIAO *(extending her hands)*:   Give it to me, let me count it again. *(Hsing gives the pouch back to her; very nimbly she manipulates the money, calculating, muttering.)*

HUA *(looking at her fiercely)*:   Ma, don't worry! Ta-hsing wouldn't give it to me.

CHIAO *(finished counting, she gives the money to Ta-hsing)*:   Take it and go, quickly! *(Suddenly she turns on Chin-tzu; in a low voice and cruelly)* Humph! You lewd, cheating fox spirit.
(Ta-hsing walks step by step towards the right.)

CHIAO: What are you looking at?

HUA: Who's looking?

CHIAO: Is it dark?

HUA: Almost.

CHIAO: Doggie. *(Calling)* Doggie! Doggie! Doggie! *(No one answers.)*

HUA: What are you doing?

CHIAO *(to herself)*: · That's strange, it's dark, he should have brought that axe back here. Dumb bastard! I wonder where he's run off to again! Come on, let's go home!

HUA *(unmindful)*:   Uh, go home. *(Extending her hand)* Let me help you.

CHIAO *(casting aside her hand)*: Go! I don't want your help, or your phony courtesy!

(Chiao walks towards the left side of the tracks; Hua, not moving, stays behind. From far away on the right Pai Sha-tzu can again be heard to start up his "Chi-cha-ka-cha, chi-cha-ka-cha", very gleefully.)

CHIAO: Chin-tzu! Why haven't you come? What are you doing?

HUA *(noticing Pai Sha-tzu's curious behavior in the distance; then laughing out loud in spite of herself)*: Ma, listen, the locomotive is coming.

CHIAO *(morbidly)*: If you don't come along, just wait 'til the locomotive crushes you to death.

HUA: No. There isn't any locomotive. It's Doggie!

CHIAO: Doggie?

HUA: Uh.

("Tu-tu-tu-tu"-ing, the "train" runs in along the roadbed from the right; Pai Sha-tzu's hands gyrate rapidly and he bellows out the "wu-wu" of the steam whistle.)

CHIAO *(hearing it is Pai; imperatively)*: Doggie!

PAI *(glancing at Chiao Ta-ma, he squints; the "train" slows and gradually stops)*: "Tu - tu - tu - tu, tu — tu — tu — tu, tu — tu — tu — tu —".

CHIAO: Doggie, where'd you go off to?

PAI *(looking at Chiao, and then at Hua)*: I . . . din't go off nowhere.

CHIAO: What about the axe?

PAI *(recalling, but is confused)*: Axe?

HUA: What are you thinking about? She asked you where the axe is.

CHIAO *(harshly)*: What about the axe?

PAI *(fearfully)*: The axe, a . . . a man took . . . took it away.

CHIAO: What?

PAI: A lame . . . lame guy took . . . took it away.

CHIAO *(in a low voice)*: Come here.

PAI *(walking up to her uncomprehendingly)*: Wha' . . . wha' for?

CHIAO: Where are you?

PAI *(giggling)*: Here!

CHIAO *(judging from the direction of the voice she slaps Pai Sha-tzu on the face)*: You dumb bastard, take me to this lame guy!

PAI *(rubbing his face, bewildered)*: You hit . . . hit me!

CHIAO: So what? *(Sha-tzu starts to wail)* Are you going or not?

PAI: I . . . I go.

CHIAO: Move! *(She lifts up the end of the staff and hands it to Sha-tzu; then with him in front and the blind woman behind they move off towards the right.)*

(A gust of wind blows so the telegraph lines whistle; the giant tree stands loftily on the plain, its leaves soughing; the frogs begin to croak again on the bank of the pond.)

(Hua leans against the giant tree, gazing at the horizon—the red clouds in the sky are now transforming gradually into black thunderheads; the surrounding vista becomes obscured as darkness slowly falls; the earth turns black. She walks onto the roadbed, squats down, picks up a stone and raps lightly on the rail.)

(From the left, behind the roadbed, Ch'ou Hu crawls out stealthily on hands and knees. In his hand he holds the pair of irons he has broken off; slowly he moves behind Hua.)

HUA *(sensing there is someone near, she stands up suddenly)*: Who is it?

CH'OU: Me!

HUA *(scared)*:   Who are you?

CH'OU *(rubbing the chains between his hands; darkly)*:   Me!—
(Slowly) Don't you know me?

HUA *(startled)*:   No, I don't know you.

CH'OU *(gruffly)*:   Chin-tzu, you've forgotten me?

HUA *(pressing closer, she scrutinizes him and gasps in astonishment)*:   Ah!

CH'OU *(angrily)*:   Chin-tzu, I haven't forgotten you.

HUA: What, you . . . you're Ch'ou Hu.

CH'OU: That's right, *(intimidatingly)* Ch'ou Hu's come
back.

HUA *(looking all around)*:   What did you come back for?

CH'OU *(suggestively)*:   I came back to see you.

HUA: To see me? *(She chuckles uneasily.)* Why see me?
I'm already married.

CH'OU *(gravely)*:   I know, you married my good friend,
Chiao Ta.

HUA: Uh. *(Suddenly)* You . . . *(Pause)* Where did you
come from?

CH'OU *(pointing to the horizon)*:   From a far, far, faraway
place.

HUA: Did you come on the train?

CH'OU: Hm, *(in a forlorn tone)* "tu-tu-tu-tu", and after
a while I got here.

HUA: How did you get off? There's no station here.

CH'OU: I jumped out the window, *(pointing to the chains)*
bringing these. *(With a clank he casts the chains onto the bank
of the pond.)*

HUA *(somewhat fearful)*:   What? You . . . you were in
trouble with the law?

CH'OU: Uh! Take a look at me! *(Stepping back)* How do I look? Huh?

HUA *(not noticing until then)*: You . . . you're lame.

CH'OU: Yeah, lame. *(Suddenly)* Does it make your heart ache?

HUA: What if it does, and what if it doesn't?

CH'OU *(smiling wryly)*: If your heart aches for me you'll take me home, but if it doesn't, I'll take you away with me.

HUA *(suddenly defiant; wildly)*: You brute, go home and look at yourself in your own piss! If you don't watch out, the train will run you right over.

CH'OU: What did you call me?

HUA: A brute, and a lame and humpbacked short-lived demon, too.

CH'OU *(in sweet, honeyed words, but spoken sincerely)*: But Chin-tzu, you don't know how I've thought of you. I haven't died all these years only because of you.

HUA *(unoffended, she giggles)*: Then, why didn't you come back before?

CH'OU: It's not too late now. *(Pressing closer, he wants to take her hand.)*

HUA *(pushing him away)*: Go away! Go! Go! Save your breath, you brute. I don't want to listen to you.

CH'OU *(craftily)*: I know you don't want to listen, you're such a proper girl. But you can't stop me from speaking my true feelings.

HUA *(casting a glance at him)*: Say what you like, so what?

CH'OU *(solemnly)*: Chin-tzu, I've come back this time to take you away.

HUA *(looking at him askance, and planting hands on hips)*: Where would you take me?

CH'OU: To a far, far, faraway place.

HUA: A very faraway place?

CH'OU: That's right. Even on the train it takes seven days and seven nights. Gold covers the ground there, the houses can fly; open your mouth and people will fill you up with food. And as you pass on the road and open your eyes, you can see it fly backwards; every day's a holiday—you eat well, you dress well, and you drink well.

HUA *(her eyes shining with envy)*: There's no point in talking about it. I knew, I knew about that all along, but Hu-tzu, you can't—

CH'OU *(pressing her)*: Not another word; I know what you mean. Take a look at this first! *(He extracts a brilliantly lustrous ring from his bosom, the top of which is inlaid with precious stones; he raises it up high)* What is it?

HUA: What, *(very surprised)* it's gold!

CH'OU: That's right, this is real gold, and look, there's more in my pocket.

HUA *(rolling her eyes)*: So what? It's yours anyway. I don't care about it.

CH'OU *(deliberately)*: I know you don't care about it, you're a very proper girl. All right, let it go, then! *(He throws it into the pond.)*

HUA *(grieved)*: What . . . what'd you throw it away for?

CH'OU: If you don't care about it, what use is it to me?

HUA *(laughing)*: You brute! You really . . .

CH'OU *(immediately following)*: I really miss you, Chin-tzu, you're the only one in my heart! There're more to be had here, whether or not you want them.

HUA *(overbearingly)*: I don't want them.

CH'OU: If you don't want them, then I'll throw them away.

HUA *(stopping him quickly)*:   Hu-tzu, don't!

CH'OU: Then, do you love me or not?

HUA: What if I do and what if I don't?

CH'OU: If you do, you'll bring me home.

HUA: And if I don't?

CH'OU: I'll jump into this pit and drown myself!

HUA: Then . . . then go ahead!

CH'OU *(intentionally taking the opposite tack)*:   All right, I'll go! *(He runs behind Hua and is about to jump off.)*

HUA *(holding back Ch'ou)*:   What are you doing?

CH'OU *(turning his head)*:   Don't you want me to jump?

HUA: Who said so?

CH'OU: Ah, you don't—then, when are we gonna do it?

HUA *(shifting moods, she stops smiling)*:   Do what?

CH'OU *(taken aback)*:   Do what?

HUA: Hm?

CH'OU: Go . . . go up to your house, and I, we can—

HUA *(altering her manner once more)*:   What'd you say?

CH'OU *(noting her displeasure)*:   I said we could have a pleasant talk about that nice, nice place I come from!

HUA *(suddenly unable to hold back, laughing)*:   Oh, that! All right, tonight.

CH'OU: Tonight?

HUA: Yes, tonight.

CH'OU *(laughing)*:   I know, Chin-tzu, ever since you were small you've been a proper girl.

HUA *(suddenly hearing the sound of a staff probing the ground, she turns her head to see; nervously)*:   My ma's coming! Come with me quickly.

CH'OU: No, let me look at her first, and see how she's changed.

HUA: No! *(Taking hold of Ch'ou Hu)* Come with me.
(Ch'ou Hu hurriedly follows Hua offstage.)
(The sky is very black. Chiao walks in from the right, the axe in one hand, the staff in the other; Pai Sha-tzu follows behind.)

CHIAO: Chin-tzu! Chin-tzu!

PAI *(vindicating himself with vigor)*:   I knew he wouldn't take the axe away. When he got done, I'm sure he put the axe there. Look, ain't I right?

CHIAO: Shut up, Doggie! *(Sternly)* Chin-tzu, remember, this is the first night that Ta-hsing is gone, so tonight you have to be real careful about the doors and windows. If a thief gets inside and steals anything, *(cruelly)* I'll plunge a needle right through your eyes and make you as blind as I am, do you hear me?

PAI: Hee! Hee! Hee!

CHIAO: Doggie, what are you laughing for?

PAI: Your . . . your new bride, she's already . . . already gone.

CHIAO *(standing behind the roadbed, in front of the giant tree; austerely)*:   What? Already gone?
(Suddenly in the distance a train rushes by, creakingly with its whistle sounding. The searchlamp on the front of the engine, like the eye of a monster, with its light rays stretching to infinity, shoots in from the right; it moves closer and closer.)

PAI *(running to the side of the tracks; jumping and dancing; calling out)*:   Train! Train! Train's comin'!
(The noise of the engine increases, and gradually the searchlamp illuminates Chiao's entire right side.)

CHIAO *(standing under the giant tree like a corpse; mumbling)*:   Humph! That fox-fairy, let the train crush her to death!
(The hastening train, as though flying, races along the plain; the wind is intense! As the searchlamp spotlights Chiao beneath the giant tree we can see her white hair and blouse being tousled in the gale.)

(FAST CURTAIN)

ACT ONE

Ten days later near evening, in Hsing's home.

It is late in the day—on the earth are drawn dark, brown shadows. The window curtains have been pulled up, and gazing out, one can see a view of a vast plain, where dense clouds, deep and black, press low upon the horizon. There is no one in the room. Blowing the distant telegraph poles, the evening wind arouses a continual and fearsome whistling sound. Outside there is a flock of crows circling round and about . . . circling round and about . . ., screaming ceaselessly. And when the noise of the wind abates slightly, one can even hear the rapid flapping of the birds' wings in the air. Gradually the wind diminishes, the sunlight fades, and an autumn mist begins to rise outside, drowning the plain in its greyness. It is unknown what the thick fog conceals, for it is dim and quiet, noiseless. Occasionally one or two crows will cry out in the void, as the dense mist envelopes the dusky wilderness.

It is a front room, flanked by two side-doors; the main door opens to the outside where one can see a hedge in the foreground and the plain in the distance, with low clouds and black smoke about the railroad bed. There is a window on each side of the main door, both of which open outward and are supported by props. From low down you can see the color of the sky, and the giant tree. Immediately above the right window hangs an expansive, half-length oil portrait of Chiao Yen-wang. He wears a captain's uniform and has thick eyebrows, cruel eyes, a nose like an eagle's beak, and a well-groomed moustache and beard. He seems to smile affably, and yet his entire face shows a menacing character. To one side is suspended a rusty sword, and next to the left door stands a black incense table, on which lies a fearful, three-headed, six-armed Bodhisattva with gold eyes, *sitting cross-legged behind a red silk curtain. Beside it is placed a Chiao ancestral tablet. In front of the table there is a* mu-yü,* *a black incense burner, candlesticks, a red kneeling mat, and a set of enormous brass musical chimes, resting on a cotton cloth of faded scarlet. When Chiao kneels in meditation and raps upon it, it gives off a dark, heavy, hollow sound, which seems to come from the mouth of the Bodhisattva. There is half a stick of incense in the brazier, burning into ashes; it glows brightly, the Bodhisattva's black face gleaming in its illumination. As the candle's wax has already been exhausted—a stump is all that remains—only the holy lamp in front of the figurine gives forth a weak flame. Along the left wall a dark-red, old-style cupboard rises loftily, the top of it nearly touching the ceiling. It has two layers, both inlaid with huge, round pieces of brass, the top layer having an old yellow lock. On the door are stuck tattered pictures of Chung K'uei apprehending demons. In front of the right window there is a spinning wheel, and on the right, a child's cradle—the baby lying in it already fast asleep. On the dark walls are hung a few miscellaneous objects, and at the back stands a square table, surrounded by a few chairs and benches.*

As the curtain rises, there is the distant, urgent sound of a whistle. Faintly a train seems to be racing past, and as the wind blows, the crows in the sky cry out as a flock. There is no one in the room.

Gradually a man's coarse voice is heard from the room on the right, lowly singing: "In the first moon I visit my love, in the first moon, the first moon; we roam, my love and I, to look at flower lamps,† but the flower lamps are only false! I'm only trying at your heart, my love." *He intersperses the song with vulgar, low laughs.*

THE MAN'S VOICE FROM WITHIN *(huskily)*:   Chin-tzu! Chin-tzu! Come here!

A WOMAN'S VOICE FROM WITHIN *(quietly)*:   No, No!

---

* Lit., "wood-fish"; a skull-shaped block on which priests beat cadence while chanting.

† A nallusion to the Lantern Festival held during the first full moon of the lunar year, at which lanterns of all descriptions are displayed.

THE MAN'S VOICE FROM WITHIN *(coarsely)*:   Chin-tzu! Sit here! *(He apparently pulls her.)*

THE WOMAN'S VOICE FROM WITHIN *(breaking away)*:   Let go of me, let go, someone's coming! *(Suddenly freeing herself from him)* Someone's coming!

(Hua walks out from the right side. Her black hair hangs in strands upon her forehead, covering half her face, making her all the more seductive. She wears a red silk jacket and black satin trousers; her bun of hair is bound with red silk threads, and the gold-colored bracelets on her wrist jingle as they sway.)

HUA *(turning her face and laughing)*:   You repulsive brute! *(She straightens her clothing and rearranges the black hair on her forehead, but it hangs down again.)* Come out of there! *(Casually looking at herself for a moment in the mirror on the wall—so attractive! Her face beams with a smile. She walks to the open window on the left, holds her breath, and gazes out. The man within sings his little ditty again; she moves deftly to the door on the right; softly)* Stop singing! There's nobody outside, get a move on! Come out here!

(Ch'ou Hu walks out from the left. He has changed his costume to a long, black satin robe with a blood-red lining, tied at the waist with a belt of blue thread; the collar is open and only a few buttons are secured; he holds an old velvet hat in one hand and kneads a red flower with the other. He enters, limping.)

HUA: Go, it'll soon be dark,

CH'OU *(lifting his head and staring at the dense clouds in the distance)*:   It sure gets dark early here!

HUA: It's been autumn for nearly a month, go on! Go to your sworn brothers and find your lair with them; otherwise you'll freeze to death when winter comes.

CH'OU: Find my lair? This is my lair. *(Looking at Hua)* Wherever you are, that is my lair.

HUA *(softly)*:   And if I went away?

CH'OU *(throwing down his hat)*:   I'd go after you.

HUA *(fiercely)*:   And if I died?

CH'OU *(clutching Hua's hand)*:   I'd go with you into death!

HUA *(intently crying out in pain)*:   Ay! *(She tries to release her hand.)*

CH'OU: What's wrong?

HUA *(suggestively)*:   You hold me so tight!

CH'OU *(not loosening his hand)*:   Does it hurt?

HUA *(flashing a bewitching glance; in a low voice)*:   It hurts!

CH'OU *(smiles)*:   Hurts—? Then, more— *(He grasps her hand with force.)*

HUA *(shouting out in such pain)*:   What are you doing, you monster!

CH'OU *(from between his teeth)*:   May you be in pain, may you never in your whole life be able to forget me! *(With heavier pressure.)*

HUA *(in such pain tears nearly flow from her eyes)*:   You demon, let go of me.

CH'OU *(tightening still more; gritting his teeth; word by word)*: This is how I will hold you, tight to me; you won't escape for a lifetime. Wherever your soul may be, I will be there with you also.

HUA *(her face having turned blue)*:   Let go of me, you're killing me. You brute.

(Beads of sweat issue from Ch'ou Hu's face; he looks sufferingly at the convulsive contractions of Hua's face and slowly releases his hand.)

HUA *(her eyes inflamed; but moving not a fiber)*:   You demon, you—

CH'OU *(slowly turning about; facing Hua directly and stiffly; painfully)*:   Do you love me now or not?

HUA *(biting her lip, nodding)*: Yes! I do! *(Looking at him cruelly; slowly and in a low voice)* This—is—the way— I— *(suddenly towards—Ch'ou Hu's face—)* love you! *(Hitting him heavily)* Get out!

(Pause.)

CH'OU *(making no move, and fixing his eyes on her, gradually he bows his head. Walking over to the square table and sitting down; in a pensive mood)*: Humph! Women's hearts change— change so fast!

(Hua stands where she is, rubs her hand, but makes no response.)

CH'OU *(standing up; his eyes unblinking)*: Chin-tzu.

HUA *(glancing over without turning her head)*: What?

CH'OU *(lifting up the flower in his hand; looking at her askance)*: This is the flower you wanted; I went five miles* to find it for you. *(He hands it to her.)*

(Hua gives Ch'ou a glance, then turns her head away again, paying no attention.)

CH'OU: Pick it up! *(Throwing the flower in front of Hua)* I'm going. *(He walks toward the center door.)*

HUA *(suddenly)*: Come back and pick it up for me.

CH'OU: I have no time, pick it up yourself.

HUA *(commandingly)*: You pick it up for me.

CH'OU: I won't.

HUA *(smiling)*: Hu-tzu, you really won't pick it up, will you?

CH'OU: No, I won't. Are you going to kill me?

HUA *(walking up to Ch'ou's face and squinting at him)*: Who'd dare to kill you! I'm asking you, do you want me?

CH'OU: Me? *(Looking at Hua; unable to do anything but shake his head)*: I can't afford you!

---

* Lit., "fifteen *li*": one *li* is equivalent to approximately one third of an English mile.

HUA *(taken by surprise)*:   What?

CH'OU *(pressing her intently)*:   I don't want you!

HUA *(suddenly enraged)*:   What? You don't want me? You
don't want me? But why don't you want me? You brute,
you monster, you one-legged, humpback, fatheaded
demon, short-lived son of monkey, you cussed thief. This
wilderness has no one near you so vile,* you turkey . . .
(Her fists hit Ch'ou Hu's iron-like chest in a torrent.)

CH'OU *(withstanding her with his hands, but she pounds away as
before like a wild drummer)*:   Chin-tzu, Chin-tzu, put
down your hands! Don't shout, listen, someone's outside!

HUA: I don't care! I'm not afraid! *(Quickly; her hair
nearly coming unbound)* You brute, you monster, you don't
want me, how dare you say you don't want me! You
don't want me, why don't you want me, I'll hit you!
I'll hit you, I'll fight you! I don't care! I'm not afraid
if someone's out there!

(Someone is outside calling indistinctly: "Mrs. Ta-hsing! Mrs.
Ta-hsing!"*)*

CH'OU *(casting her aside, he runs to the window and gazes out)*:
Look, someone, someone's calling at the hedge gate!

HUA *(stops suddenly)*:   Who is it? *(Stepping rapidly along the
wall to the window)* Who could it be at this hour?

CH'OU: Stop yelling, listen!

*(There is an apparently drunken man singing bunglingly with a
voice like a broken gong*: "I went with my lover o'er yonder
gate, and I asked of my lover so plain, 'When will you
come back? Whether yes or no, just send me a note, so
I'll not worry for you.' " *He sings all but the last line and
then stops abruptly, raps upon the hedge gate, and calls out,* "Mrs.
Ta-hsing! Mrs. Ta-hsing! Open the gate!"*)*

---

* Lit., *shun*—a Peking dialectal word for which no Chinese graph has
been devised; the author uses the National Phonetic Alphabet to render the
phoneme in dialogue. *Shun* refers to a kind of ugly bird.

CH'OU: Listen, he's calling you!

HUA *(unable to see clearly; puzzled)*: Who is it? *(The man outside calls again,* "Mrs. Ta-hsing! Open the gate!"*)* Ah, it's him! The old fool's drunk too much again.

CH'OU: Who?

HUA: Ch'ang Wu!

CH'OU *(surprised)*: What, that old codger's not dead yet?

HUA: That's him all right. *(Disgusted)* I don't know what it is he's come here to spy on again.

CH'OU: Spy?

HUA: He's been coming around here the last couple days with no particular business to speak of. It could be Ma has put him up to spying on me, to see what I'm doing here!

CH'OU: All right, Chin-tzu, I'm going in, get rid of him fast.

HUA *(grabbing hold of him)*: Don't mind him, don't go now! *(Glancing at him)* Humph, so you're going away just like that, are you?

CH'OU *(understanding what she means; deliberately)*: What's the matter?

HUA *(pointing to the flower on the floor)*: Pick up the flower for me!

CH'OU: No, I won't.

(Outside there is an urgent knocking.)

HUA *(calmly)*: Listen!

CH'ANG WU OUTSIDE *(irritatedly)*: Mrs. Ta-hsing, Mrs. Ta-shing, open the gate! Open the gate! I'm coming in!

CH'OU *(listening intently, glancing at Chin-tzu)*: He wants to come in!

HUA *(unreasonably)*: If you don't pick it up, then I'll open the gate and let him come in and grab you.

CH'OU *(vehemently)*:   How vicious you are!

HUA: Vicious? Ha! My viciousness is yet to come!

CH'OU *(surprised)*:   "My viciousness is yet to come!" Good! It sounds like you're taking after me. *(He glances at her.)*

(Outside there is shouting again.)

HUA *(hands on hips)*:   Ch'ou Hu, are you going to pick it up or not?

CH'OU: Now look, *(bending)* it's not that . . . *(picking up the flower and handing it to Hua)* You asked me to pick it up, so I picked it up. What of it?

HUA *(grabbing the flower with one hand)*:   I know there's nothing to it. But that's just me: I want my way. *(Beckoning)* Come here!

CH'OU *(walking up to her)*:   What for?

HUA: Pin it on for me. *(Ch'ou Hu pins the flower on securely for her, but suddenly she embraces Ch'ou Hu strangely.)* You wild demon! My brute, you've made me suffer these ten days, you've made me suffer! I love you to the death, you rascal! *(While she talks, she kisses Ch'ou's neck and cheek with apparent unmindfulness.)* How could you say today you don't want me? Not 'til now did I know I was living; how could you say you don't want me? *(Kissing Ch'ou Hu longingly; indistinctly)* Uh—

CH'ANG WU OUTSIDE *(drawn out)*:   Mrs. Ta-hsing! What are you doing? Quick, open the gate!

HUA *(still embracing Ch'ou Hu; then closing her eyes and slowly pushing him away. Suddenly she turns around toward the center door and calls, one phrase at a time in a sustained manner)*:   Don't rush me, Uncle Ch'ang Wu. I'm chanting the sutras. Just wait a minute and I'll be finished.

(Ch'ang Wu outside sighs a long sigh.)

CH'OU *(rolling his eyes)*:   Chanting the sutras? What sutra?

HUA *(pushing him)*: Never mind, go on in, I'll deal with him. These last couple days my ma's been around a lot looking for him. I don't know what's in the head of this blind hag. Maybe I can sound out something from him. Listen quietly at the door, and watch how I get him to talk, just listen! *(While she speaks, she searches about for things and finds a half-embroidered child's shoe, a flat basket with tinfoil [for ritual sacrifice] mostly folded. She sets a volume of the sutras in place and straightens a chair; all in order, she enumerates the items, mumbling.)* The baby's shoes—the tinfoil, the flat basket—the sacrificial money—the chair, all's in order . . . *(Finding nothing in error; to Ch'ou Hu)* How about that?

CH'OU *(admiringly; lifting his thumb)*: Great! If I become an emperor, I'll appoint you my chief-of-staff.

HUA: All right, I'll go open the gate. Go on in the room there and start making out like a king. *(She slips quickly out through the center door.)*

(Pause.)

CH'OU *(looking all about him; then, his breast full of hate, he stares frozenly and directly at the half-length portrait of Chiao Yen-wang above the left-hand window. In a deep voice he forces his words through his teeth)*: Humph, what are you staring at me for? I'm your worthy friend. I gave you my word I'd come back and here I am. I haven't forgotten a one of the kindnesses you treated me to. It's been ten years! I've waited 'til my eyes wept blood; it's today I've been waiting for! Yen-wang, open your eyes wide and look at me again. *(Striking his chest)* Ch'ou Hu has come back. *(Pointing at the portrait)* Don't look askance at me, I've repaid your kindness, you old devil. The first thing I did when I came to your house was to sleep with your daughter-in-law! Huh, Yen-wang, aren't you ashamed? How can you still laugh at me? *(Maliciously)* You just wait, this is only the first blow! "My viciousness is yet to come", old devil, open up your eyes and look at me. I mean what I say. Today I'm returning your favors— *(suddenly hearing someone outside talking; he turns around for a glance; again he lifts his head towards Chiao Yen-wang and laughs evilly)* I go now to the room of your daughter-in-law to make out like an emperor. Ha!

(Ch'ou Hu goes into the room on the right. Immediately Hua appears via the center door, Ch'ang Wu following behind her. Ch'ang Wu is about sixty years old and a short, fat man. Hitherto he has passed through good times, and although he is not now as in the past, still he is quite content with his present station in life. Always garrulous and merry, he is never quiet and loves to brag. His memory is not good, and oftentimes he does not know what he is talking about. Nevertheless, he is quite straightforward and honest, and because he enjoys drinking, he speaks out foolishly and quite uninhibitedly about his former excesses. He was once something of a "squire's son"*, and even though he is no longer what he was, he still keeps to his old habits. His beard is very distinctive, and the top of his head is already showing. He carries a small bird cage, which, because it is late, he has covered with silk. Also, he wears an old and ragged, brass-colored satin robe with a vest. Being of high spirit and very agreeable temperament, he treats his bird and dog as he would his own son and daughter.)

(Having had a little evening wine to drink and being in an exhilarated state, he steps in through the center door.)

HUA: Come in, Uncle Ch'ang Wu!† *(Indicating the chairs next to the square table)* Please sit down.

CH'ANG: No, I'll say my piece and then go.

HUA: Well, then put down your bird cage and relax a bit.

CH'ANG *(laughingly)*: All right, I'll let my bird sit a while first, let her rest her legs, but I'm really not tired. *(He puts the bird on the table.)*

---

* Connoting an impractical, spoiled son, or spendthrift.

† "Uncle" is a term of respect here, rather than a term of family relationship.

Hua: I'll pour a cup of tea for you. *(She pours the tea.)*

Ch'ang: No, you don't need to, you don't need to. *(Suddenly thinking a moment)* But a cup of water might be good, for my bird here; she's been with me all day, and should drink some water. *(Hua hands the water to him. He takes it and pours it into the bird cage's basin as he talks.)* It sure isn't easy calling at your gate; really, what's the use of a lock on a hedge gate? All your mother-in-law's worries are just a lot of hullabaloo about nothing. I called for so long . . . Mrs. Ta-hsing, what were you doing? You said just now you— *(He suddenly sneezes, nearly spilling the water; he puts the cup on the table and chuckles to himself)* Ha, goodness! Ha, *(sneezing again)* ha, goodness gracious! *(Another)* Ha, goodness gracious alive.* See, these three sneezes make me an emperor.

Hua *(becoming nervous; calming herself for a moment; then titteringly)*: You're the emperor, and I'm your chief-of-staff.

Ch'ang *(taking the privileges of an elder)*: Yes, yes, I appoint you chief-of-staff of the Imperial Presence, to rule over my three palaces and six harems.

Hua: Uncle Ch'ang Wu, you must have caught a cold. I'll bring you some millet wine to chase the chill away.

Ch'ang: No, you don't need to, I just drank a few cups of evening wine. The weather turns cool during these fall mornings and evenings. And when people get on in years, it's a little hard to ward off this bit of cold. But, no matter, I'll be fine just to rest in this room a while. If I start drinking a lot, I'll get to talking, which doesn't matter much, but then again I won't be able to walk, I mean, I won't be able to get home.

Hua: What does it matter? Drink some wine, and if you have too much, I'll call Doggie to take you home.

* Lit., in order, *pai sui* ("one hundred years old", i.e. long life), *ch'ien sui* ("one thousand years old"; epithet for a brother of the emperor), and *wan sui* ("ten thousand years old"; epithet for the emperor).

CH'ANG (*looking at Hua; he wants to drink but is a little hesitant; in an embarrassed way*): So, you want me to have a couple?

HUA (*beguiling him*): We have an excellent Fen-chiu in the house, which we saved from the wedding. Uncle Ch'ang Wu, do have a few cups.

CH'ANG (*very accommodating*): All right then, I'll have a cup!

HUA: Good, (*preparing the cups and wine*) have a seat!

CH'ANG (*sitting next to the square table*): Mrs. Ta-hsing, what was it you said you . . . you were chanting?

HUA: Ah, just now? I was chanting the sutras. (*She puts down the cup.*)

CH'ANG: Chanting the sutras?

HUA: Uh-huh! (*She pours the wine.*)

CH'ANG (*taking out a handful of peanuts from the purse at his waist*): By good fortune, I just bought a bag of peanuts. (*He sips a mouthful of wine, and shucks the peanuts.*)

HUA (*bowing her head, and gathering her eyebrows*): Excuse me, Uncle Ch'ang Wu! (*She walks to the incense table, kneels on the red mat and kowtowing once, starts to pray. Rapping the musical chimes and softly striking the* mu-yü, *she reverently intones.*) "Namo, omitopoya,* totagatoya, todiyata, omilido popi, omiyado, sidanpopi, omilido, pigalandi, omilido, pigalando . . ."

CH'ANG (*curious; standing up and approaching Hua*): What are you chanting?

HUA (*shaking her hand, more devoutly*): " . . . gamini, gagana, jidogalirapoko." (*She raps twice again on the musical chimes and bows deeply three times; then she stands majestically.*) Uncle Ch'ang Wu!

---

* "I put my trust in Amida Buddha. . . ."

CH'ANG *(with deep respect)*:   You mean you were chanting this before I came?

HUA: Yes.

CH'ANG: What is it?

HUA: I'm chanting a Buddhist prayer to release the soul of my father-in-law from suffering!

CH'ANG *(smacking his lips in admiration, and shaking his head; praisingly)*: So filial a daughter-in-law, you want to release Yen-wang's soul from suffering?

HUA *(her face filled with kindness)*:   My father-in-law murdered people when he was alive.

CH'ANG *(laughing candidly)*:   Well, go ahead, but I don't think it'll be of any use. Yen-wang really should go to Hell and boil in the cauldron of oil just the same.

HUA: Yo, Buddha! What are you saying? How can we children listen to such a thing?

CH'ANG: Pardon me, pardon me! Mrs. Ta-hsing, Yen-wang was a friend of mine for twenty years, but what I say is true nonetheless. *(Shucking a peanut)* Your ma hasn't come back yet?

HUA: She's been going out in the afternoon these past few days. She won't be back 'til dark.

CH'ANG *(suggestively)*:   Do you know what she's doing?

HUA *(docilely)*:   The affairs of an elder. We of the younger generation dare not ask about the affairs of our elders. *(Inquisitively)* But I've heard that she often goes to see the old nun at the temple, who can tell fortunes by incense and put people to death with a curse.

CH'ANG *(drinking a mouthful of wine)*:   I saw her in the temple, too. Strange, what's she doing there with the nun? Chanting and muttering God knows what. There's something I just can't figure about the Chiao family. On the outside everything looks fine, but I just can't tell what act you're putting on inside. I don't like to see this—of course, Chin-tzu, you're an exception; you're a decent and proper girl. Still, you must be careful, you're very young, and you've grown as pretty as a flower; if you're not careful, you'll be—uh, Ta-hsing still hasn't come back yet?

HUA *(gravely vigilant, looking at him)*:   He's just been gone for two days. How could he be back so soon?

CH'ANG *(looking all around, in a low voice)*:   Mrs. Ta-hsing, let me ask you something. How does your mother-in-law treat you?

HUA: Ah, *(blinking her eyes, calculating inwardly)* you're asking me how my mother-in-law treats me?

CH'ANG: Eh?

HUA *(crisply)*:   Well, of course; she treats me very well! She treats me exactly the way she would treat her own children.

CH'ANG *(coughing)*:   But I . . . I always feel there's some kind of disagreement between you.

HUA: Who said so? *(Taking the baby's shoe in hand and starting to sew)* We've had peaceful days together; who would say such a thing?

CH'ANG *(coughing again, and shaking his head)*:   Strange, strange, there's no way of understanding your family. You speak well of your mother-in-law, and your mother-in-law's spoken well of you, too, the last couple days. But in the background, in the background there's always— *(Suddenly shaking his head)* Well, I'd better keep my mouth shut.

HUA *(putting down her needle and thread; laughing)*:   Say it, Uncle Ch'ang Wu. *(Looking at him stealthily)* What's to fear in speaking of family matters?

CH'ANG *(gradually becoming more inebriated)*:   No, no, it's no good. If I say anything, I'll just be a big gossip. My long tongue—I really don't want to meddle in other people's business.

HUA: Uncle Ch'ang Wu, *(walking to the square table)* you're not a stranger. I'm young, I've just become a daughter-in-law; if anything's wrong and you don't come and guide me, who else will do it? Come, *(pouring a cup of wine)* Uncle Ch'ang Wu, have another cup.

CH'ANG *(all smiles)*: All right, all right, I'll drink, I'll drink.

HUA: Uh, *(expectantly)* Uncle Ch'ang Wu, what did you say my mother-in-law is doing behind my back?

CH'ANG *(looking at her)*: Your mother-in-law's asked me —uh, I think I'd better not say. If I do, your mother-in-law will complain.

HUA *(stopping; angrily)*: All right, if you won't say, then don't say. *(She walks back again to pick up the needle and thread.)*

CH'ANG *(timidly)*: You want me to say it?

HUA *(all smiles again)*: As you like, Uncle Ch'ang Wu.

CH'ANG *(unable to hold it in any longer)*: All right, all right. I'll say it. I'll say it, *(babblingly)* but remember, you made me say it.

HUA *(doing her needlework)*: Uncle Ch'ang Wu, I couldn't make you say anything.

CH'ANG: All right, all right, I'm saying it of my own free will. I tell you, I'm not making mischief. But your mother-in-law told me to watch you.

HUA *(coughing; slowly)*: Ah, you see. *(Bitterly)* How she cares for me!

CH'ANG: Not to look after you, you heard me wrong, it's to watch you. She said that lately there's suddenly been some—some kind of trouble in your house.

HUA: Ah! *(Alert)* Trouble?

CH'ANG: Eh, some trouble. She said she's alone and blind, and that's why she's worried.

HUA: What trouble in the house?

CH'ANG: That's what she said. But I can see *(looking all around)* everything's very nice and quiet. How could a virtuous bride like you hide a man in her house?

HUA *(rolling her eyes)*:   Eh, well, but you just can't tell.

CH'ANG *(startled)*:   What?

HUA *(warning him)*:   Aren't you the first one to believe her and come running to our house to investigate?

CH'ANG *(blushing)*:   Heh, how could you say this? Who says I believe her? *(Pointing)* Her words go in one ear and out the other. Heh, how could you say this!

HUA *(slowly)*:   It's good that you don't believe her. You are a respected and virtuous man; one word from you is worth ten thousand from any of us.

CH'ANG *(stroking his beard)*:   You're right. I always speak the truth. A virtuous wife like you, chanting the sutras and keeping the house all alone, is truly one in a thousand, one in ten thousand.

HUA: You're too kind. Uncle Ch'ang Wu, have another cup.

CH'ANG: All right, all right, I'll help myself.

HUA *(purposely startled)*:   Goodness, the wine is cool, look at me, really! I'll heat it up for you.

CH'ANG *(more pleased)*:   No need, no need. It's fine, it's fine. Chin-tzu, you really are a good daughter-in-law, intelligent and understanding, and obedient. Huh, if my son had married such a bride, I would have no regret when I die *(Having another half-cup of wine)* Later, Chin-tzu, when Ta-hsing comes back, I certainly must say a few kind words on your behalf.

HUA *(surprised)*:   What, what did you say?

CH'ANG *(staring at her fixedly)*:   I mean, I want to say a few kind words.

HUA *(anxiously)*:   Did you say Ta-hsing will be back in a while?

CH'ANG: Uh? You didn't know— *(Suddenly realizing)* Ah! *(Knocking his head)* Your mother-in-law told me not to tell you. But I let it out again. It's not my fault, though. *(Excusing himself)* When I drink a little, I talk a lot, what can I do?

HUA *(taken unaware)*:   Who told him to come back?

CH'ANG *(indiscreetly)*:   I did, of course! No, it was your mother-in-law! She had me go and tell Ta-hsing to hurry home.

HUA: So you told him to come back?

CH'ANG *(resignedly)*:   Uh, what could I do? It's all because I'm so easy-going and talkative! If you'd told me to go, I would've gone just the same, you . . . you can't blame me for this either.

HUA *(restraining her laugh)*:   Ta-hsing's coming home is good news, why would I blame you? Ah, *(apparently casual)* Ta-hsing didn't say exactly when he'd be back, did he?

CH'ANG: No, he didn't. Maybe tonight, maybe tomorrow night, and then again maybe this very minute.

HUA: Ah! *(Deep in thought)* Darn, this needle doesn't work at all. Ah, when my mother-in-law told you to do this, didn't she ask you to carry some message?

CH'ANG: She didn't . . . didn't say anything in particular. She only said it was very noisy in the house, as though someone had gone in during the night.

HUA *(startled, turning pale)*:   Oh, someone came in? *(The needle pricks her thumb; crying out in pain)* Yo! *(She puts down the needle and thread.)*

CH'ANG: What's the matter?

HUA: The needle pricked my hand, it's nothing! Hm, *(quietly)* who could that be?

CH'ANG: That's what she said! She said she wanted Ta-hsing to hurry back, that there had to be someone who could see in the house, and only then could she find out.

HUA *(again picking up the needle and thread, chuckling)*: Am I not able to see?

CH'ANG: That's what I said! Look, *(pointing at her)* don't you have eyes? *(Pointing to himself)* And don't I have eyes? Really, what she says is topsy-turvy, she's talking a lot of nonsense. Your mother-in-law's blind and she's *so* suspicious. You just can't help it.

HUA: Do you think, *(lifting her head)* my mother-in-law might be a little crazy?

CH'ANG *(very definitely)*: Uh, yes! Yes! A little!

HUA: That in the middle . . . the middle of the night someone would come into the house, isn't that gibberish!

CH'ANG: Uh, gibberish! Who would believe it? But Chin-tzu, you must still be careful, you're young, and pretty. Besides, you haven't any neighbors around— *(He suddenly coughs, looks all around, coughs heavily again.)*

HUA: What's the matter?

CH'ANG *(in a low, secret voice)*: Do you—you have somebody in the house?

HUA *(apprehensive)*: Somebody?

CH'ANG: It's strange, there's something peculiar about this room. I have to ask you, are you hiding someone in the house?

HUA *(maddening)*: Hiding who? In broad daylight, me, a woman, who would I be hiding?

CH'ANG: Who said it was you? Mrs. Ta-hsing, I think if you haven't been careful enough, some robbers might've slipped in.

HUA: Robbers? Would robbers dare to steal into the house of Yen-wang?

CH'ANG: Chin-tzu, don't you know about this robber who's come around looking specially for your house?

HUA: No, who could that be?

CH'ANG *(pointing to Hua's embroidery work)*: Who? I ask you, what are you embroidering?

HUA: The baby's shoes.

CH'ANG: No, I mean your embroidery pattern?

HUA: Oh, this?—a tiger?

CH'ANG *(in a low voice)*: That's him—the tiger's come back!

HUA: Tiger? Who's that?

CH'ANG: Don't you understand? The tiger! Ch'ou Hu's come back!

HUA *(pretending ignorance)*: Ch'ou Hu? What about this Ch'ou Hu?

CH'ANG *(amazed)*: Don't you know? Ch'ou Hu? You almost married him, how could you *not* know?

HUA: Uncle Ch'ang Wu, drink, just drink, don't talk such nonsense.

CH'ANG: But it's true! Some ten years ago your papa had you engaged to Chou Hu!

HUA: Oh?

CH'ANG: Later on, Ch'ou Hu's family fell into some bad luck and was brought to court, so he changed his mind and married you to Yen-wang's son. Such an important matter, and yet you know nothing of it?

HUA: When my parents were living they never mentioned it.

CH'ANG: I'm telling you, this time Ch'ou Hu's come back to settle his accounts with your Chiao family. So you mustn't provoke him. Your father-in-law ruined him and his family, and the great wrongs that Yen-wang inflicted you people'll have to pay for now.

HUA: Isn't Ta-hsing coming back?

CH'ANG *(picking up the bird cage)*: Yes, yes, but he's not going to be any help either, is he? The nincompoop, how can he stand up to Ch'ou Hu? *(Suddenly turning his head)* Have you seen Ch'ou Hu?

HUA: No. Have you ever seen him?

CH'ANG: I should say. I tell you, if you want to see something ugly, he's it—humpbacked, with a face like the God o' Kitchen's. And he's so gross—his body's covered with black hair. If you see him, let me know; we'll hand him over to the posse for a big reward, you hear?

HUA: Yes, of course. Are you leaving?

CH'ANG *(walking to the door; thinking; in a low voice)*: Do you know who told me that Ch'ou Hu's come back?

HUA: Who?

CH'ANG: Your mother-in-law.

HUA *(alarmed)*: What, she! How did she know?

CH'ANG: She said people on the railroad told her. She said Ch'ou Hu was hiding around here, and that a posse was looking for him.

HUA: Oh! *(The baby cries out.)* Uncle Ch'ang Wu, the baby just woke up. I need to look after him, so I can't see you out. *(She walks to the cradle and lightly rocks it.)*

CH'ANG: Oh, the baby! *(Walking to the side of the cradle)* Huh, this child certainly looks like his dead mother, very pitiably the same. *(Yawns)* I'm going now. *(Walking to the door)* Oh, Chin-tzu, take advantage of your mother-in-law's being away and fill up that wine bottle with water. Don't say I was here drinking free wine. And I haven't said anything while I was here, you hear? Hee. Hee. *(He opens the door; outside it is covered over with an autumn fog.)* Ha, what weather, the mist comes up so unexpected.

(Ch'ang Wu picks up the bird cage and walks exuberantly out of the center door. As he goes you can hear him singing, "I went with my lover o'er yonder gate . . .")

(The child is no longer crying; Hua walks hurriedly to the window and gazes out; suddenly she walks to the right door.)

HUA: Ch'ou Hu! Ch'ou Hu!

(Ch'ou Hu walks out by the right door.)

CH'OU *(exasperated)*: Is he gone?

HUA: He's gone. *(Staring at Ch'ou Hu's face)* Did you hear it all?

CH'OU: Every word. *(Sullenly)* It's better they know I've come back. *(Looking at Yen-wang's portrait)* Yen-wang, you hurt me once, and you can hurt me again. Come on! Ch'ou Hu is waiting to die!

HUA: Waiting to die? Waiting to die? *(Fidgeting, she mumbles.)* Why waiting to die? *(Shaking her head)* No! No! No! We, we must— *(Slowly lifting her head and looking up; suddenly—)* Ch'ou Hu, Ch'ou Hu! Look, look . . .

CH'OU: What?

HUA *(running to Ch'ou Hu's side)*: Look! *(Calling out frighteningly)* Look, look up.

CH'OU: What?

(Outside the sky is darker.)

HUA: The portrait! The portrait! *(Turning pale)* He's looking at me, he's looking at me!

CH'OU: Who?

HUA *(bowing her head; and shrinking in upon herself)*: Yen-wang, Yen-wang's eyes were moving, —he—he lives, he lives!

CH'OU *(embracing Hua; looking at Chiao Yen-wang's portrait in the darkness)*: Nonsense! Nonsense! It's just a painting, don't scare yourself.

HUA: It's true! It's true! *(Gradually recovering her discernment)* Hu-tzu, didn't you see it? It's true, I really saw him laugh at me just now; he called to me . . .

CH'OU: Phooey! *(Spitting into the air)* Yen-wang, if you really live, come on down, Ch'ou Hu is waiting for you! *(Pushing Hua)* Look, does he still move or not?

HUA *(lifting her head stealthily and looking again)*:   He . . . he's not moving anymore.

CH'OU *(warning her)*:   From now on, Chin-tzu, don't cry out so foolishly.

HUA: I haven't before, but just now I really saw—

CH'OU: Chin-tzu, don't say it again.

HUA: Hu-tzu, I . . . I'm a little scared. Hu-tzu, go to the window and take a look.

CH'OU: What is it? *(Walking to the window and looking out)* I don't see anything out there, it's so foggy.

HUA: Foggy?

CH'OU: Uh, very foggy.

HUA *(vacantly)*:   I'm so scared!

CH'OU: Scared of what?

HUA *(in deep thought)*:   I'm scared because my mother-in-law has called Ta-hsing back!

CH'OU: Huh?

HUA *(lost in thought)*:   I don't know what she's going to tell Ta-hsing.

CH'OU: Humph, what more has he to say? He took you away from me.

HUA *(bowing her head)*:   No, it wasn't him, it was his papa. He didn't want me at all at first.

CH'OU: Humph.

HUA: Hu-tzu, go now, go quickly, don't let him see you when he comes back.

CH'OU: All right, I'll go. But, Chin-tzu, don't forget what you said to me just now . . .

HUA *(lifting her head)*: What?

CH'OU: You said you wanted to leave this place.

HUA: Yes . . . I want to go away. When autumn comes it gets so very foggy here. There's just my blind mother-in-law and me, and she hates me, and I hate her. Ta-hsing's just a ninny, he's useless. He's a mama's boy, not my husband.

(From far away in the fog comes the sound of a train whistle; a rushing train gradually approaches from the distance.)

CH'OU: Chin-tzu, where do you want to go?

HUA: Far, *(longingly)* far, far away— *(supporting her lower jaw)* that place you talked about where gold covers the ground.

CH'OU *(smiling sadly)*: Gold? I was only fooling about that.

HUA *(shaking her head)*: No, you don't know, there is such a place. People've told me. There is such a place! I've dreamed about it.

CH'OU: Chin-tzu, when Ta-hsing comes back—

(Gradually the train in the fog moves farther and farther away; distantly there sounds a remote, sharp whistle.)

HUA *(day-dreaming)*: Don't talk, listen. You ride on the train to go there. "Tu-tu-tu-tu, tu-tu-tu-tu", you ride the train and go straight away, go and go and go, way over the horizon. Humph, I'd die rather than stay here.

CH'OU: Chin-tzu, you know, when Ta-hsing comes back—

HUA *(suddenly)*: D'you remember when we were small? When one day I was combing my two shiny pigtails and reeling thread under that little window back home, waiting for you?

CH'OU *(his eyes brightening)*:   Eh, my father was still living
then, and every day I'd tend cattle and look after the
fields with him.

HUA: I still remember the song I used to sing when I was
reeling the thread: "The barley is green and glossy, the
red sorghum spreads over the hilltop, I still cannot see
you from the window, my heart is so sad, so—"

CH'OU *(suddenly toughened up)*:   Stop it, have you forgotten
that Ta-hsing's coming back?

HUA *(awakened from her reminiscing)*:   Uh, yes, yes. Hu-tzu,
go, quickly.

CH'OU: Chin-tzu, do you really want to go away?

HUA *(recovering her usual vigorous manner)*:   You think I'm
lying?

CH'OU: Then I'll be back later.

HUA: Later? No, you can't! Ta-hsing might be back soon.

CH'OU: Oh?

HUA: And the blind one's sure to be home.

CH'OU: So what?

HUA: So what? She'll take you right to the posse, and
you'll have to go back just like you ran away.

CH'OU: Humph, *(in deep thought)* that blind hag! Blind
hag! *(Sitting down determined)* I won't go then! What can
she do to me?

HUA *(grabbing Ch'ou's arm)*:   What're you going to do?

CH'OU *(standing up suddenly)*:   All right, we'll just go on
back to the room there and sit a while, have some more
good time together. *(He pulls Hua's hand.)*

HUA: No, go, don't be crazy!

CH'OU (*turning his head toward the center door*): Ha! That blind hag and I are a good match, like a long grub meetin' a long centipede. I'm gonna tell her now that Ch'ou Hu is here, 'cause I've come openly and I'm not sneaking away. I'm telling her out straight, so she'll be ready.

HUA: No, no, Hu-tzu, you must listen to me, listen to me—listen—listen to my—

(*The center door opens slowly and Hua fearfully turns her head around. Chiao, supported by a staff, walks in, her face looking as if it is covered with a layer of heavy frost. She stands silently in the doorway, holding a red cloth-wrapper in her hand. Her ears seem to substitute for her eyes in detecting her surroundings.*)

HUA (*sighing a long sigh*): Oh, Mama.

(*Ch'ou Hu stops where he is.*)

CHIAO (*coldly*): Humph, what are you chattering about?

(*A pause; Ch'ou Hu thinks of strutting towards Chiao, but Hua gestures hastily, begging him quickly to enter the door on the right.*)

(*Ch'ou looks at Chiao, then at Hua, and then walks off toward the right.*)

CHIAO (*suddenly*): Stop! (*Ch'ou stops abruptly where he is.*) Who is that?

HUA: Who is that? (*Laughing anxiously*) It's me! (*She suddenly affects embracing the baby; as she walks she sings a lullaby.*) Oo—oo—oo! Be . . . be good now, oo—oo—oo! (*Looking beseechingly at Ch'ou Hu who again wants to approach Chiao*) You little precious, you must be good now. (*Glancing once more at Chiao*) Be good now and sleep, oo—oo—oo! (*Looking at Ch'ou Hu*) Someone loves you, you good, precious little one, oo—oo—oo! (*She turns and sees Ch'ou Hu stepping through the right door. Her strained face has a slight smile as she looks toward Ch'ou Hu's receding image.*)

Good, baby, good, oo—oo—oo! *(Looking at Chiao)* You good, precious little one, you're falling asleep now, oo—oo—oo.

CHIAO *(listening carefully for a moment; suddenly)* :   Chin-tzu, what are you doing?

HUA :   I'm just comforting the baby! *(In a low voice; the "baby" gradually falls into slumber)* Oo—oo.

CHIAO :   Comforting the baby?

HUA :   Ma, hold your voice down a little. The baby just fell asleep! *(More gently)* Oo—oo—oo.

CHIAO *(realizing her deception, and pointing to the cradle in front of the window)* :   Huh, the baby's over here, I know, my dear! *(She is about to walk towards the cradle.)*

HUA *(concealing)* :   I just picked up the baby, you didn't see.

CHIAO *(unable to do anything; sternly)* :   Your mother be damned! What are you doing leaning against the edge of the table?

HUA *(resolutely)* :   I'm thirsty, I'm going to drink some water now.

CHIAO :   Drink what, there's no water on the table!

HUA *(not realizing she knew that clearly)* :   Uh, no—there isn't—but—

CHIAO *(putting her head awry)* :   Your mouth is full of fox-spirit lies! *(Coldly)* Come here.

HUA *(slowly)* :   Yes! *(Defiantly, yet leisurely, she adjusts the flower inserted upon her head.)*

CHIAO *(walking to the incense table and putting the red cloth-wrapper upon it)* :   Come here!

HUA *(looking furiously at Chiao; softly)* :   Coming.

CHIAO: Come, quickly. *(Pounding her staff reverberantly on the floor)* Come here! *(She sits on a chair next to the incense table.)*

HUA *(coldly)*: You want to scare the baby? *(She walks toward her.)*

CHIAO: I'm touched indeed! *(Pointing to the cradle)* He's not your son.

HUA: Yes, Ma. *(Dragging herself to Chiao's side)* Ma, I'm here.

CHIAO *(pulling at her hand)*: Let me feel you.

HUA *(startled, but—)*: Go ahead!

CHIAO: What are you wearing?

HUA *(looking straight ahead)*: A large red jacket and black satin trousers. *(Emphatically)* Ta-hsing had them made for me for the holiday.

CHIAO *(hatefully)*: Ah, what's on your hand?

HUA *(looking askance)*: A gold-plated bracelet! And a silver ring! Ta-hsing bought them for me during the holiday.

CHIAO *(detestfully)*: Humph! *(Exploring her head and feeling Ch'ou Hu's flower; suddenly)* Oh, what's this?

HUA *(unable to help feeling frightened)*: This?—a flower, Ma.

CHIAO *(pressing her closer)*: A flower? Who gave it to you? Who gave it to you?

HUA *(rolling her eyes)*: Who gave it to me? *(Intentionally counter-questioning)* Ha, did it fall from the sky? Did it bore its way out of the earth? *(Looking askance)* I bought it at the gate all by myself.

CHIAO *(having been counter-attacked, but still there comes a peculiar burst of fire)*: You bought it? What'd you buy this for?

HUA *(looking at her)*:   I dreamed yesterday that **Ta-hsing** had come back home—

CHIAO: Who told you Ta-hsing was coming back home?

HUA: No one told me, didn't I say I dreamed it?

CHIAO: Dreamed it, dreamed what?

HUA: That Ta-hsing came to the gate and took a bad fall there; and after that I began wearing a red flower, for good luck.

CHIAO: Humph, you have a dream, and then you want to wear some flower! Throw it away! Don't you wear it again 'til I'm dead. Since Ta-hsing married you his soul still hasn't come back to him, and now you want to bewitch him even more by wearing flowers. Throw it away!

HUA *(with delay)*:   Oh! *(Looking at Chiao's stern countenance, she takes down the flower.)*

CHIAO *(sternly)*:   Where did you throw it?

HUA *(helpless; casting the flower at her feet and glancing at Chiao poisonously)*:   At your feet. *(Giving an indication with her foot)* Here!

CHIAO *(rising suddenly and trampling upon the red flower fiercely)*:   Now wear it! Wear it! *(Bending and picking up the flower)* Take it and wear it! *(Taking the crushed flower and tossing it at Hua, hitting Hua right in the face)* You shameless bitch, go ahead, wear it! Bring it along with you to marry the King of Hell.

HUA *(being so angry her face has turned blue; cowering to one side, gritting her teeth, and in a mumble)*:   If I ever become the King of Hell's wife, the first thing I'd do is send big-headed demons after you, you old hag!

CHIAO *(not hearing clearly)*:   You're muttering something again?

HUA: I was muttering how good my mother-in-law is, that for as long as you live the King of Hell will never invite you to a feast.*

CHIAO *(guessing the meaning)*: Oh, I'll not die, my witch. You just wait, I shall live as long as Heaven lives. Your curses will not make me die. I'll take all of you into your coffins.

(Distantly a train roars along the roadbed in the wilderness, its whistle ceaselessly wailing.)

HUA: Ma, listen! Listen! *(She looks at Chiao.)*
(The train whistle sounds in the distance.)

CHIAO: Listen to what? Chin-tzu, your mind's flying again; you want to ride the train, fly over the horizon and die there.

HUA: Who says I do? *(Thinking hastily of a way to make her leave)* Don't you want to ride away? Look at the train, flying in the fog, isn't it beautiful?

CHIAO *(pounding the floor with her staff)*: How can I see? I ask you, how can I see?

HUA *(remembering; making excuses)*: Didn't—didn't you say that even blind you could see better than anybody with eyes?

CHIAO *(hinting)*: Oh, I can see better, I can see that you're a calamity for the Chiao family; that your heart changes eighteen ways in a single day. I'm telling you, the train is a dragon that spouts poisonous fire; one day he's going to eat you up, and take you to face Buddha in the Western Heaven.

HUA *(disgusted)*: Don't you want something to drink? How about a bowl of tea?

CHIAO: No you don't, I'll get it myself. Stop putting on airs with me. I don't want any of your put-ons.

---

* That is, you will never die.

HUA: Well then, I'll go back to my room.

CHIAO: Go. *(Hua rapidly walks half-way to the door.)* Wait, Chin-tzu, I want to ask you something.

HUA: Yes, Ma?

CHIAO *(slowly)*: What kind of sounds have you been making in your sleep these last couple nights?

HUA: What do you mean?

CHIAO: During the night, what were you mumbling about all alone here in the house?

HUA: Ma? I wasn't mumbling.

CHIAO *(suspiciously)*: You weren't? There was a lot of commotion in your room one night. But when I came to the doorway, it stopped. What was the matter?

HUA: Oh, *(pretending to understand)* you mean that! *(Laughing)* That was a rat; I got up in the middle of the night to catch a rat!

CHIAO *(in a low, low voice)*: Well, if you ever see another rat, you just tell me. Do you see this? *(Pointing to the iron staff in front of the incense table)* I'll just use this iron staff here and beat him to death.

HUA: Yes, Ma. *(She is about to walk towards the room on the right.)*

CHIAO: Don't go. Sit down.

HUA: O.K. *(She stands there.)*

CHIAO *(coldly)*: Sit down.

HUA: I'm sitting. *(She still stands there.)*

CHIAO *(sternly)*: No, you're not, I know. *(Pounding urgently on the floor with her staff)* Sit down.

HUA *(looking vehemently at Chiao; sitting down reluctantly)*: Yes, Mama.

CHIAO *(letting out a menacing smile, hinting)*: I'm gonna tell you something.

HUA: Yes, Ma?

CHIAO: Last night I had a nightmare.

HUA: Oh, you had a nightmare, too?

CHIAO*(taking up the tinfoil, and slowly folding it into mock ingots; a phrase at a time)*: I dreamed your father-in-law was alive again—

HUA: Father-in-law, —alive?

CHIAO *(calmly)*: It seemed as though he had come back from a long, long way, but he was wearing white mourning clothes, and from head to foot he was covered with blood—

HUA *(disturbed)*: Blood?

CHIAO: Yes, blood! He saw the baby there, and without saying a word, he picked it up and he wouldn't let it go. And the tears flowed down from his eyes.

HUA: Oh!

CHIAO: I went to him to quiet him down, but as soon as I called to him, all of a sudden he changed into a tiger, a wild tiger—

HUA *(startled)*: A tiger?

CHIAO: Yes, a wild tiger, and he took the baby and he ran away with it as though he had seen an enemy.

HUA: Oh, this dream sounds like bad luck, very bad luck.

CHIAO: That may be. "When a savage tiger nears the gate, the house must have a spirit of hate." I think something bad is going to happen in this house very soon. Chin-tzu, what do you think?

HUA: I've been very happy here, what would go wrong?

CHIAO *(standing up, and picking up a stick of incense from the incense table; to Chin-tzu, in an apparently casual manner)*: Chin-tzu, do you know where Ch'ou Hu is?

HUA: Ch'ou Hu?

CHIAO: Don't pretend you don't know. My adopted son Hu-tzu's come back, how couldn't you know that? Come here, Chin-tzu, *(lifting up the incense)* light this.

HUA *(nervously taking up the "eternal lamp" on the table and shakily lighting the incense; the two women facing each other)*: I *did* hear Ch'ou Hu had come back, but who knows where he might be hiding out. *(The glow from the incense reflects brightly against Chiao's cadaverous face.)*

CHIAO: Chin-tzu! *(She grabs hold of Chin-tzu's wrist.)*

HUA *(alarmed)*: Ma, what is it?

CHIAO *(like an evil spirit)*: Your hand is trembling.

HUA *(her voice having a slight waver)*: It got burned by the incense, Ma.

CHIAO: Hasn't he come to our house?

HUA: Who, Ma?

CHIAO: Ch'ou Hu!

HUA: How dare he come? *(She twists the incense around; the flame brightens.)*

CHIAO: He hasn't come to see you, eh? Do you know that you were close to being man and wife once? *(Pointing to the incense burner)* Put it in the burner.

HUA *(while putting in the incense, she speaks)*: Ma, don't make such accusations! That brute, who wants him anyway? If he should come by I'll just call the posse to take him away.

CHIAO: You said it.

HUA: Uh.

CHIAO: And your father-in-law *(pointing to the portrait over the right window)* up there could hear it, too.

HUA: Uh.

CHIAO: Go on now. *(Hua walks to the doorway on the right; but Chiao has thought of something suddenly.)* Chin-tzu, your birthday's the ninth day of the fifth month, isn't it?

HUA: Yes, *(becoming suspicious)* what about it?

CHIAO *(warmly)*: And weren't you born around midnight?

HUA: Yes, why do you ask?

CHIAO *(not minding her)*: I'm just asking, yes or no?

HUA: Yes, Ma.

CHIAO *(evilly)*: I'm asking because I want to know from your horoscope whether you'll have a son or not.

HUA *(sharply)*: Don't bother.

CHIAO *(suddenly with gentleness)*: All right, go to your room, go on.

HUA: Uh. *(She eyes Chiao strangely, then turns about and enters the door on the right.)*

CHIAO *(hearing Hua walking out of the room; then sighing heavily)*: Humph, such a she-devil!

(Outside in the fog, crows circle round, cawing dismally, as the telegraph poles sob in the distance.)

(Chiao walks lightly to the doorway on the right, listens a moment, and hearing nothing walks dejectedly to the incense table. She suddenly turns her head toward the door on the right, but no one enters. She undoes the red cloth-wrapper on the incense stand, which encloses a wood-carved female figurine with large eyes, a combed coil of hair, and red rouge besmeared on its face. The carving is crudely done, but one can still make out Chin-tzu's features. On the abdomen of the wooden figure is attached an incantation on plain yellow paper with Chin-tzu's birth-date characters written upon it, and at the heart there is a vermilion charm; seven iron needles have already been pierced into the figure. She feels the face with her hands and mouths a few mysterious, indecipherable words.)

CHIAO (*stroking the surface of the wooden figure, muttering*): It might not be cut like her, (*slowly*) hmm, but the birthdate characters are right. (*Reckoning with her hands*) Fifth—month—the ninth. (*Nodding*) Around midnight —she was born. Yes, that's right, it's correctly written. (*She supports the wooden figure high in her hands and raises it three times. Nodding thrice, she places it in offering upon the incense table, sounds the musical chime thrice heavily, and kneels before the table. Kowtowing three times, with a grave expression, she kneels as before and chants some words. With a final kowtow, she faces the wooden likeness; in a low voice*) Chin-tzu, you yourself lit the incense, you yourself told me the birthdate characters. If you should die of a heart attack some day, Chin-tzu, you can't blame me. (*She bows deeply, rises, raps once on the musical chime, and walks to the incense table. Raising the wooden figure, she plucks an iron needle from her hair and directs it toward the heart; calling out in a low but brutal voice*) Chin-tzu, Chin-tzu. (*With a third "heng!"*, she plunges the needle in*) Chin-tzu! (*Sighing as though unusually fatigued; slowly counting the needles and lifting her head*) Already they're eight needles. (*Victoriously*) There's only one left, Chin-tzu. (*She places the wooden figure properly in front of the incense table, and covers it with the red cloth-wrapper.*)

(*Outside the telegraph lines moan; indistinctly there is the sound of someone approaching in pursuit of a herd of sheep. Chiao walks in through the left door without a word.*)

(*Immediately Hua steps in by the door on the right.*)

HUA (*softly within the right-hand door*): Don't come out now; listen for my cough.

(*Hua goes to the center door, opens it and looks out. Outside is a mass of heavy fog; no one can be seen. She turns around and looks at the red cloth-wrapper before the table. Hurriedly she moves near and uncovers it to view. She picks up the wooden figure and inspects it; suddenly she understands and replaces it disgustedly on the table.*)

HUA *(toward the door on the left; viciously)*: Humph. *(She covers the wooden figure. Suddenly she remembers Ch'ou Hu at the door on the right; she coughs lightly. Ch'ou Hu appears in response at the doorway, and is about to move toward the center door—)*

(Chiao hurries out sternly from the door on the left.)

CHIAO *(fearing Hua has walked in)*: Stop!

(Hua lightly coughs again and Ch'ou Hu nervously stands in front of the right door. Gesturing, she orders him to go back in.)

CHIAO *(slowly walking to the center door)*: Who is it? Who's there?

HUA: It's me, Ma.

CHIAO *(loudly)*: Who else?

HUA: Who else? *(indicating to Ch'ou Hu with her eyes not to make any sound)* There's also— *(smiling at Ch'ou Hu)* a ghost!

CHIAO: Ah!

(Hua instructs Ch'ou Hu to leave. He looks at Chiao glaringly and hatefully walks out.)

CHIAO *(at a loss; pausing)*: I thought the tiger had really come.

HUA: Ma, why don't you go to your room and rest a while?

CHIAO: Never you mind. I want to sit here in the main room a while.

HUA: All right, sit. *(Discontentedly she enters the door on the right.)*

(Chiao waits until she goes out, and then, walking to the incense table, she rubs the wooden figure under the red cloth-wrapper; she is pleased. Once more she mouths a few unintelligible words.)

(Just then there comes a sudden startling cry from the cradle; she walks to the side of the cradle and enfolds the baby in her arms, sadly caressing its head.)

CHIAO *(patting the child's back lightly)*:   Little precious is dreaming! O—oo! Dreaming that the tiger will come and eat you up, oo—oo. The tiger won't eat you, oo—oo! Don't be afraid, oo—oo, your grandma will protect you all your life, oo—oo! Don't be afraid, oo—oo. *(She carries the baby into the room on the left.)*

(Outside there appears to be a herd of sheep scampering clamorously by, baaing sorrowfully. Following the sheep's cacophony is a very gleeful voice: "Da, da, da—di—! Da-di-da-di-da, Da-da-da-da! Di-da-da-da-da-da-da! Da—da-di-da, Di-da-da-da-da-da-da-da!" *(More enthusiastically)* "Da, da, da—di—. Da-di-da-di-da, Da-da-da, Da-di-da! Di-da-da-da-da-da-da!" *Accompanying the variable pitches of a bugle, Pai Sha-tzu orally strikes up a martial drum, his tongue rolling.* "Drr—chiang, chiang, chiang! Drr—chiang, chiang, chiang! Drr—chiang, chiang—Drr-chiang!" *(With all his energy)* "Drr—chiang, chiang, chiang! Drr—chiang, chiang, chiang! Drr—rr, chiang, chiang—Drr—chiang!" *With much pride he marches in the center door with triumphant flourish.* "Drr—chiang, chiang, Drr—chiang!" *His two hands roll imaginary drumsticks in downward striking motions, with hot perspiration flowing from his head. So engrossed is he that he enters without seeing Chiao Ta-ma. He walks in by the door on the left, still mimicking the bugle:* "Da, da, da—di—!"*)*

CHIAO *(suddenly calling from Pai's right)*:   Who is it?

(Pai is startled and the drum stops. He sees Chiao. Sticking out his tongue he turns about suddenly and starts to run.)

CHIAO *(standing up)*:   Stop! Who is it?

PAI *(halting where he is)*:   It, it— *(swallowing hard)* it's me!

CHIAO: Me? *(Surmising who it must be)* Who's "me"?

PAI *(stuttering and blinking rapidly)*:   Dog—doggie! Chiao Ta-ma. *(Finished speaking, he wants to flee again.)*

CHIAO: Don't run off! You aren't tending your sheep, what'd you come here for?

PAI: No—nothing. I . . . *(gazing with big eyes)* I come to see the new bride in our family.

CHIAO: What business do you have with the new bride?

PAI *(chuckling; chanting in rhyme)*: "If the bride's a pretty girl, Sha—Sha-tzu'll go into a whirl; but if the bride's an ugly ma'am, Sha—Sha-tzu'll turn away and scram."

CHIAO: You like to look at pretty girls, too?

PAI *(rolling his eyes; looking at Chiao Ta-ma)*: Uh! *(He sniffs, drawing back two long green strands of mucus into his nostrils.)*

CHIAO: Doggie, don't look at her, our family's new bride is a whore; she's a tiger and she can eat people.

PAI: Tiger? *(Incredibly)* Oh! I've seen her!

CHIAO: You've seen the tiger? Then why do you keep coming around?

PAI *(the mucus runs down again and the tip of his tongue unconsciously turns up to lick it off)*: If I come to see her, will she eat me up? *(He rubs some more mucus away.)*

CHIAO *(pitying him)*: Doggie, do you want a tiger to come and eat you someday?

PAI *(honestly)*: If . . . tigers are all like that, then may— maybe tigers are good.

CHIAO *(distressed)*: Sha-tzu, don't marry a pretty wife. "Beautiful wives, a family will ruin; 'cause you throw away Ma when you wed a fair woman."

PAI: Naw . . . that don't matter, my ma's already dead.

CHIAO *(looking at Pai; with a long sigh)*: Uh, when children grow up, they're all this way, their hearts change.

PAI: What?

CHIAO *(in a muffled voice; painfully)*: They forget their mother. They don't remember any of the hard times. *(She bends her head down.)*

PAI *(confused)*: What . . . what you say?

CHIAO *(bending her head down and knocking the floor with her staff; suddenly)*: Nothing. Oh, Sha-tzu! Do you hear somebody talking in the other room?

PAI *(stretching his neck, and listening a moment; then shaking his head stupidly)*: N—no.

CHIAO *(pointing to the room on the right)*: No! I mean in the west room.

PAI *(definitely)*: Oh, I see! *(Still shaking his head)* N—no.

CHIAO *(unbelievingly)*: Go to the room and take a look.

PAI *(nodding)*: Oh, all right. *(He walks a step.)*

CHIAO *(grabbing hold of him; in a low voice)*: Walk quietly, do you understand?

PAI *(not liking her prattling; with an impatient manner)*: I know!

CHIAO *(anxiously)*: Doggie, what are you seeing there?

PAI: Uh?— *(Just then realizing)* What? Who knows what you want me to see?

CHIAO *(in a low voice)*: Go and see if anybody else is in the room.

PAI: Oh, oh, *(appearing to understand fully; nodding)* all right. *(Going to the door on the right, looking up and down, turning around, walking a couple of steps, then shaking his head)* Door—door locked. I can't . . . can't open it.

CHIAO *(rising in surprise; urgently)*: What? The door's locked? You can't open it? Push it open, break it in!

PAI *(shrinking back)*: I'm afraid—I—

CHIAO: Afraid of what! If anything goes wrong, I'm here.

PAI : I'm afraid the tiger'll eat—eat me.

(Immediately Chiao draws out an iron staff from beside the incense table.)

CHIAO *(to Pai Sha-tzu)*: You come with me. If there's somebody else besides Chin-tzu there, catch him for me.

(Pai nods; carefully and reverently he follows Chiao. They walk to the door on the right. Chiao raises her staff and is about to pound on the door.)

(Hua runs out through the right door.)

HUA *(shouting out)*: Ma, what are you doing? *(Holding up Chiao's hands with her own)* Ma, put it down, who is it you want to hit? *(She coughs.)*

CHIAO *(sensing something tricky about her)*: You cheap whore, *(pushing Hua away with force)* let go! *(Hua is thrown to the floor.)*

HUA *(crying out)*: Ma!

CHIAO: Sha-tzu, come with me! *(She enters the door on the right alone.)*

HUA *(coughing; calling out loudly)*: Ma! Ma!

(In the room on the right there are sounds of Chiao's iron rod falling to the ground and of someone dodging her.)

CHIAO'S VOICE *(shrieking, she grits her teeth, raises her iron staff, and strikes downward)*: Damn! Damn! Damn you!

(In the room on the right there appears to be someone pushing Chiao fiercely; Chiao calls out loudly, but stumbles and falls prone. The man then breaks a window and jumps out.)

(Sha-tzu is so scared he can only watch Hua fixedly; it seems he has grown roots into the floor.)

CHIAO'S VOICE *(shouting)*: I've been knocked down! Sha-tzu, someone's broken the window and gotten away, after him quick, Sha-tzu! Get him, Sha-tzu! Sha-tzu . . .

PAI *(not knowing what to do; trembling)*: Oh, Oh, I know, I know. *(But he remains motionless as before.)*

(Hua, hearing that the man inside has fled, immediately runs up to the center door, but Ch'ou Hu has already entered from outside.)

HUA *(grasping Ch'ou's hand; in a low voice)*: Are you all right? Did you fall?

CH'OU: Damn, the window was too small, I broke it, my leg busted off a piece.

HUA: What about her?

CH'OU: I gave her a shove. She fell to the floor.

CHIAO'S VOICE *(inside)*: Chin-tzu! Chin-tzu!

HUA *(giving answer, and about to go to the right-hand room)*: Ma!

CH'OU *(grabbing her)*: Don't go! *(Points at Pai)* Look! Him!

PAI *(rubbing the top of his head, he looks at Ch'ou Hu; mumbling very softly, unconsciously)*: "Chi—cha—ka—cha", *(even lower)* "tu—tu—tu—tu".

HUA *(speaking at the same time as Pai)*: That's Dog— Doggie!

CH'OU: He knows me, be careful of him.

HUA: Oh!

(Chiao walks out by the door on the right; her face is bleeding.)

HUA: Ma!

CHIAO *(ignoring her)*: Sha-tzu! Sha-tzu! Sha-tzu!

(Pai dares not answer. Immediately Ch'ou escapes quietly through the center door.)

HUA: Ma! Ma!

CHIAO *(gnashing her teeth)*: You cheap whore!

HUA *(uneasily)*: Ma, did you get hurt?

CHIAO *(raging)*: Sha-tzu! Is Sha-tzu here?

PAI (*looking directly at Hua; with no alternative*): I'm—I'm here. What is it? (*He looks again at Hua.*)

CHIAO (*gnashing her teeth in rage*): Doggie! Did you see anything?

PAI: I saw, saw (*putting his forefinger in his mouth*) the tiger here.

HUA (*greatly alarmed*): Who says so?

CHIAO (*loudly*): You dead whore, don't interrupt. Who else is there? Sha-tzu, speak up!

PAI (*looking apprehensively at Hua*): There's still—there's still—there's still the— (*Suddenly Hua scurries in front of Sha-tzu; her expression is strange, beguiling. She kisses him ever so gently on the cheek; Sha-tzu stands there seemingly transfixed, in a trance.*)

CHIAO (*harshly*): There's still a what?

PAI (*having never been kissed by anyone before, he caresses his kissed cheek*): There's still the—tiger—the tiger!

CHIAO: You fox spirit, what are you doing?

HUA: I'm not doing anything.
(*The baby cries out very softly from the room on the left.*)

CHIAO: Tell me, Doggie! (*Pounding her staff on the floor*) What are you two doing?
(*Hua gives him another affectionate kiss.*)

CHIAO: Doggie, are you dead?

PAI (*not knowing what to say*): —No! The tiger will eat— eat me.
(*The baby cries loudly through the left door.*)

HUA: Ma, listen, the baby's awake.

CHIAO: Never mind. Doggie, speak up, who else is there?
(*Inside the baby cries more fearfully. It bawls for some time, while the three people listen quietly.*)

HUA (*anxiously*): Ma, maybe the baby is sick. (*Purposefully*) Ma, you can keep on with him; I'll go take a look. (*She is about to go.*)

CHIAO *(harshly)*: Don't you go! You witch! Don't you dare murder my little baby with your poisoned hand! *(Walking a couple steps toward the left room)* I'll go. Doggie! Don't go away, I've got more to ask you later on.

(Chiao goes into the left room; one can hear her comforting the baby.)

HUA *(seeing Chiao has entered the door, she walks to a bench beside the square table and sits down; beckoning to Pai seductively)*: Doggie! Come here!

PAI *(uncomprehendingly)*: What—what for?

HUA: Come here, *(in a low voice)* I want to have a word with you.

PAI *(putting a forefinger in his mouth; becoming instinctively bashful)*: What—what for? *(He approaches in a rather embarrassed manner.)*

HUA *(vacating a place beside her, holding his hand)*: You sit beside me. Now put down your finger.

PAI *(putting his hand down; glancing at her blushingly and chuckling foolishly)*: What—what for? *(Unconsciously he puts his hand in his mouth again.)*

HUA *(eyeing him)*: Put your finger down! Now listen real careful to me! I want to talk seriously with you.

PAI *(putting his finger down again)*: Uh, all right, you talk! *(The tip of his tongue unconsciously curls around to lick his upper lip.)*

HUA *(gently)*: Doggie, listen, when Ta-ma starts asking you things later on, and wants to know if you saw anybody, you, you just say—

PAI *(blinking, as though studying something. Bringing his tongue to his upper lip, he licks it across and rolls it back. Suddenly he makes a great discovery; jumping up)*: New—new bride! *(Unusually joyful)* Guess, guess what snot taste like.

HUA *(unexpectedly)*: What? Snot?

PAI *(urgently)*: Tell me! Is it sweet, or salt?

Hua *(angrily)*:   I don't know.

Pai *(happily slaping his rear end)*:   It's salt! Salt! You didn't guess it. *(Making another swipe with his tongue)* Just a little salt.

Hua *(standing up)*:   Damn you, foolish stupid bastard.

Pai *(chuckling)*:   Hee, hee, did you—you tell me t'do somethin'?

(Ta-hsing, with his eyes filled with the cares and confusion of travel, worriedly and very wearily steps across the center-door threshold, shouldering a cloth bundle and holding a wooden stick in his hand.)

Hsing *(a smile appearing on his face)*:   Chin-tzu! *(He puts down the cloth bundle.)*

Hua *(insipidly)*:   Oh, it's you.

Hsing *(a little relieved)*:   Where's Ma? *(He wipes the dust off of himself.)*

Hua *(looking at him)*:   I don't know. *(Pai cowers to one side and looks on curiously.)*

Hsing *(putting the stick down and rubbing his face with his handkerchief)*:   I'm home! *(Lifting his head to look at Hua)* How are things here? *(Concerned)* Still all right?

Hua *(frigidly)*:   Ta-hsing, who told you to come back?

Hsing *(laughing unnaturally)*:   No—no one. I wanted to come back myself and take a look.

Hua *(suddenly)*:   What for? Did you think there'd be someone in the family who'd run away?

Hsing *(guessing that the old woman and his wife have been squabbling again; apologetically)*:   I don't understand, Chin-tzu, what's the matter now?

Hua: Nothing's the matter. I'm screwing around with men in my own house; I'm so happy I can hardly stand it.

Hsing *(evasively)*:   Who says so! Don't talk that way! This is *our* home, if Ma hears—

HUA: If Ma hears, so what! I've let her see everything.

HSING *(weakly)*:   Chin-tzu, when you came into my house, surely you weren't going to have the same comforts you had before as a young lady. But I've never made any complaints; everything I've thought of was for you. I've bought this and that, so why is it when you see me, you bowl me over with these terrible words?

HUA: Humph, terrible words? I've done things even worse to you! This is not the first time I've slept with somebody, you know. I had another man the very night I married you. When you're away, I'm out for a man every day, walking the streets, hunting for 'em, hanging on 'em. I—

HSING *(painfully)*:   Chin-tzu, what are you saying?

HUA: What I'm saying's the real truth; you know what I am. I just couldn't be cooped up, even in my parent's family—my name was bad to begin with—but I didn't want your family either; it was Yen-wang, your father, who wanted me to come. When I married you, one man wasn't enough; two weren't enough; even three weren't enough—

HSING *(distressed)*:   Chin-tzu, what's wrong with you? *(He sits down droopingly.)*

HUA: There's nothing wrong with me, it's the man who comes back as soon as he's left who's got something wrong with him; it's the man who comes home blind with suspicion; it's the dupe who believes anything he hears; it's that "bleary-eyed" man who thinks he knows what he sees—he's the one who's sick. I'm telling you, there's nothing wrong with me!

HSING: Really! How strange! What was it I suspected? What *did* I see! The moment I come in the door you "blister" me with this crazy idiotic jabber. Now look, am I suspicious, or are you the one?

HUA: Oh, I'm the one who's suspicious, I'm the one who doesn't trust anybody; I'm the one who suspects my daughter-in-law of screwing around with somebody in her own house, never faithful to her own man.

HSING: But who said anything about that? Did I hear something? Or did I see something just now?

HUA: You couldn't see anything, and you couldn't hear anything either.

HSING *(unable to conceive a solution)*: Then, Pai Sha-tzu, did you hear anything, or see anything just now?

PAI *(pointing at himself)*: Me—Me—

HSING *(accommodating Hua)*: That's right, I was away just now. Tell us, what did you see?

PAI *(stuttering)*: I—I just—s—saw—saw a—

HUA *(hastening to Pai's side)*: Go away! Go! Go! The words of the living are hard enough to figure out without your listening to the dead.

PAI *(showing off)*: But just now I—saw—saw— a—

HSING *(incredibly)*: Speak up, what?

PAI: I . . . I saw a—

HUA *(suddenly slapping Pai's face)*: Go on! Go on! You foolish dumb bastard.

PAI *(dumbfounded)*: You hit me? *(He rubs his cheek.)*

HUA: So, I hit you, what of it?

PAI *(grimacing; then crying out)*: Ah, Ma! *(Lamentably)* You—you really are a tiger. *(He sobs and walks toward the center door.)*

HSING *(taking a look at Hua, he can only comfort Pai Sha-tzu; sympathetically)*: Go on, Doggie, go quickly, and don't come here again tomorrow.

(Doggie wipes his tears away with the back of his hand and exits by the center door; in a while one hears again the sounds of a herd of sheep bleating and tramping along.)

HUA *(wildly)*:   Wonderful! *You* don't get suspicious, oh, not at all! But come back home, then you start asking around about everything, trying to figure out from this fool Doggie all about what I've done wrong. Well, all right, go ahead and stick the blame on me, all o' you, come on you two, put an end to me, why don't you? *(Ta-hsing tries to interrupt several times, but she speaks on without pause.)* I have to tell you, Chiao Ta-hsing, that since I married you, you haven't given me a day of happiness, what with your mother grinding me down all day without let-up, and then you, coming around—you stick by your ma, and then you go and beat on me. *(Weeping and sobbing)* We have to get things settled now; what do I owe your family from my past life? If I haven't paid up, then I'll just have to pay you back by dying for you. *(Wiping her nose)* I'm a slut and a whore, I'm huntin' for men all day; I'm a bitch, without shame. A prostitute—what kind of life is that? Oh, God! *(She collapses on the table, beats her breast and stamps her feet; she starts to cry.)*

HSING *(not knowing how best to console her)*:   But, Chin-tzu, who said that? Who would say that? Weren't you the one who asked me all those questions? Who made you talk this way? Hey, look, I've brought you a lot of good things, don't cry, O.K.?

HUA *(still sobbing)*:   I don't care, I won't look.

HSING: But the way you talk, you spill blood on yourself, you call yourself a slut, and a whore—

HUA *(still sobbing)*:   I didn't say it, I didn't say it. Your ma said it, your ma said it.

HSING *(unbelieving)*:   Ma? How could Ma say such terrible things to you?

HUA: Your ma thinks I'm a "nail in the eye"; she can't wait for me to die; she's made up her mind I . . . I'm screwing around with men at night; she cusses at me, and calls me all kinds of shameful things. "You slut! You cheap thing! You demon! You whore!"—all this your ma said; she said it all.

HSING *(explaining)*:   I don't believe it, I don't believe my ma would—

(Chiao walks out through the left door.)

CHIAO *(pounding her staff heavily on the floor; sternly)*:   Ah! *(They turn their heads.)* Yes! I said it all right. Chin-tzu, tell your husband, that's just what I said.

(Pause.)

HSING *(fearfully)*:   Ma! *(He walks toward her to help her.)*

HUA *(suddenly feeling isolated; standing up unconsciously)*: Ta-hsing!

CHIAO *(severely)*:   Out with it! Say right out what you think, tell your husband plainly what I am, Chin-tzu, go ahead! Out with it! You're pretty, and you can speak well enough. Your husband bought you flowers today, tomorrow he'll buy you face powder; you're the center of your husband's life. Say it, put the blame on me. I'm old, I've got no home, no property, my son is my only possession, and now he belongs to you.

HSING *(grievously)*:   Ma.

CHIAO *(sourly)*:   I just have one son, he's the only thing that belongs to me; but now you've taken him away. I'm an old woman now, I'm blind, I can't see, and I jabber on and on; I'm a bother to you. I know I should die, I should've let you bury me alive long ago. Chin-tzu, say it, put the blame on me, I'm waiting for the swing of your knife!

HUA *(apprehensively)*:   But, Ma, I haven't said anything about you at all. Ta-hsing, you heard what I said just now, Ta-hsing, you—

CHIAO *(exploding; harshly)*:   You whore! You cheap thing!
You fox spirit! You just can't cheat people enough, can
you? Do you still make him a fool to my very face?
Shameless, your cheeks are like your ass; you're a demon
with a mouth full of lies. While I'm here you can be
on your best behavior, for then you can bewitch your
husband; but when my back is turned, oh if Ta-hsing
would only kill me! You think I don't know, don't you,
you fox-spirit? Don't rely on your husband's good faith,
speak from your own good conscience. What were you
doing last night? And what were you doing just now?
Speak up, why do you close your door in broad daylight?
Who were you whispering to behind closed doors? Who
was that wild bastard who jumped out the window and
got away when I broke into the other room? Tell your
husband here, explain it to us, just how am I abusing
you? How am I persecuting you?

HUA: Who heard somebody talking in my room? Who
says I closed the door? Who got away through the
window? Ma, you better not snort at people with a
bloody mouth, you could—

CHIAO *(so angered she loses control of herself; trembling)*:   You
bitch, may lightning strike you down! *(Turning her head)*
Doggie, Doggie, you saw it, speak up!

HSING: He just left, Ma.

CHIAO: He's gone? *(suddenly)* Doggie, Doggie! *(She
walks hurriedly out the center door.)*
(Outside one can hear Chiao calling Sha-tzu.)

HSING: Chin-tzu!

HUA: Go on, believe her!

HSING *(darkly)*:   Go to the west room now.

HUA: What for? I won't go!

HSING: Chin-tzu, don't rile her now. Listen to what I
say, go now.

HUA *(staring at Ta-hsing)*: All right, so you two talk. You two have your little conference. Scheme against me as you like! I'll go! I'll just go! *(She leaves by the door on the right.)*

HSING: Chin-tzu!—

(Chiao enters by the center door.)

CHIAO *(tremulously)*: That foolish stupid bastard's disappeared again, run away. *(Returning to her principal subject; sharply)* Good, the two of you have had your little talk, and you've got a mind to scheme against me, I suppose. *(She conjectures that Chin-tzu has been muttering something behind her back just then; acridly)* Uh, Chin-tzu, you're an upstanding person; all that just now was a lot of blind talk, calling you a nail in the eye and like that. Your husband's come around now and you can put on your best show. *(Exploding; fiercely)* Chin-tzu, you slut! I told Ta-hsing before: you have to be careful, don't listen to your father about Chin-tzu. "Beautiful wives, a family will ruin; 'cause you throw away Ma when you wed a fair woman"—

HSING: Ma, Chin-tzu isn't here.

CHIAO: She's gone? Where'd she go?

HSING: She went back to her room.

CHIAO: Oh, you were afraid she'd have to bear up under my anger; you told her to go.

HSING: No, Ma. I was afraid seeing her would make you uncomfortable and very angry; so I kept her from bothering you.

CHIAO: I ask you, how could I see her? How could I see her? Ta-hsing! Now the both of you are bent on teasing me about how blind I am. You make me so depressed—

HSING *(unable to stand anymore)*: I wasn't thinking that, don't be so blindly suspicious.

CHIAO *(bursting out)*:   I'm not blind and I'm not suspicious. Huh, you dupe, you've been infected by your wife's poison.

HSING: Ma, rest a while, don't get all mad! She's no good and she makes you angry. I'll beat her later on for doing that.

CHIAO: I'm not mad; I just get angry at hen-pecked husbands.

HSING *(at a loss)*:   Yes, Ma. I've brought along a little refreshment for you, the kind you like!

CHIAO *(smiling cynically)*:   No need, be an obedient husband and take it to your wife. I don't care for it.

HSING *(sighing)*:   Ma, if this is the only way you think, how can I talk to you? It hasn't been easy in our house, the old one has her old ways, the young one her young ways; the husband's out all day and there aren't any neighbors or relatives around; just the three of us and the baby in the family, and yet we're all so petty, that—

CHIAO: Ta-hsing, who're you talking to? Who?

HSING *(with an apologetic laugh)*:   Ma, I don't dare to chide you.

CHIAO: Oh, am I petty? I think you're too big-hearted.

HSING: All right, all right, Ma, what's going on with her anyway? Tell me!

CHIAO: Ask yourself.

HSING *(a little shaken)*:   Ma, she really . . . really did it . . . while I was away.

CHIAO: The last couple of evenings, about the middle of the night, I've heard somebody talking outside under the big tree.

HSING: With Chin-tzu?

CHIAO: Yes, about the middle of the night, Chin-tzu and somebody else.

HSING: What was she doing?

CHIAO: What was she doing? She dragged the man inside.

HSING: Dragged him inside?

CHIAO: Dragged him into the house, and the two of them whispered half the night.

HSING: 'Til midnight?

CHIAO: Midnight? 'Til sun-up.

HSING *(somewhat doubtful)*: Then why didn't you nab them?

CHIAO: Me? *(Intentionally speaking wryly)* You really think I'm so blind as not to know it wasn't the two of you? If the man in the middle of the night wasn't you, you ninny, who else would it be?

HSING: Me?

CHIAO *(continuing to interrogate him, however; intimidatingly)*: Why did you keep it from me about coming back home? How have I ill-treated you so you had to make such a secret out of it?

HSING *(frightened)*: That man wasn't me.

CHIAO: Oh? *(Feeling that he is gradually being convinced; grinning)* It wasn't you?

HSING: No, it wasn't.

CHIAO: Then who was that man just now.

HSING: What, there was another man?

CHIAO: You mean it wasn't you?

HSING *(painfully)*: No! No!

CHIAO: Oh?

HSING *(suddenly)*: Ma, is what you say true?

CHIAO *(calmly)*: It's true. Have you really caught your wife's poison!

HSING *(his heart burning)*:   How could she? How could Chin-tzu do that? I've gone to so much trouble for her, and gotten angry so many times because of her. She swore an oath to me that she'd start behaving herself . . . she . . . she . . .

CHIAO *(cruelly)*:   She swore an oath, isn't that a laugh! I knew that man was in here just now; I broke in the door and he was about to escape through the window. I grabbed him by the lapel, but that son-of-a-bitch knocked me down with one blow and jumped out. Pai Sha-tzu saw him; Chin-tzu was still talking to him at the door, all casual-like. Look, this is where my face got hurt from the fall; go in the other room there and take a look, the window's all broken out. You see, when you're not at home, the house turns into a brothel. Ta-hsing, how could I not call you back? I'm telling you, you young fool, *(fiercely)* that your wife is a whore, a wanton woman. There's no one now who doesn't cuss at you, or mock you, or call you a—

HSING *(so frantic he beats the table)*:   Ma! Ma! Don't say anymore, I've had enough, I've heard enough.

CHIAO *(again enraged; pounding heavily on the floor with her staff; vehemently)*:   Then why don't you call her out and ask her, force her to admit it, beat her to admit it; she must confess to it with her own lips, confess it!
(Hsing collapses onto the table; his whole body shakes.)
(Hua emerges by the door on the right.)

HUA *(with a stern countenance)*:   You don't need to call me. *(With abrupt coldness)* There's no need for both of you to yell, I'll come out on my own.

CHIAO: Fine! It's nice that you've come! Very nice indeed! Ta-hsing, there's a whip behind the door that your father used to beat people with. Ta-hsing! If your heart softens again, you're no longer my son. *(She walks behind the door and gropes for the leather whip.)*

HUA *(defiant)*:   Humph!

CHIAO: That's right, go ahead and grunt! Ta-hsing, here's the whip. I'll lock the door for you. You make her answer! Do it! Do it! *(She locks the center door securely.)*

HSING *(taking the leather whip; his hand trembling)*:   Chin-tzu—

CHIAO: Make her answer now! Now!

HSING: Ma, I'm trying! I'm trying!

CHIAO: Make her kneel and face the ancestral tablet!

HUA: What?

CHIAO *(thunderously)*:   Kneel!
(Hua kneels.)

HSING *(holding the leather whip; his face perspiring)*:   While I was away, did . . . did you . . . you do that?

CHIAO: Speak up, I tell you to speak up, you demon.

HSING *(pointing at her with the whip; without pity)*:   You—say it.

CHIAO *(harshly)*:   Talk!

HUA *(looking at their faces; hatefully)*:   Ha! *(A cold laugh)* Go ahead and beat me, beat me! *(Suddenly in a high voice)* I did it! I did it; I'm a slut! A whore! I won't take this slop from you anymore, I want to die. What are you going to do to me?

HSING *(getting pale)*:   What? You—you admit you—

HUA: Yeah! I admit it. Everything your mother said is true; she doesn't accuse me wrong. I'm a slut, all right; when I came into your family, I had no idea of living properly with you. It was your father who forced me to be his daughter-in-law and ever since then your mother has hated me, and cursed at me, and shamed me, and ruined me; she didn't even treat me as a human being. I'm telling you, Ta-hsing, you're a nice chump, but with a mother like yours, I'd rather die than live with a sop like you. A slut is what I am. Even if you'd treat me better I'd have to get away from you sooner or later. I'm telling you I don't like you; you're a good-for-nothing whipping-post, fall guy for your mother's tricks. You don't deserve to have a wife like me. Go ahead, beat me, beat me 'til I'm dead! I confess. But, look at your mother, there isn't any woman under heaven more deadly than she is. She isn't anybody's mother-in-law, look at her—

HSING *(simultaneously)*:　Chin-tzu, don't say anymore!

CHIAO *(desperately)*:　You demon, you have to keep talking, don't you!

HUA *(running to the incense table, unwrapping the cloth bundle, and holding up the wooden figure pierced with steel needles)*: Ta-hsing, look! This is what she did. Look, she wants to kill me! She thought up this shameless way of destroying me. Look, look both of you. *(She throws the wooden figure to the floor.)*

CHIAO:　You . . . you . . . you! Ta Hsing, aren't you going to kill this slut? Hit her—hit her—hit her!

HSING *(disconcerted)*:　Mama!

CHIAO *(like thunder)*:　Kill her! Kill her!

HSING:　Uh, *(getting numb)* uh, kill! Kill! *(He raises the leather whip and wants to strike Chin-tzu—but he seems to have frozen into ice, his hand lifted in mid-air, his tears overflowing; he looks dumbly at Hua's cold unfeeling eyes. He is silent. Suddenly he throws down the whip, falls to his mother's feet and cries.)* Oh, Mama!

CHIAO *(shoving her son away; cursing)*:　Are you still a man? *(She swings up her staff and bats in Hua's direction. Hua intercepts it with one hand.)*

HUA *(with all her might)*:　You . . . you dare—

CHIAO *(desperately)*:　I'll kill you first—

(Outside someone is knocking very urgently at the door, calling out, "Open up! Open up!")

HSING *(between the two women)*:   Who is it? Who is it?

THE VOICE OUTSIDE: It's me, me!

CHIAO *(putting down her staff; hearing something queer in the voice; stopping)*:   You? Who are you?

THE VOICE OUTSIDE *(a chilling laugh)*:   Ch'ou—Hu! I'm Ch'ou—Hu.

CHIAO: What? Hu-tzu.

THE VOICE OUTSIDE: It's me, Kan-ma!*

HSING *(alarmed)*:   Strange, Hu-tzu's come here? *(He opens the center door.)*

(Ch'ou Hu enters; they all look at one another apprehensively. There is a long pause.)

CHIAO *(darkly)*:   Hu-tzu, what'd you come here for?

CH'OU *(venomously)*:   To pay respects to my kan-ma.

CHIAO *(gloomily)*:   Pay respects—?

CH'OU *(nodding his head)*:   Yes.

HSING *(walking up to Hu-tzu; happily)*:   Hu-tzu, how'd you get out?

CHIAO *(despondently)*:   Ta-hsing, come here! Come with me to this room here.

HSING *(not quite understanding)*:   Mama?

CHIAO *(harshly)*:   Come here.

(Chiao walks towards the room on the left leaning on her staff; Ta-hsing follows behind. The mother and son enter the left room.)

(A long pause; Hua looks fearfully and dumbly at Ch'ou Hu.)

HUA *(in a low voice)*:   Who told you to come back?

CH'OU *(looking out; gloomily)*:   There's somebody after me out there.

HUA: Who?

---

* Lit., "adopted mother".

CH'OU: The fog's too heavy. I can't see. *(Suddenly)* Blow out the candle.

HUA *(startled)*:   Why? *(She blows out the candle flame in front of the incense table.)*

(The room darkens ; looking out from the two windows, one can see a mass of grey, thick fog. Faraway a train is heard rushing along, and the sound of a lonely whistle. Ch'ou Hu paces to the window and gazes out.)

HUA *(in a low voice)*:   What is it? You—

CH'OU: Don't talk, I think there's somebody walking outside the gate. Listen!

HUA *(listening attentively)*:   No, it's the wind.

CH'OU: Oh.

HUA: The wind is blowing the wild grass.

CH'OU *(turning his head and looking at the left room)*:   Strange, what have they been doing in that room all this time?

HUA: Who knows?

CH'OU: Uh. *(Suggesting gloomily)* I think something's going to happen tonight.

HUA *(nodding)*:   I feel it.

CH'OU: Chin-tzu, are you afraid?

HUA *(turning her head)*:   Afraid? *(Twisting her head to the front)* No!

(FAST CURTAIN)

ACT TWO

The same day, at nine in the evening, in the front room of the Chiao house as before. There burns a dim and dispirited kerosene lamp on the square table; the black shadows flicker, bursting forth haphazardly upon the window sill, crawling up the surrounding dusky walls. The windows are draped deeply, and the enormous dark-red cupboard stands awesomely against the wall, posing mysteriously as the inscrutable controlling force of the house. In front of the incense table the light of the candle diminishes; the three-headed, six-armed Bodhisattva is hidden in the darkness, with only a thread of glimmering light from the holy lamp reflecting against its oily-bright, black face; it appears repulsive, fearful.

Chiao stands beside the incense table, her countenance somber. Her wide, pupilless eyes stare forward, her thoughts unknowable. Imperceptibly she taps the musical stone; it sounds majestically, as though issuing from the idol's huge mouth. Before the table stands a plump, earthenware cistern, within which sacrificial paper blazes brightly to persuade the sacred spirits—"ghost money" to pray for safety from calamity and the blessings of good fortune. The ashes rise after the sparks, as the dancing flames soar upward. The red light spurts upon Chiao's craggy face in flashes, like a tsou-ma-teng.* Shadows drift to and fro across Chiao Yen-wang's cruel likeness, now black, now light; intermittently you catch a glimpse of Yen-wang's glaring countenance, like that of a spirit of death.

One apprehends a subtle tension here, bordering upon illusion, wriggling into the arteries, stiffening the body fluids.

---

* Lit., "running horse lantern". It consists of a paper drum with horses or human figures drawn on it and a candle inside, mounted so that the ascending hot air-current causes the drum to revolve.

The blind one rolls up the yellow paper and fills the bowels of the earthen jug with it; the flames leap more violently. She mumbles a Buddhist incantation and faces the Bodhisattva, apparently in prayer.

It is quiet for some time, and then suddenly from a corner of the room in darkness there is a tender cry, a fearful choking; it is the baby in the cradle awakened from a nightmare. Seeing also the shadows on the wall, it cries out more anxiously. The blind grandmother walks to the cradle and picks up the fightened child to console him in a low voice.

CHIAO *(lightly patting the child)*:   Don't be afraid, oo—oo—what did you dream about, my little precious? Oo—oo—oo—baby, come home quick—oo—oo. Come home and sleep, oo—oo. Don't be scared, oo—oo. Gramma will protect her little grandson for as long as she lives, oo—oo. You're Grandmama's life, oo—oo—oo. No one will dare come and bother you! My little grandson, don't be afraid, oo—oo—oo.

(The baby still chokes with sobs at first, then gradually falls asleep.)

(Chiao is about to put down her grandson when Chiao Ta-hsing enters from the left room. His cheeks are slightly red, his expression is uneasy; he closes the left door, takes a look back, then coughs suddenly.)

CHIAO *(in a low voice)*:   Who is it?

HSING *(in a rasping whisper)*:   Me, Mama. *(He walks toward Chiao.)*

CHIAO *(putting down the baby)*:   Easy there. The baby's just fallen asleep.

HSING *(walking to the side of the cradle and looking at his son)*: Is the baby a little better?

CHIAO *(stroking its slender, small head; concerned)*:   His little head's still warm. He woke up frightened just now and bawled for a long time.

Hsing *(annoyed)*:   Cry! Cry! Cry! What's the matter with this child today? Really, he seems to be mourning my death.

Chiao *(picking out another piece of sacrificial paper and kindling the fast-expiring fire)*:   "When a savage tiger nears the gate, the house must have a spirit of hate." Yes! A fox-spirit hides in the right room, and a wild tiger hides in the left. The baby's eyes are very sensitive; he must have seen these two bogies, so that his soul's been scared from his body. Why wouldn't he cry?

(Just then in the left room a man imitates a woman's voice, intermittently sharp and coarse. Oppressively he sings a folk-opera aria, with each phrase so very distinct: " . . . On the first and fifteenth the temple gate opens, the ox- and horse-headed demon-messengers align on either side. . . . The Judge of Hades before the temple officiates the registers of the living and the dead. . . . The blue-green-faced ghostling holds warrants for the seizure of spirits. . . .")

(Chiao harkens anxiously. Ta-hsing sits next to the square table and stares at the flames in the earthen jar.)

Chiao: Listen, he's singing again. *(Softer)* Listen, he's singing this in our very house. Listen! *(Ch'ou sings gloomily:* ". . . His Highness Yen-wang sits in the center; a gust of chilly wind wafts in a female spirit. . . .") Ta-hsing, he's putting a curse on us, isn't he?

Hsing *(arguing in Ch'ou Hu's defense)*:   He's happy, he hasn't seen me for many years. Today he sees me, he drinks a lot, and so he wants to sing something, so he sings something. Why should we mind him?

Chiao: But he's so sure that your father killed his family. *(Lowly)* You still don't understand? Do you think he's come to bring us good will?

Hsing: Mama, come on now, don't be so suspicious. He spoke with me just now, and said he'd just stay a couple nights and then go away.

CHIAO *(incredulously)*:   And then go away?

HSING: He's your adopted son, and he's been my friend since I was little; he's made a special trip just to see us. We haven't got any hate or gripe between us. How come you've got the idea he wants to hurt us?

CHIAO: You just don't understand—no use arguing with you. Ta-hsing, listen. *(Inside Ch'ou sings dejectedly again:* ". . . His Highness Yen-wang sits in the center, a gust of chilly wind wafts in a female spirit. . . .") He always sings those two lines, always those two lines.

HSING: Hu-tzu's got no home, no property now, he's feeling bad; let him sing it out.

CHIAO: But why does he—?
(Within Ch'ou repeats the song from the beginning: ". . . On the first and fifteenth the temple gate opens, the ox- and horse-headed demon-messengers align on either side. . . .")

CHIAO: Listen, does he do this on purpose—?
(The baby bawls out suddenly. Chiao hastens to the side of the cradle and comforts the child; inside the singing has stopped again.)

CHIAO *(hatefully)*:   Listen, he's doing this on purpose. When the baby wakes up, he doesn't sing anymore. *(The baby bawls continually.)* Ta-hsing, be a father and burn some money for your baby, to drive away the evil spirit; I'm going to call the baby's soul again.
(Hsing stands unwillingly, then walks to the incense table and burns the sacrificial paper. Chiao lightly pats her choking grandson by the cradle.)

CHIAO *(very distantly, in a frigid voice that seems to emit from the wilderness)*:   Come on home—, baby! Come on home, baby soul—baby! Come on home quick, soul—, baby! Gramma's waiting for you to sleep—, baby! Come on home, soul—, baby.

(The child is again silent; all about it is quiet; there is only blind Chiao's voice calling in a kind of lullaby; Ta-hsing's eyes gaze at the fire in the earthen jug.)

CHIAO *(suddenly)*: Ta-hsing, look at the baby's eyes, is he really sleeping?

HSING *(lifting his head and glancing at the baby)*: His eyes are closed. *(Strangely)* The way the child sleeps, it's so scary.

CHIAO: What?

HSING *(in a low voice)*: —He seems almost dead.

CHIAO *(blurting out)*: Nonsense! He's a good baby, what are you cursing him for? *(Again stroking the baby)* Baby, don't be afraid, your papa's only joking with you. You stay here, don't you worry, we'll give you food and shelter. Our house is your house, baby, stay here, don't go away.

HSING: But, Mama, can't you see that small face, the wrinkled eyebrows, the hollow cheeks? *(Softer)* With his eyes closed, really, he looks like—.

CHIAO *(apprehensively)*: Don't be ridiculous, you've drunk too much today. *(Thinking)* Still, it's strange, when we were eating a while ago, why did the baby start to wail all of a sudden?

HSING *(spiritlessly)*: I don't know. I was just now looking at the child's eyes, and it seemed like the baby saw something, and then it cried out in terror.

CHIAO *(suddenly)*: I think we have to get rid of 'em fast. The sooner gone, the better.

HSING: Just like that?

CHIAO: Yes.

HSING *(plaintively)*: No, Mama, wait a minute, let me think about it.

CHIAO: Think about what? The sooner our bad luck's gone the sooner things'll get better.

HSING: But, there's no one in her family now; you want her to go right away, this . . . this isn't—

CHIAO: What can I do about it? I only beg that there be peace in my house. It's too late today, tomorrow at daybreak we'll let him go.

HSING: Mama, we can't do that.

CHIAO *(coldly)*:   Then, Ta-hsing, how would you do it?

HSING: Mama, you can't chase her out like that. She's the one who's wrong this time; she's—she's the one who's disgraced us, but now you just want to send her away; wouldn't that make her do only one thing, to go looking for that—that man of hers? *(Painfully)* Mama, I know this time she's really got—no shame, for doing this ter—terrible thing to me, but Mama, do you mean to say we aren't just a little wrong, too? Do you mean we—

CHIAO *(with a stern countenance)*:   You ninny, what are you thinking about. Who are you talking about?

HSING *(irresolute)*:   Don't you mean Chin-tzu?*

CHIAO: Chin-tzu! Chin-tzu! *(Sighing)* You stupid worm! Death will soon be on us, and yet all you can think of is Chin-tzu, Chin-tzu. Ta-hsing, I'm telling you, the tiger's already in the door, and I mean the tiger in this very room. The tiger's been eating in your house, and he's already been in your room, making . . . *(Stopping suddenly)* Ta-hsing, why did you have to drink so much tonight?

HSING *(without energy)*:   Yes, Ma, I've been drinking.

CHIAO: I told you not to drink and still you drink. What devil's gotten into you today? You've changed.

HSING: Yes, I want to change. *(He pounds on the table heavily with his fist.)*

---

* The misunderstanding arises from the fact that "he (him)" and "she (her)" are homonyms in Chinese.

CHIAO *(compassionately)*: Ta-hsing, my son, come here.

HSING *(walking over)*: What for, Mama?

CHIAO: Ta-hsing, are you sad?

HSING *(looking at Chiao and biting his lips)*: No, Mama.

CHIAO *(taking Hsing's hand)*: You can't be without Chin-tzu, am I right?

HSING *(wanting to withdraw his hand; annoyingly)*: Who said so? *(As though he is afraid to expose his weakness, he becomes more irritated.)* Who said so? Who told you?

CHIAO *(understanding her son, she skillfully aggravates his sense of chagrin)*: Yes, yes it's true, she's just a slut; she wants any man she sees. *(She feels that Ta-hsing is in a troubled state, that he wants to interrupt her, but she lightly rubs his hand; slowly—)* If I were a man— Let her go, she's lucky I didn't kill her!

HSING *(suddenly withdrawing his hand, alarmed)*: Mama!

CHIAO *(startled)*: Ta-hsing, you——

HSING: Mama, tell me, who is it? Who is that man, I must know, I have to know. Ever since I was little, you've hidden everything from me, but now I'm Chin-tzu's husband. Who is that bastard? *(Repeatedly hitting upon the table)* Who is it? Who? Mama, are you so hard-hearted that you hide even this from me?

CHIAO *(stopping; standing up; heavily)*: Ta-hsing, your hands are trembling

HSING: My—my heart's on fire. *(Striking his chest)* It's all . . . all on fire here! It burns so badly.

CHIAO *(closing her eyes; pityingly)*: Child, you're a thin blade of grass, you just can't take the wind and frost.

HSING: But . . . but . . . *(mumbling)* I should still know who he is.

CHIAO *(as if she can really see)*: Child, why is your face so pale?

HSING *(hatefully)*:   Mama, if you love me, then you should tell me.

CHIAO: Your eyes, why do they stare?

HSING *(turning his head)*:   How, how do you know?

CHIAO *(shaking her head)*:   Your mother's blind, but she can always see her own son. But, *(turning her head toward Ta-hsing)* Ta-hsing, why are you staring at me? You're afraid to look at me, aren't you?

HSING *(nervously)*:   Mama, no, no.

CHIAO *(definitely)*:   You are! You are! Ta-hsing, what are you thinking now?

HSING: I . . . I'm not thinking about anything!

CHIAO: No, Ta-hsing, you're hiding something from me again. I can see you, I see your heart; you've always hated me, haven't you? Hated your mother?

HSING: No, Mama.

CHIAO *(somberly)*:   You hated me for coming between the two of you, you hated me for telling you the truth, so you couldn't close your eyes and be blind.

HSING: No, Mama. I hate, I hate only that one person. But you won't tell me who he is.

CHIAO: Why don't you ask Chin-tzu?

HSING: Chin-tzu's been taken in by that man, she won't say.

CHIAO: She still doesn't talk?

HSING *(earnestly)*:   Mama, you saw him, why don't you tell me!

CHIAO: Ta-hsing, you forget, I'm blind.

HSING *(suddenly standing up)*:   Mama, I'm going out.

CHIAO *(worriedly)*:   It's nearly midnight, where're you going?

HSING: I can't stay in this room anymore, not anymore.

CHIAO: Why?

HSING *(toward Chiao Yen-wang's portrait on the wall)*: Mama, come here, come here quickly and look.

CHIAO: Me, look?

HSING: Yes, look! Look how Father's laughing at me on the wall.

(Ta-hsing runs out through the center door.)

CHIAO *(pursuing him, shouting)*: Ta-hsing! Ta-hsing! *(Exiting the center door)* Ta-hsing!

(Once more a man sings rudely and hoarsely in the left room: "On the first and fifteenth the temple gates open, the ox- and horse-headed demon-messengers align on either side, . . . His Highness Yen-wang sits in the center, a gust of chilly wind wafts in a female spirit.")

(Far away a train rumbles past.)

(From the right room emerges Hua. Her expression is calm, and a skein of hair hangs down at her temple. Her eyes are watchful; as she walks on, she tiptoes toward the left room.)

HUA *(in a low voice)*: Hu-tzu! Hu-tzu!

(Chiao enters by the center door.)

CHIAO *(sternly)*: Chin-tzu!

HUA *(straining to be casual)*: What is it?

CHIAO: Where are you going?

HUA *(stepping back)*: I'm not going anywhere.

CHIAO: Chin-tzu, *(slowly)* what are you two gonna do?

HUA *(startled)*: Us?

CHIAO *(speaking unequivocally)*: You and Hu-tzu.

HUA *(bluntly)*: I don't know.

CHIAO: There's no use pretending, I know it's Ch'ou Hu.

HUA: I'm not pretending. Once I do things I'm not afraid if anybody knows.

CHIAO: Chin-tzu, why's he in the house all by himself, without saying anything, or even coming out?

HUA *(blinking her eyes)*:   You're asking me?

CHIAO: What idea's Hu-tzu got in his head now? What's he going to do?

HUA: I don't know.

CHIAO *(biting her teeth)*:   You don't know? You're the worm in his belly, his heart's——

HUA *(warningly)*:   Be a little mindful of what you say. If you decide to bring things into the open, I can be just as nasty.

CHIAO *(apparently understanding why Hua was suddenly unyielding; intently)*:   Ah, you probably know Ta-hsing just left.

HUA: Yes.

CHIAO: Hu-tzu's in the other room. There's only me, a blind old woman left in this family now, so you can—

HUA: Don't scare me with your tricks! I know, our fate's in your hands, isn't it?

CHIAO: Chin-tzu, *(sighing)* why don't you go now?

HUA: This late?

CHIAO: Yes.

HUA: Where are you going to send me away to?

CHIAO *(significantly)*:   As you will!

HUA *(having sensed something in her words)*:   As I will?

CHIAO: Yes. *(Deeply)* Are you going?

HUA: No!

CHIAO: Chin-tzu, don't you have any feeling left?

HUA *(detestfully)*:   I'd like to ask you that, too!

CHIAO *(though offended, she decides to bear up with her)*:   All right, I won't argue with you now, I give up, you've won this time. But, Chin-tzu, I've had a family and property, and I've raised a son; you haven't. You can't realize what thoughts go around in a mother's mind night and day. *(In a low, conciliatory voice)* Yes, Chin-tzu, just see how old I am—this grey head of hair—shouldn't you give in just a little? Perhaps I made a mistake before, by treating you badly, as you say, by grinding you down, by pushing you, by making life in our house miserable for you. But now, you, you've done this thing, and you've caused us so much pain, and still we Chiaos have done nothing to you. Now, when our Chiao family *(her head turning unconsciously towards the left room)* is—is in trouble, do you want to stab us in the back, too?

HUA *(looking at Chiao)*: Mother, don't be coy with me. I understand well, "A country has its laws, and a family has its rules." Since I've done what I'm not supposed to do, I know, of course, what's to become of me.

CHIAO *(suggestively)*: You do?

HUA: I'm no fool.

CHIAO: Then, tell me. What are you two going to do?

HUA: Us?

CHIAO: Yes, you and Ch'ou Hu. He didn't come to my house for nothing.

HUA: Naturally, "when a savage tiger nears the gate, the house must have a spirit of hate." But how can I know for sure what he's up to?

CHIAO *(admonishingly)*: Chin-tzu! Even though you don't want to be a part of the house of Chiao ever again, still you've carried the Chiao name. Ch'ou Hu's back now, to destroy us; how can you look on without a grain of pity, without giving us a little help?

HUA *(smiling coldly)*: You want me to think up something?

CHIAO: Eh, you've always been ready with an answer.

HUA: The road is straight ahead of you, why don't you walk it?

CHIAO *(concerned)*: What? Tell me.

HUA: Report him to the posse; they'll shoot him.

CHIAO *(understanding Hua's wry remarks but pretending ignorance)*: You know I can't do that. Hu-tzu's my adopted son, after all.

HUA *(acridly)*: Your adopted son? Oh, I forgot, you recited prayers for compassion for nine years, and burned sacrificial money for ten years; you're the very incarnation of the Goddess of Mercy, how could you do such a thing?

CHIAO *(swallowing the insult)*: No, I can't do that.

HUA: Well then, *(very seriously)* I must ask Ch'ou Hu's birth-date characters for you.

CHIAO: Why?

HUA *(fiercely)*: So you can make another wooden doll and stab him to death!

CHIAO *(bursting out)*: You slut, you whore, *(propping herself up)* you—. *(They face each other a moment; then Chiao suppresses her anger.)* Ah! I will not get mad, I must not get angry. Chin-tzu, I want to be quiet and talk with you.

HUA: Talk about what? Your son is still your own, the Chiao estate was yours in the beginning and it'll keep on being yours. What more do you want to talk with me about?

CHIAO: Chin-tzu, you think of me as a "nail in the eye", I know that; and you know how I see you. Chin-tzu, you hate me with a passion, but you always seem to forget that both of us love the same man. *(Hua is about to refute her.)* You don't need to say it, I know. You want to say you're finished with Ta-hsing now, right? But after all, you and Ta-hsing have been husband and wife, and he's been good to you.

HUA: I know.

CHIAO: And, how about you to him?

HUA: I pity him because he's never grown up, he's always been a baby, cringing at his mother's breast.

CHIAO: All right, these things are over and done with; we won't talk about them. I beg one thing of you now; help me and you can help him and yourself.

HUA: What? Go on.

CHIAO: Whatever Ta-hsing should ask you when he comes back, don't say that man was Hu-tzu.

HUA: Huh, why would I tell him?

CHIAO: But if Ta-hsing sees you he's sure to ask, so however he tries to scare you, don't tell him.

HUA: Why?

CHIAO *(terrified)*: He might've gone out just now to borrow a gun.

HUA: What? *(Unbelievingly)* He'd dare borrow a gun to kill Hu-tzu?

CHIAO: Huh! After all, he still has part of me in him.

HUA *(uncertainly)*: Oh, you mean when Ta-hsing comes back he'll look for—

CHIAO: Chin-tzu, don't pretend! Hu-tzu must've told you—

HUA: Told me what?

CHIAO: Ha! I've figured him out; he has such a poison heart, he'd have you tell Ta-hsing it was him.

HUA: That's crazy!

CHIAO: Crazy? He wants to have Ta-hsing make the first move to force him out. Then he can kill him, kill his sworn brother without mercy. Ha! Such a good brother he is!

HUA: Yes! Such a good brother! *(Sternly)* Such a good brother he is that he took his land—

CHIAO (*so soft she is almost inaudible*):   What?

HUA (*closing upon her previous words*):   —Broke his legs, sold his sister into prostitution, killed his elders.

CHIAO (*alarmed*):   What, who told you this?

HUA: He told me everything!

CHIAO (*trembling with fear*):   But, Ta-hsing didn't do this; it was Yen-wang, Yen-wang . . . (*pointing to the portrait on the wall; suddenly altering her words*) Yen-wang's rotten friends, his rotten friends have made—rumors. No, it's not true.

HUA (*incredibly*):   It's not true?

CHIAO (*suddenly determined; severely*):   No! It's not true. (*Again softening*) So, Chin-tzu, promise me!

HUA: What?

CHIAO: No matter what Ta-hsing does to you, don't tell him it was Hu-tzu. Help us and you help yourself.

HUA: Help myself?

CHIAO: Yes, talk Ch'ou Hu into leaving tomorrow. You can go with him, neither of us'll mention the past.

HUA: You're letting me go with Hu-tzu?

CHIAO: Yes, I'm letting you go. If you haven't got enough money, I'll help you.

HUA (*blinking her eyes in disbelief*):   You'd help me?

CHIAO: Yes, I'll help you! Tomorrow morning I'll help you steal away with Hu-tzu.

HUA: Yeah, (*looking at her askance*) and then you'll quietly tell the posse how to follow us.

CHIAO: Why?

HUA: Because when Ch'ou Hu has left the house of Chiao, and is no longer able to harm your grandson or your son, then you can take the two of us with one stroke—Ch'ou Hu for kidnapping, and me for running off with him. Then, will Heaven or Earth be our witnesses, or must we rely on your word?

CHIAO *(menacingly)*: Chin-tzu, you really are poison; if you were the mother-in-law, your heart would be more vicious than mine.

HUA *(snorting)*: To say things you don't like—I've lived with you long enough to know your ways.

CHIAO: But this time you've guessed wrong. I really did want to report him, but I saw Ta-hsing and I changed my mind. I don't want my son suffering from Yen-wang again; I won't have my grandson being hated by an offspring of the Ch'ou. Hate is easy to gel, but hard to dispel. Why would I make it so my children couldn't even live in peace? Unless Ch'ou Hu is dead, then every day he's alive will be unsafe for the Chiao family.

HUA: So you must have him dead.

CHIAO: No. Since he can't be killed by the law, why would I want him to keep on hating us more and more? Believe what you like, Chin-tzu, but what you don't want to believe is still the only thing you should believe. Call Hu-tzu here for me now. I'll speak to him myself.

HUA: But, you—

CHIAO *(changing her mind)*: Ah, don't go, I'll go myself. *(Calling out towards the left room)* Hu-tzu! Hu-tzu!

HUA *(toward the left room, in a low voice)*: Hu-tzu!

CHIAO: He doesn't answer. Chin-tzu, go to your room now, I'll call for him myself. *(Walking to the left door)* Hu-tzu! Hu-tzu!

HU-TZU'S VOICE WITHIN *(slowly)*: Eh?
(Ch'ou Hu enters by the left door. As he emerges he sees Hua and stops short. Pointing at her mother-in-law, Chin-tzu warns him to be careful. He glances with enmity at Chiao and waves his hand to direct Chin-tzu out of the room.)

CHIAO *(sensing that Hu-tzu has already come out)* :   Chin-tzu, go on in.

HUA :   Uh. *(She exits by the right door.)*

CH'OU *(evilly)* :   Kan-ma, your adopted son is here.

CHIAO *(calmly)* :   Hu-tzu, *(indicating a bench next to her)* sit down and we'll have a little chat.

CH'OU *(realizing that what is to follow will be serious)* :   All right, let's chat. *(He sits on a bench at a distance from her.)*

CHIAO *(a pause, then suddenly)* :   Did you have enough to eat just now?

CH'OU *(rubbing his chin; inspecting Chiao)* :   Oh, yes. Seeing you, Kan-ma, why wouldn't I have enough to eat?

CHIAO :   Hu-tzu! *(Pointing once more to a bench next to her)* Sit down!

CH'OU :   I am sitting down. *(He looks again at her.)* *(Outside there is a distant sound of a train whistle.)*

CHIAO :   It's late.

CH'OU :   Eh, it's late, why aren't you asleep?

CHIAO :   When people get older they can't sleep at night. *(Straining to be pleasant)* Hu-tzu, how have you been?

CH'OU :   I'm still alive, Kan-ma.

CHIAO *(to allay the purport of his words)* :   Why do you talk with such bad omen?

CH'OU :   Ha! When you're on the road, you couldn't care less for that sort of superstition. *(Again he looks her over stealthily.)*

CHIAO :   Come here!

CH'OU :   Why? *(He approaches uneasily.)*

CHIAO :   Stretch out your hand.

CH'OU *(suspiciously)* :   What for?

CHIAO :   So we can have a nice talk A blind woman doesn't feel safe unless she can rub a hand as she chats.

CH'OU: Ah, *(recalling her former habits)* your ways haven't changed. *(He extends his hand and she grasps it. Ch'ou Hu sits down easily on the bench alongside of Chiao; they face the audience.)*

CHIAO: No, they haven't. *(She stares straight forward.)*

CH'OU: Your hands are icy.

CHIAO *(mysteriously)*: Hu-tzu, close your eyes.

CH'OU *(looking at her doubtfully)*: I've closed them, Kan-ma.

CHIAO *(shaking her head)*: No, you haven't.

CH'OU *(staring at her; intently)*: This time you guess wrong, I did close them.

CHIAO *(nodding)*: Now we two blind ones can talk and get to know one another better. *(Suddenly)* Hu-tzu, do you feel that broad light in front of you?

CH'OU *(looking apprehensively at her)*: Eh.

CHIAO *(sullenly)*: What do you see?

CH'OU *(looking all round unconsciously)*: I can't see, can you?

CHIAO *(slowly)*: Yes, I can see. Hu-tzu, *(sternly; pointing to her front and rear)* I see ghosts standing by you, who have died unjust deaths; their faces are dark. And your face is filled with murder.

CH'OU *(perceiving that she is speaking falsely)*: You have fine eyesight, Kan-ma.

CHIAO: But can you guess what else I see about you?

CH'OU: What else do you see?

CHIAO *(releasing her hand)*: I see your father's spirit beside you.

CH'OU: Ah, my father's spirit? *(Sneeringly)* No doubt His Highness Yen-wang gave him a holiday, so he's happy, smiling at his kinfolk.

CHIAO: No, no. His face is covered with tears. I see him *(standing up)* next to you, *(pointing)* right here, kneeling to you, kowtowing, kowtowing, kowtowing.

CH'OU: What for?

CHIAO: He begs you to protect the last member of the Ch'ou family, and not to lose your own head, because it'll do no one any good. But you don't listen! *(Ch'ou Hu looks up at Chiao, amused by her mischief.)* Your face is filled with a viciousness. Ah, I see, the mist is rising, it's a very dark sky. Oh! I see your head roll off, and fresh blood spurting out at the neck.

CH'OU *(detestfully)*:   Kan-ma, you speak with better omen than I.

CHIAO: Hu-tzu! *(Taking hold of Ch'ou Hu's hand once more; warning)* Look, your hand is boiling, the demons are in you, your blood is hot; you must be careful.

CH'OU *(standing up suddenly)*:   But Kan-ma, your hands are cold. *(Smiling fiercely)* I'm not afraid that my blood is hot, but that your blood is cold; you must be careful, too.

CHIAO: Hu-tzu, *(making an effort to flatter him)* you really have learned a lot, Hu-tzu. You've learned to be thoughtful of me after all.

CH'OU *(alert)*:   For eight years, Kan-ma, you've been always on my mind.

CHIAO *(forcing out a laugh)*:   Good son! But, Hu-tzu, *(weightily)* I didn't treat you bad in the past.

CH'OU: I didn't say you were treating me bad now.

CHIAO: Hu-tzu, do you see who's hung on the wall?

CH'OU *(biting his teeth)*:   Yen-wang, my kan-tieh.*

CHIAO: Your kan-tieh, how does he look at you?

CH'OU: He smiles at me.

* Lit., "adopted father".

CHIAO: And how do you look at him?

CH'OU *(making a fist)*: I want to cry.

CHIAO: Why?

CH'OU: Because I didn't come early enough to show my affection to him as a son these eight long years.

CHIAO *(laughing unnaturally again)*: Good son! Can you guess what I'm thinking about now?

CH'OU: You're thinking about your adopted son, of course.

CHIAO: About you?

CH'OU: That's right! *(Putting on a smile)* Perhaps you feel sorry for me as a bachelor, lonely and lonesome——

CHIAO: So?

CH'OU *(mockingly)*: Perhaps you want to marry me off to some fine lady.

CHIAO *(taking him to be serious; laughing with satisfaction)*: Hu-tzu, you have a magical wisdom now. You're right. *(Significantly)* I *was* thinking of giving you a good wife.

CH'OU *(cunningly)*: A good wife?

CHIAO *(suggestively)*: So, are you going?

CH'OU: Where?

CHIAO: If you want a cart, I've got one.

CH'OU: I don't need a cart.

CHIAO: If you want money, I've got some.

CH'OU *(firmly)*: I've got money.

CHIAO *(feeling a tension in the air)*: Ah, *(tersely)* then, if you want the life of your kan-ma, her life is right here.

CH'OU *(pretending to be respectful)*: I don't dare, Kan-ma. May you live to be a hundred; we all must die, but you cannot.

CHIAO *(unable to tolerate anymore; despondently)*: Hu-tzu, be frank. No matter what kind of game you want to play, just name it. I'll be at your service.

CH'OU *(glaring at her, but his voice is tender)*:   Your adopted son doesn't feel that way. I only want to take advantage of Ta-hsing's homecoming to stay here a couple days, to show my filial respect for you.

CHIAO *(gradually succumbing to his sternness)*:   "Filial respect"! Hu-tzu, you'd better understand, Kan-ma hasn't mistreated you. *(Apprehensively)* If you must mention these words, then do so to the dead; those who are living can look at you without shame.

CH'OU *(indistinctly)*:   I didn't say there was anyone in the Chiao family who has mistreated me.

CHIAO: Hu-tzu, Ta-hsing's been your childhood friend.

CH'OU: Ta-hsing means well, I know that.

CHIAO: He went to the yamen himself because of your lawsuit, to plead and bribe for you, giving money and clothes to those he thought could help you.

CH'OU: He can face me without shame, I know.

CHIAO: Even me— I cried myself to death for you many times.

CH'OU: Yes, I understand.

CHIAO: Your kan-tieh pleaded with the yamen officials all the time to take good care of you, and asked them to treat you as our own son.

CH'OU: Yes, I remember.

CHIAO: You don't seem to agree, Hu-tzu, you—

CH'OU: Kan-ma, I'm only a fool, I speak whatever comes to my head.

CHIAO: Uh, *(continuing)* but your father, his tragic death—

CH'OU *(his animosity stimulates ridicule)*:   Ha! The old man sure died cheap—buried alive, saved us buying a coffin.

CHIAO *(defensively)*:   But you can't blame Ta-hsing's father; he risked his life bargaining with Hung Lao, but they made no deal; after the time was up, Hung Lao just killed him.

CH'OU *(forcing himself to be restrained)*: My father made friends blindly; for that he must blame himself.

CHIAO: Who do you mean?

CH'OU *(altering his words)*: I mean Hung Lao, that bastard.

CHIAO: That's right! Hu-tzu! And then your younger sister, her unjust death, a fifteen-year-old girl, being sold into that kind of place, tortured and ground to death . . .

CH'OU *(making a fist)*: That was the fate she was meant to have.

CHIAO: Such a poor child, but to speak of her, how can you blame Ta-hsing's father. Ta-hsing's father beat that pimp half to death because of your little sister. But no one could find her—a fifteen-year-old girl being made to live in that kind of place—so what could be done?

CH'OU *(trembling)*: Kan-ma, don't talk about it anymore.

CHIAO: What are you afraid of?

CH'OU: If you talk too much, *(menacingly)* take care your adopted son's mind isn't touched by devils.

CHIAO *(obstinately)*: No, Hu-tzu, white's white, and black's black; I have to make everything clear; I can't have you feeling so cheated. You told me how unfair the law-suit was, and how you were wrongly accused.

CH'OU: Eight years of serving time; I got a lame leg, and I lost my land.

CHIAO: Yes, and in those eight years your kan-tieh pleaded with them, and asked around for favors, only there wasn't anybody to look to for help. He spent money pleading with them, but still he couldn't get you out.

CH'OU *(hatefully)*: Yes, I haven't for one moment forgotten the good things Kan-tieh did for me.

CHIAO *(making one last effort)*:   And as for your family's land, Hu-tzu, you can't say your kan-tieh's intentions were bad. Your father loved to eat and gamble until he was cleaned out, and then he'd come around to your kan-tieh's door. Your kan-tieh bought your land for three times what it was worth, so your father still got a double profit.

CH'OU: Yes, my father took a profit from Kan-tieh.

CHIAO: Uh! *(Her mouth and her tongue are dry; she expects some effect from her persuasion; attentively)* Well, what do you think?

CH'OU *(nodding; casually)*:   Huh? Think what?

CHIAO *(suspiciously)*:   Hu-tzu!

CH'OU *(looking obliquely)*:   Yes, Kan-ma?

CHIAO *(suddenly resigned)*:   Hu-tzu, all this time I've tried talking to you, but at heart you just don't believe a word I've said.

CH'OU: Who says I don't? *(His expression darkens.)*

CHIAO: Then, what'd you come here for?

CH'OU: Like I said, *(emphatically)* to pay you my debts.

CHIAO *(despairing)*:   Pay your debts? *(Suddenly)* Hu-tzu, I heard you came back some time ago. Why did you wait by yourself and not come out before Ta-hsing came back?

CH'OU: It's been a very long time since we two brothers have seen each other; I waited 'til he came back so I could see you together—

CHIAO *(anxiously)*:   Together?

CH'OU *(hastening to change his words)*:   Sure, it'd be more an event that way! More an event!

CHIAO *(as though she suddenly recalls)*:   The way you talk, are you thinking of staying here for good?

CH'OU: To serve you on your way to the Western Heaven. *(Noxiously)* When you've gone back to Heaven, then I'll go.

CHIAO (*pausing for a long time*): So devoted you are, I must've earned this in a past life.

(*Pause; the wind blows the telegraph lines, making a crying sound like the low moan of a woman weeping in distress.*)

(*An old frog calls out coarsely.*)

CH'OU (*seemingly bored; in a cutting voice, gloomy and harsh, he sings with severe majesty*): "On the first and fifteenth the temple gate opens, the ox- and horse-headed demon-messengers align on either side. . . ."

CHIAO (*afraid to listen*): Don't sing, (*standing up*) it's time for you to go to bed.

CH'OU (*looking at her and continuing to sing*): " . . . The Judge of Hades before the temple officiates the registers of the living and the dead. . . ."

CHIAO (*somewhat fearfully*): Please don't sing, Hu-tzu!

CH'OU (*as though he hasn't heard*): " . . . The blue-green-faced ghostling holds warrants for the seizure of spirits. . . ." (*He walks away.*)

CHIAO (*all about it is silent as death; rising suddenly with indefinable apprehension*): Hu-tzu! (*In a high voice*) Hu-tzu! Where are you? (*Groping around her*) Where are you?

CH'OU (*looking at her coldly*): Here, Kan-ma. (*Moaning more sadly*) " . . . His Highness Yen-wang sits in the center; a gust of chilly wind. . . ."

CHIAO (*frightened and full of anger and vexation*): Hu-tzu, don't sing! Don't sing!

CH'OU: " . . . Wafts in a female spirit!"

CHIAO (*trembling with great hate*): Hu-tzu, who taught you to sing that?

CH'OU (*intently; deeply*): My unjustly murdered little sister, Kan-ma.

CHIAO: Ah! (*Unconsciously she suddenly picks up the iron staff at a corner of the table.*)

CH'OU *(smiling with hatred)*: Do you want to hear it again?

CHIAO *(curtly)*: No. *(She leans upon the iron staff.)*

CH'OU *(seeing the iron staff)*: Ah, Kan-ma, you're still so strong.

CHIAO: Oh?

CH'OU: Your staff, *(trying to clutch it lithely)* is still made of iron.

CHIAO: Yes! *(Feeling Ch'ou Hu's grasp and lightly snatching it away)* Iron! *(Unmoved)* Because I use it to beat wild dogs.

CH'OU *(understanding)*: Wild dogs?

CHIAO *(repeating)*: Yes, to beat wild dogs. *(Groping for her iron staff suddenly)* Hu-tzu, it's such a pity, you're so thin.

CH'OU *(curiously)*: Me, thin?

CHIAO: But you're still so strong.

CH'OU: How do you know?

CHIAO *(slowly tightening her hold on the staff; strangely)*: Have you forgotten how you kicked me in Chin-tzu's room?

CH'OU *(alerted)*: Ah, I haven't forgotten, Kan-ma. I also haven't forgotten how well you swing your staff. *(He laughs loudly and fiercely.)*

CHIAO *(also laughing loudly along with him; her face muscles contracting unnaturally, but making an effort to seem casual)*: You naughty child, come here, Hu-tzu, you still haven't seen the sore on your kan-ma's face—

CH'OU *(cautiously)*: Yes, I'm coming— *(He walks straight ahead—)*

CHIAO *(suddenly standing up and grabbing her iron staff; urgently)*: Hu-tzu, where are you? *(She is about to raise the iron staff—)*

Ch'ou *(at nearly the same time drawing out a pistol and pointing it at her; in immediate response)* :   Here, Kan-ma. *(He glares at Chiao and the two of them stand opposite each other, motionless. Ch'ou Hu thrusts his words out gruffly between his teeth, one at a time.)* Hu—tzu—is—here, Kan-ma.
(Silence.)

Chiao *(perceiving alertly that her opponent is prepared, she slowly puts down the iron staff)* :   Ah! *(With a long sigh, she sits down calmly.)* Hu-tzu, do you really want to stay here for good?

Ch'ou *(slowly replacing his pistol also)* :   Of course. The two of us should have a real family reunion.

Chiao *(suddenly standing up again; severely)* :   Hu-tzu, you can't! *(With great hate)* Tomorrow morning you must get out of here.

Ch'ou *(jeeringly)* :   The way you talk, Kan-ma—you don't seem to like me, do you?

Chiao *(also jeeringly)* :   Don't like you? I'm giving you a wife, to make you happy.

Ch'ou: Giving me a wife?

Chiao: Yes, Chin-tzu. We don't want her; you may take her and go.

Ch'ou: Take her and go?

Chiao: Yes.

Ch'ou *(suspicious; laughing in contempt)* :   You're so very generous, aren't you?

Chiao: Don't worry, Hu-tzu, I won't track you down.

Ch'ou: But what if I don't want to go?

Chiao *(viciously)* :   Then you'll go back where you came from. I'll tell the posse to come and get you.

Ch'ou: Get me?

Chiao: So, what about it?

Ch'ou: I'm afraid—

CHIAO: Afraid of what?

CH'OU *(threatening)*:   I'm afraid you—wouldn't—dare.

CHIAO: Wouldn't dare?

CH'OU: "A barefoot man fears no one shod." I have no shoes to lose. You seem to forget that a lot of ghosts follow me. When I escaped from the mouth of death I didn't intend to go back there alive. Kan-ma, "if a dog is pushed too hard, he'll jump the wall." And when people get pushed too hard, then—I suppose there's no use talking, you understand.

CHIAO: Ah, *(mumbling)* so, my adopted son, you've already made up your mind to die.

CH'OU *(fiercely)*:   I've made up my mind, I— *(stopping suddenly; altering his tone)* Well, let me think.

CHIAO *(listening)*:   Then, you mean we can still make a deal?

CH'OU *(looking at her askance)*:   Yes, we can—make—a deal.

CHIAO: Good, I'll call Chin-tzu. While Ta-hsing's gone, you can make plans together. *(She walks to the right.)*

CH'OU *(mockingly)*:   You really love me, don't you? You don't even mind giving up Ta-hsing's wife to me.

CHIAO: Chin-tzu! Chin-tzu! *(Suddenly turning her head toward Ch'ou Hu)* There's something else: you understand, of course, that you mustn't let Ta-hsing guess that you're sneaking away together.

CH'OU: Why would I do that, my kan-ma?

CHIAO: Hu-tzu, you really are my understanding child. *(Turning her head)* Chin-tzu! Chin-tzu! Chin-tzu!

(Chin-tzu emerges from the right door.)

HUA: What is it?

CHIAO: Chin-tzu, burn a stick of incense for me, to honor the Bodhisattva. I'm going to the other room there to fix up some bedding for Hu-tzu. I'd also like to chant some sutras, so don't let anybody in, do you hear?

HUA: Yes.

CHIAO (*walking to the left door and then slowly moving over to where Ch'ou Hu is*): Hu-tzu, I'm going in; you talk it over with her.

(*Chiao exits by the left door. Ch'ou and Hua look at each other; pause.*)

CH'OU: Did you hear?

HUA: Yes.

CH'OU: She's letting us go.

HUA (*unbelievingly*): Do you think she'll let us off so easy?

CH'OU (*mysteriously*): Maybe.

HUA (*in a low voice*): Hu-tzu, I'm afraid we've already fallen into her trap.

CH'OU: We won't. Ha! She hurt me once, do you think she can do it again?

HUA (*concerned*): You—you shouldn't have shown your face.

CH'OU (*with great pain*): No, I have to show my face. I came openly this time and I will not sneak away. Ch'ou Hu has ten years of hate in his heart—my poor papa, my unjustly murdered little sister, my lame leg. Just look what I'm doing now, Chin-tzu. If I start slinking around again, I'll die with regrets.

HUA: But, (*in a low voice*) Yen-wang is dead.

CH'OU (*viciously*): Yen-wang's dead, all right. But he's got a son, hasn't he?

HUA: But Yen-wang's son hasn't hurt you.

CH'OU (*looking cruelly at the portrait on the wall*): Yen-wang hurt me. (*Suddenly in a low voice; slowly*) Chin-tzu, tonight you must help me.

HUA (*covering his mouth*): Hu-tzu!

CH'OU: What is it?

HUA *(looking stealthily from the corners of her eyes)*:   Be careful, she can hear.

CH'OU: She closed the door.

HUA: No, he's still here, isn't he?

CH'OU: Who?

HUA *(trembling)*:   Yen-wang. *(Both of them look back; Yen-wang's eyes shine sternly upon them; Chin-tzu, fearfully)* Oh, Hu-tzu, *(throwing herself into his bosom)* do you really want me, or don't you?

CH'OU *(passionately)*:   Chin-tzu, you're—you're my life. Chin-tzu!

HUA: Then, let's go, quickly, I can't stay here anymore. Hu-tzu, I . . . I'm worried now; I'm afraid if we wait any longer, something will happen.

CH'OU *(prophetically)*:   Something will happen.

HUA: I know. But . . . may . . . be, maybe something will happen to us. *(Suddenly begging of him earnestly)* Hu-tzu, when are we going? Hu-tzu, tell me, tell me!

CH'OU *(very low)*:   Midnight.

HUA: So let's go, let's go.

CH'OU *(his eyes flashing hate; to his front)*:   No, let's finish things here!

HUA: But—but isn't it late?

CH'OU: If we run out now there'll be no train.

HUA: Train?

CH'OU: When we're finished here, we'll go. It's very foggy out there; when we run out, nobody'll see us going through the dark forest—

HUA *(somewhat anxious)*:   The dark forest?

CH'OU: Yes, the dark forest, and after about three miles, before the sky is light, we'll be at the station; and when we see the railroad, it'll be a road to life, a road to life!

HUA *(half-aflame with expectation)*:   A road to life!

CH'OU: Yes, a road to life; and there'll be friends to meet me over there.

HUA: And then we'll be gone away. *(Longing becomes true hope.)* We'll go away to that faraway place, riding the train. *(Slightly quieter, but quite affectionately and light-heartedly)* "Tu—tu—tu—tu—tu—tu—tu—tu—" *(Her heart has already been taken away by the train; her eyes look straight ahead.)* We'll go away to that gold-covered land—

CH'OU: Yes, *(he can only go along with her)* that gold-covered land.

HUA *(dreamily)*: Houses can walk, and people can fly . . .

CH'OU: Yeah, yeah.

HUA: And for big people and children, too, everyday's a New Year's Day!

CH'OU: Yes, *(dispirited)* every day's a New Year's Day!

HUA *(grasping Ch'ou Hu's hand)*: Hu-tzu!

CH'OU *(suddenly)*: No, don't move!

HUA: What is it?

CH'OU: Listen!

HUA: What?

CH'OU: There's someone out there. *(In a low voice)* There's someone out there!

(They both hurry to the window.)

HUA: Who is it? Who is it? *(Listening carefully, but no one responds)* There's no one! No—one. *(Looking at Ch'ou Hu)* What's wrong with you today?

(Just then, on the plain outside the window, a "cuckoo" calls softly and merrily.)

CH'OU *(looking anxiously)*: Strange, I always get the feeling there's somebody outside the window, somebody outside the window following me.

HUA *(consoling him)*:   How could that be? How— *(The calling of the "cuckoo" gradually attracts her attention)* Listen! Listen!

CH'OU *(grabbing his pistol)*:   What?

HUA: No, no, not that. Listen, what's this? *(Imitating the calling of the "cuckoo")* "Ku-ku, ku-ku"!

CH'OU: Ah, *(laughing)* that! He says: "A bachelor's harried so he goes and gets married."

HUA *(beaming with smiles, she's forgotten her present misery; imitating him)*:   No, he says, "He's gone and got married, so he's even more harried, even more harried."

(The two of them laugh at one another.)

HUA *(feeling sad again after her brief happiness)*:   Later on I'm afraid I won't be able to hear the "ku-ku, ku-ku".

CH'OU *(surprised)*:   Why?

HUA *(happily)*:   Aren't we going away?

CH'OU *(suddenly remembering)*:   Ah, going away, yes. *(Despondently)* But at midnight—

HUA *(her face is again covered by a shadow; fearfully)*:   Mid— midnight—?

(She sighs.)

CH'OU: What's wrong?

HUA *(complaining)*:   God, why is this gold-covered land so hard to get to?

CH'OU: You said—

HUA *(painfully)*:   Why must we kill people, and break the law to get there?

CH'OU *(suspicious)*:   Chin-tzu! Are—are you already afraid?

HUA *(grievously)*:   Afraid of what? *(Suddenly in a firm manner)* If things are going to be that way, then that's the way they'll be!

CH'OU: Good! *(Sticking out his thumb)* That's the spirit!

Hua: How much longer is it?

Ch'ou (*looking up at the sky as he thinks*): I think we've got only a couple hours yet.

Hua (*somewhat softer*): A couple hours—the time goes fast.

Ch'ou (*doubtful; thinking of testing her*): But what if it didn't go so fast?

Hua (*grasping Ch'ou's hand*): Hu-tzu, I've already given my life to you!

Ch'ou (*moved*): Chin-tzu, you— (*Tears well up in his eyes.*) I feel my father here beside me; and my dead little sister's here. She—they can protect you.

Hua: But, (*sighing*) why today?

Ch'ou: What?

Hua (*sympathetically*): It's a pity that Ta-hsing should come just now.

Ch'ou (*darkly*): That's what I've been waiting for!

Hua (*timidly*): But Hu-tzu, wh—why must it be Ta-hsing? Isn't a blind woman enough?

Ch'ou: No, no! Death would be a blessing for her. (*Wickedly*) I want her alive, alive and alone!

Hua (*softly*): But Ta-hsing is a nice man.

Ch'ou (*nodding*): That's right, he won't even step on an ant. But— (*battling within his heart*) but, he's Yen-wang's son!

Hua (*more softly*): Ta, Ta-hsing's been good to you; when you were in jail he always spoke of you to me. He's been your friend since you were little, Hu-tzu.

Ch'ou (*nodding*): Yes, he used to look up to me as his own older brother. (*Biting his lip; spouting out suddenly*) But now, he's Yen-wang's son.

Hua (*impatiently*): No, Ch'ou Hu! It's not right, you can't do this to Ta-hsing; he's been so good to me, too.

CH'OU *(rushing forth)*: Then I want to kill him even more! Because he— *(deeply, painfully)* he's Yen-wang's son.

HUA *(suddenly)*: Then why don't you kill him now? Why not!

CH'OU *(with effort; slowly)*: Yes, kill him, I will kill him. *(Nodding)* Yes, I have to kill him, I must kill him.

HUA *(compelling him further)*: But you can't, you can't, you don't have the heart to do it, Hu-tzu.

CH'OU *(denying vigorously)*: No, no, Chin-tzu.

HUA: Hu-tzu, tell the truth, your heart is soft.

CH'OU *(looking into space)*: No, no, my father. *(Woefully)* My heart isn't soft, it can't be soft. *(He lowers his head.)*

HUA *(earnestly)*: Hu-tzu! You're a good man! I know you're a good man in your heart, let him go!

CH'OU *(slowly looking forward; gloomily)*: Chin-tzu, it can't be, it—can't—be. I made an oath, I made an oath to my father. *(Raising his fist towards the sky)* Two generations, two generations of hate! I can't forgive them.

HUA *(making a final supplication)*: Then, Hu-tzu, let him go, for my sake!

CH'OU *(suspicious)*: For your sake?

HUA: Yes, *(heedlessly)* for my sake!

CH'OU *(suddenly laughing with ferocity; slowly)*: Ah, now you want to speak in his defense, do you?

HUA *(startled; seeing the jealousy in Ch'ou Hu's eyes)*: Why— why do you look at me that way? You—

CH'OU *(suddenly grabbing her arm, holding it with all his might; painful wrinkles appear on his forehead)*: Now I see, from the beginning it was for him that you—

HUA *(closing her eyes and gritting her teeth; in the greatest of pain)*: Let me go, Hu-tzu, you're killing me.

CH'OU *(releasing his hand, he pants; one can see his chest rise and fall; he wipes the sweat from his brow; looking at her)*: You were for him from the beginning, that's why you were so nice to me. Now your true feelings come—come out.

HUA *(looking at him)*: Why is it you don't understand people?

CH'OU: Don't understand?

HUA *(suddenly; very sincerely)*: Do you think I'm not human? Just pinch me and I'll tell you it hurts; poke me and I'll tell you it tickles; curse me and I'll get mad at you. Do you think, if someone's good to me, I wouldn't have some feeling towards him? When he's here, sure, I feel a kind of disgust for him in the pit of my stomach; I can't look at him, I don't even like him. But when he's gone, I think of him, and I can't help pitying him. *(Lighter but rapidly)* There's nothing you can do about him. *(Laughing sympathetically)* Sometimes I hope after I'm gone someone else will come along who'll really love him. *(Looking at Ch'ou)* But for me to grow old with him as husband and wife, I just can't. Still, it's different to see him— but how can I be so unfeeling? And you—Hu-tzu, how can you be so hard-hearted?

CH'OU *(sighing)*: Yes, Chin-tzu, you're right. Ta-hsing thinks of me as his good friend, he hides nothing from me. Even now he's— *(stopping suddenly)* huh, if it weren't for that honest face of his, a couple of hours ago, I—

HUA *(pulling at Ch'ou's hand)*: Then, let's go now; if you leave him—

CH'OU: No, no, how could I face my dead father and sister with honor? No, it wouldn't be right! That, that would be too good for Yen-wang.

HUA *(helplessly)*: Hu-tzu, then, what are you going to do?

CH'OU *(deep in thought)*: I'm thinking, I'm trying to think how I can have Ta-hsing make the first move; if he makes the first move, then he can't blame me.

HUA *(startled)*:   What? Have him come—come and kill —kill you first?

CH'OU: Yes, 'cause I know I can kill him with one hand, like a lamb. But, *(sighing)* my hand just—just won't do it.

HUA *(thinking of what Ch'ou Hu has said; fearfully)*:   But, Hu-tzu, if you weren't careful, and you let him get you first, then—

CH'OU *(stroking his head)*:   That couldn't be, don't worry, that couldn't be.

HUA *(suddenly very much afraid, embracing Ch'ou Hu and cowering in his bosom)*:   No, it's no good, Hu-tzu. My Hu-tzu, if you— then I'd be so miserable.

CH'OU *(consoling her as he pushes her away)*:   Don't, don't, don't. Chin-tzu, don't be this way. *(Suddenly)* Chin-tzu, listen.

HUA: What? *(She abruptly pushes him away.)*

CH'OU: Somebody's there!

HUA *(apprehensively)*:   Could it be Ta-hsing!

CH'OU: We'll see!

(The center door opens and Chiao Ta-hsing enters. Somewhat nervous, he looks to his left and right. Jealousy burns in his breast—his eyes are bloodshot, his hair is in disarray, and his voice is a little hoarse. He senses that people are laughing at him now behind his back, as though Chin-tzu had already blurted out their story in revenge. He looks at Chin-tzu with hate, and with a bitterness spawned by unrequited love—emotions which convulse his mind and make both his countenance and behavior somewhat abnormal. He gazes at the two people in the room without moving a fiber; miserable and despondent, he stands in the doorway, hiding a knife at his chest. Espying Chin-tzu, his hand gropes awkwardly for the knife, but it seems even to him that his conduct is strange and he drops his hand. He seems to laugh and cry at once, seeing these two gaping people before him. Ch'ou Hu looks at him and instinctively goes for the pistol in his pocket.)

Hsing *(to Ch'ou Hu)*: So, the two of you are here.

(Ch'ou looks at Chin-tzu and says nothing.)

Hsing *(looking at Chin-tzu)*: Where's Ma?

Hua: In her room. *(She lowers her head.)*

Hsing *(suspicious)*: What've you been telling Hu-tzu?

Hua: Nothing.

Hsing *(plopping down next to the square table; making a long sigh)*: Ah! *(Looking at Ch'ou Hu in anguish)* Hu-tzu, *(feeling Chin-tzu near him; looking at her)* bring me some wine!

Hua *(exhorting)*: Ta-hsing!

Hsing: Bring me some wine!

(Hua picks out a wine bottle from behind the incense stand and puts it on the table.)

Hua *(anxiously)*: Brother Ch'ou, *(hinting to him)* Ta-hsing's had a lot to drink, look after him a bit.

Ch'ou *(nodding and watching her with care)*: Don't worry, Sister-in-law.

Hua *(looking at Ta-hsing)*: Ta-hsing, I'm going.

Hsing: *(Looking at Hua; but making no reply.)*

Ch'ou: Go—go on, Sister-in-law.

(Hua exits by the right door.)

Hsing *(waiting for her to go out)*: Hu-tzu, sit down now. *(Without waiting for him to take a seat; suddenly)* Hu-tzu, what was the meaning of the way you looked at me just now?

Ch'ou *(calmly)*: Nothing.

Hsing *(thinking that Hua has related her grievances to Ch'ou Hu, allowing some of the recent ugly affair to leak out; doubtfully)*: Then, what were you looking at her for?

Ch'ou *(surprised)*: Me? *(Heavily)* Are you talking about your wife? Why?

HSING *(clutching his forehead painfully)*:   Oh, my head, I'm all mixed up inside. *(Pouring the wine)* Hu-tzu, while I was away just now, what did my mother tell you?

CH'OU *(gazing at Yen-wang's portrait; decidedly)*:   We talked about you, about me, and even about Chin-tzu!

HSING *(as if receiving a shock)*:   Ah, Chin-tzu! *(Standing up)* What'd she say? What'd she tell you?

CH'OU *(no alternative)*:   What's the matter?

HSING *(his hand flailing aimlessly in mid-air; chattering)*:   Chin-tzu, Chin-tzu, she—she— *(seeing no reaction on Ch'ou Hu's face)* then, didn't she mention to you that today while she was in her room, in her room, she— *(unable to stand any more, and pounding on the table with a low thud)* Hu-tzu, tell me, how could she . . . she . . . she have done this to me? Tell me, *(rapping against his head)* what can I do? What can I do?

CH'OU *(slowly)*:   What, what did you say?

HSING *(looking at Ch'ou Hu, then waving his hand; mortified)*:   Nothing, nothing, I've drunk too much. *(He drinks another cupful.)*

CH'OU: Ta-hsing! You can't get rid of things by drinking.

HSING: I know. But you don't understand. When I saw her just now, I felt a chill, as if death were upon **me**.

CH'OU *(surprised)*:   Why?

HSING *(sighing an alcoholic breath)*:   I—I don't know. *(Suddenly; furtively)* But, did you see the expression Chin-tzu had on her face when she looked at me?

CH'OU *(lowering his head)*:   I didn't see.

HSING: She— *(in a low voice)* she looked at me with disgust, I know.

CH'OU: Why?

HSING: We'd only been married three days when suddenly she got cold with me; I knew then what had happened, but I didn't say anything. I was always good to her; I got this for her and bought that for her; I went to a lot of trouble because of her. But today she, she said right—right to my face, she said, there's another man now . . . she wants to go away! *(Slapping the table, bitterly)* This is too—too much, too much. *(He again pours some wine.)*

CH'OU *(urging him on)*: Ta-hsing, act like a man now. You have to do what a man is supposed to do.

HSING: You mean I've got no guts? *(Putting down the wine bottle and looking at Ch'ou Hu; inebriated)* Look who I am!

CH'OU *(deeply)*: Who are you?

HSING *(pointing to the portrait on the wall)*: Yen-wang's son.

CH'OU: Then, what are you going to do?

HSING: I'm going to find that man.

CH'OU: What'll you do when you find him?

HSING: I'm going to *(swiftly taking out his dagger; deeply)* kill him! *(He sticks the knife into the table, then raises his wine cup.)*

CH'OU: Ta-hsing, put down that wine cup!

HSING *(not understanding)*: What for?

CH'OU *(loudly)*: Put it down! *(Somberly)* Look at me, take a good look at me. Who am I?

HSING *(putting down the wine cup; then looking at Ch'ou Hu up and down)*: Who *you* are?

CH'OU *(nodding)*: Uh.

HSING *(frankly)*: You're my—good friend. *(Looking at him a long time; suddenly understands)* Ah, Hu-tzu, you want to help me; you want to help me get him, don't you? You're afraid I can't do anything, you're afraid I'm still a *(jeering at himself)* coward like before. *(More vehemently)*

Am I still a "whipping-post" who's even afraid to step on an ant? Humph, this time I want Chin-tzu to see that I'm not like that, I'm not. With one stroke I'll— look, I want to have her see what kind of a man Yen-wang's son is.

CH'OU: But, Ta-hsing, you don't understand—

HSING *(gratefully)*: I understand, I understand. Hu-tzu, we've been *(using his hand to make a comparison of height)* friends since this big. I know you're a hot-tempered man. You were charged as a criminal, you were crippled, but still you had no complaints. Your own affairs aren't settled yet, but still you want to take on my problems as if they were your own.

CH'OU *(unable to endure his speaking on)*: I, I, Ta-hsing—

HSING: After you were charged, Papa only let me see you twice. When I looked for you again, you'd been moved some place else. For ten years after that I couldn't find you anywhere. But now that I see you, you're the same sincere older brother of mine you always were. But Hu-tzu, don't you want to give me a chance to be myself? Hu-tzu, this is my humil—humiliating business, I don't want anybody else settling it for me. But when I find him and if I can't deal with him, if I can't do it, then after I'm dead you've got to take revenge for—

CH'OU: Yes—but—

HSING: You don't have to say it, I know. If anything happens to me, Hu-tzu, I—

CH'OU: But you should know who he is, shouldn't you? Why don't you . . . you ask Chin-tzu?

HSING *(hatefully)*: Chin-tzu protects him, she won't say. But I'll ask her anyway in a while. If she doesn't say, then Pai Sha-tzu'll tell me by and by.

CH'OU: What's that? Were you just now looking for Pai Sha-tzu?

HSING: I had a man go looking for him; he'll be back soon. Then Pai Sha-tzu and I'll go out and try to find him; Sha-tzu knows who he is.

CH'OU: Ah, *(hesitating)* when's he coming?

HSING: He'll be back soon.

CH'OU: And when he comes?

HSING: Then we'll go.

CH'OU: Just like that? I think you've had too much to drink; you're giddy.

HSING: Giddy?

CH'OU: You don't need to do all that, you don't understand.

HSING *(incredibly)*: So, do you understand?

CH'OU: Yes.

HSING: Then, tell me.

CH'OU *(looking askance at the dagger stuck into the table)*: First put that gruesome thing away somewhere; the way you stuck it there, it makes me nervous; I can't talk.

HSING *(looking at Ch'ou Hu, and thinking he is joking, he even laughs out loud)*: Ha, you're joking! *(He casually places the dagger at his waist.)*

CH'OU: Joking? Take it as a joke, if you like. But it wasn't to make you laugh. *(Suddenly speaking gravely)* This joke . . . *(heaving a long sigh)* Ta-hsing, we two brothers must have a cup of warm wine together. *(Holding up a wine cup)* Drink this cup of wine, to our friendship, after that, *(slapping Ta-hsing on the shoulder)* Ta-hsing. . . .

HSING *(picking up the wine cup curiously)*: How do you mean?

CH'OU: Well, it's just like this wine here, *(gesturing to simulate its flow into the stomach and its evaporation)* it changes into whatever it will. Ta-hsing, drink up!

HSING *(not knowing his intention; in a lower voice)*:   Drink up!

CH'OU: Ta-hsing, once upon a time there was a pair of good friends, who grew up in the same place, just like you and me.

HSING: Ah, were they brothers, too?

CH'OU: Yes, brothers! Both of them were good men. Unfortunately, the younger brother's father was a tyrant, an evil landlord, who used his power to cheat others. He saw that the older brother's father had a piece of nice property, so he connived with some bandits to kidnap the older brother's father; after that they buried him alive, and they took away from him that big plot of good land.

HSING: Who are you talking about?

CH'OU: Just listen! After that, the younger brother's father was worried that the dead man might have a strong son, so slyly he bribed the magistrate there to frame the dead man's son as a bandit and take him off to prison. And the dead man's daughter he sold into another county, as a prostitute.

HSING: But what about the friend, the younger brother?

CH'OU: I don't know, he's a dolt. He lets his parents fool him, so he doesn't have any idea what really happened. Naturally, his elder brother wouldn't want to look for his help.

HSING: What you . . . you say, what's it got to do with us now?

CH'OU: Be patient! After that the older brother got desperate, so he made an escape and came back, even though he was crippled in the leg. *(Hsing looks unconsciously at Ch'ou Hu's leg.)* Yes, just like my leg is now.

HSING: How did he manage to come back?

CH'OU: With two generations of hate in his heart, even the sky would open up if he chopped at it. He wanted to kill all his enemies, the whole family of them.

HSING *(not having guessed his intent)*: Didn't he want to keep his friend?

CH'OU *(exasperated)*: Friend? What can he call a friend in this world? He's come up against this kind of thing at every turn; he suffered ten years in prison, ten years of hell! Whatever heart he had was already dead. When he came back he had only one thing in his heart.

HSING *(hypnotised by Ch'ou Hu's passion)*: What?

CH'OU: Hate! He came back there, and suddenly he saw that the girl he was once engaged to had married the son of his enemy.

HSING: The younger brother?

CH'OU: Yes.

HSING *(unaffectedly)*: Your joke is getting more and more unreal.

CH'OU *(blinking)*: Who said it wasn't real?

HSING: If it was real, how could the younger brother want her?

CH'OU *(coldly)*: He doesn't know.

HSING: He doesn't know?

CH'OU: That's right, *(looking at Hsing)* it doesn't seem right to me either! But his mother thought of him as just a baby, and his father treated him like a little girl. *(He glances at Ta-hsing's earring; Ta-hsing rubs the earring unknowingly.)* His wife won't tell him the truth either, because from the day she married him, his wife's looked down on him; she's just fed up with him.

HSING *(sympathetically)*: What, she's fed up with him, too?

CH'OU: Yes, listen. The very first day the man came back and saw this little bride, the very first day, *(with ferocity)* he slept with her!

HSING: What? This . . . this friend?

CH'OU *(bursting forth)*:   Friend? He ran out of friends a long time ago! His friends are only his enemies, I'm telling you, *(boiling with emotion, and so agitated he nearly cannot speak)* there's only hate in his heart. He just waited to cut— *(rapidly)* then the guy came back, *(looking at Hsing)* and the two men met each other, but the younger brother's *(insanely)* a stupid fool! His friend and his wife, they—they slept together, and still he hasn't figured it out; he still talks like a friend to him, talks of friendship, he still—

HSING *(standing up and leaning against a corner of the table; vexed)*:   What, you—

CH'OU *(clenching his fist; vehemently)*:   Ta-hsing, I'm telling you, I'm just like that older brother, and you're just like—
(Hua runs out from the room on the right.)

HUA: Hu-tzu, don't say it, *(pointing to Hsing)* he, he—

HSING *(dazed)*:   What, you . . . it's you! Hu-tzu!

CH'OU *(looking at him; darkly)*:   Don't you see?

HSING: It can't be, it can't be. Chin-tzu, *(grasping her upper arm; shaking)* tell me, tell me, is it him?
(Hua stares at Hsing but remains silent.)
(Outside Doggie is shouting, "Chiao Ta-ma! Chiao Ta-ma!" He runs in by the center door carrying a lantern.)

PAI: Ta-ma! Ta-ma! There somebody lookin' for you!
(He runs directly to the left room.)

HSING *(grabbing onto Pai Sha-tzu)*:   Doggie, why didn't you come before? Look, *(pointing to Ch'ou Hu; trembling)* is—is it him?

PAI *(it feels strange for him to run into Ch'ou Hu here; as though meeting an old friend, he is startled at first and then pleased; his mouth opens wide)*:   Ah, yeah, chi-cha-ka-cha, it, it's him! *(Finished speaking, he turns his head toward the left room.)* Chiao Ta-ma, Chiao Ta-ma! *(He exits by the left room.)*
(Pause.)

HSING *(suddenly taking out his dagger)*: Hu-tzu, you—

CH'OU *(on guard)*: Ta-hsing, come at me now.

HUA *(leaning on Ch'ou Hu)*: Ta-hsing, put—put down the knife.

HSING *(spurting out from between his teeth)*: Chin-tzu, so, so you love him!

HUA: Yes, *(defiantly)* I do love him. *(She closes her eyes and waits for Ch'ou to make his move.)*

HSING *(injured)*: Chin-tzu, give the knife to him. What you say is more painful than being stabbed with a knife.

CH'OU *(in spite of himself)*: Ta-hsing!

HSING *(waving his hand; to Ch'ou Hu)*: Go—go away from me now. *(He droops onto the bench.)*
(Pai emerges from the left room.)

PAI *(shaking his head; in astonishment)*: Chiao Ta-ma, she's not—not in the room.

CH'OU: Humph, she was in the room just a while ago.

PAI *(shaking his head)*: No! She's not.

CH'OU: What is it?

PAI *(scared)*: No, nothing.

CH'OU: Speak up!

PAI: Somebody! Somebody's looking for her.

CH'OU: Who?

PAI: He doesn't want me t'tell you.

CH'OU: You come with me. *(Pulling Pai, they exit together by the center door.)*
(Pause.)

HSING: Well, what—what do you have to say now?

HUA *(disappointedly)*: Nothing.

HSING: Chin-tzu, what are you going to do now?

HUA *(numbly)*: I want to go away.

HSING *(standing up suddenly)*: What, you want to go away? Chin-tzu. *(He pulls her hand.)*

HUA *(turning a face toward Ta-hsing; his resentment and hatred grow more intense; Ta-hsing's hand touches her; she shouts out as though his touch has given her scabies)*: Don't—don't touch me.

HSING *(surprised)*: What's the matter?

HUA: I'm disgusted with you! *(Suddenly)* Why didn't you fight him?

HSING: Chin-tzu!

HUA: You dolt!

HSING: Huh, don't pretend with me, you love him.

HUA: No, I don't. *(In a low voice)* I was being insolent just then, only you didn't make the first move, the first move—

HSING *(there seems to be a ray of hope that he can recover a love he has already lost)*: Chin-tzu, then was what you said just now untrue?

HUA *(spitefully)*: Untrue? Heaven may be untrue, and earth may be untrue, but is it untrue that your wife has slept with other men?

HSING *(intensely bitter)*: Ah, you shameless pig, you fox fairy. *(He picks up the dagger and comes toward her.)*

HUA *(lifting her head)*: Go ahead! If you can't do it, you're not your father's son.

(Ta-hsing walks up to her.)

HSING *(raising the dagger evilly, his eyes wide open)*: Chin-tzu, you see me wrong. Look, *(slashing downward)* I strike—

HUA *(feeling her position dangerous, she instinctively impedes his wrist with her hand. But he has already sliced the back of her hand; she bleeds and cries out)*: You— *(She pushes his wrist away and runs.)*

HSING *(sweat issuing from his face)*: I really— *(He pursues her.)*

(Hua goes around the table in retreat; Hsing follows behind.)

HUA *(shrieking as she runs)*: Hu-tzu, Hu-tzu!

HSING *(speaking as he pursues her)*: You can't get away, he's gone, he doesn't want you anymore!

(Ta-hsing forces Hua into a corner and clutches her.)

HUA *(screaming)*: Hu-tzu! Hu-tzu!

HSING *(with blue-green veins jumping out on his forehead)*: You— you still call for him! You still call for—him! *(He raises the dagger, then downward—)*

HUA: My, my Ta-hsing, you're so bad to me to— *(She closes her eyes.)*

HSING *(looking down at Hua's face; unable to lower his hand and shaking his head pitiably)*: Ah, Chin-tzu, it's you who's the bad one. *(Slowly putting the dagger flat against his chest)* How—how can you treat me this way? How can you be so unfeeling to have betrayed me?

HUA *(opening her eyes slowly)*: Ta-hsing, what's the matter?

HSING *(raising the dagger again, Hua closes her eyes once more)*: I want to cut your heart out— *(Suddenly wilting he lets go of the knife; Hua looks at him; suppliantly)* Ah, Chin-tzu, I beg of you, you can't be so callous.

HUA *(understanding what kind of man he really is)*: What is it?

HSING *(looking pleadingly at her)*: Don't go.

HUA: I'm your wife, where can I go?

HSING: I mean, your heart mustn't go.

HUA: Ah, you want—

HSING: Chin-tzu, won't you listen to what I say? Chin-tzu, you mustn't do these things, I've been good to you. Chin-tzu, I beg of you, let bygones be bygones, only promise me you're finished with him from now on, finished.

HUA: Finished?

HSING: Yes, finished; tomorrow I'll make him go away and then there'll be no more of this. Chin-tzu, I'll go along with anything you want. If you want clothes, I'll go buy them from town for you; if you want jewelry, I'll have someone bring it to you; if you want money, I'll give you all my money.

HUA: Yes, but—

HSING: You don't know, without you, without you I have nothing. You can't be of two minds with me. If you're against Ma, we'll work something out, we'll think of a way. I—I could tell her to mind her own business. I could have it out with her. I could even ignore her. If you're still not happy, we'll go away together. I'll leave her! Yes, I'll even leave her for your sake.

HUA: But, *(in despair)* what do you want me for?

HSING: Ah, I . . . I do want you, you don't know how much—

HUA: What for? I'm unhappy here, and if I'm unhappy, then you are, too, aren't you. If you're unhappy, wouldn't I be, too?

HSING: Then, Chin-tzu, you don't want to do what I say?

HUA: It's not that. I'm only thinking for your sake. I know you can't leave your mother and your mother can't leave you. And your mother and I are such bitter enemies, you know that. Today she quarrelled with you about me, tomorrow I'll quarrel with you about her. Day and night it's like that; she hates me, and I hate her; how can you stand being in the middle at the of both mercy sides?

HSING: Then, you really want to go away, don't you!

HUA: I didn't say that.

HSING *(bitterly)*:   You really want to go with him, don't you?

HUA: I . . . I don't.

HSING *(resentfully)*: You're lying to me.

HUA *(helpless)*: No.

HSING *(obstinately)*: Say what you feel; I want you to say what you feel: what are you going to do with me? Don't lie to me anymore.

HUA: You want me to speak from my heart?

HSING *(trivially)*: Tell me what you would do with me. What would you do with me? What would you do? What? What?

HUA: You want me to say it?

HSING *(obstinately)*: Yes.

HUA: Well then, *(looking at Ta-hsing)* I love you, I adore you. I can't stand not to hug you every day, to call you, and pet you, to bid you, and kiss you, and lick you. Every night I hold you to my bosom. All year long, day after day, from morning 'til night, I can't put you out of my thoughts; I dream about you, I'm reminded of you, I think about you, I look at you, I long for you, I speak of you, I talk about you . . .

HSING *(slapping the table)*: That's enough! Enough! Chin-tzu!

HUA: Now doesn't that sound nice?

HSING *(looking forward)*: Oh, God! Why must a man always put up with such things from a woman?

HUA: Ask yourself, but if I were you . . .

HSING: What, Chin-tzu!

HUA: I'd kill her for sure.

HSING *(disconsolate; shaking his head)*: Then, you're not a man.

HUA: Then turn away from her, let her go.

HSING: Let her go? No, I couldn't, Chin-tzu, you can't go. You still have a motherless child.

HUA: I didn't bear the child.

HSING: Then, Chin-tzu, you still have me. I want you, I'm yours, *(gulping)* your husband; you can't go.

HUA: I didn't pick my husband.

HSING: Then, aren't you afraid that people will talk about you, or curse you, or that the posse will come and take you away?

HUA: There's no use preaching to me. If you don't want to let me go, then come at me again with your knife; I can't get away. But you can't push me around with that thing all the time; I'll still be wanting to go away sooner or later. Ta-hsing, I was born in the wilderness and I grew up in the wilderness, and maybe I'll even die in the wilderness. A person only lives once, Ta-hsing. In the Chiao family I'm dead.

HSING: Then you don't care about anything, you don't think of anything? But Chin-tzu, you must always remember the little affection I've felt for you. I've been good to you, you know that.

HUA *(nodding)*:   I know.

HSING: Then, I ask you again. *(Solemnly)* This time, Chin-tzu, I kneel to ask you. Chin-tzu, you're so beautiful, your heart couldn't possibly be bad; it can't be you have no feeling at all. Look, *(kneeling down; with great pain)* a big man like me kneeling down in front of you. Think again, think about the things you've done, things a wife should never do. But, Chin-tzu, the debts I owed you in a past life, I'll pay back to you in this life; I still beg you, I beg you, don't ever go. What you've done, is all forgotten. Hu-tzu has done me wrong, but I'll even forget that; I'll give him money and let him go. Now it's up to you, it's up to you!

HUA: No, get up.

HSING *(standing up)*:   What is it?

HUA *(determined)*:   No.

HSING *(pleadingly)*:   But, Chin-tzu, how can you love him so. That brute, that monster with a head like a big winter melon, he's like a mangy frog, and lame, and—

HUA: You don't have to say anymore, I know all that; I love him and I still want to go with him.

HSING: What, you still want to go with him?

HUA: Yes.

HSING: Why?

HUA: He's good to me.

HSING *(dully)*:   Ah! In only ten days?

HUA *(defiantly)*:   Yes, only ten days and I can't leave him.

HSING *(mechanically)*:   You can't leave him?

HUA: No.

HSING *(suddenly in madness)*:   Then, if you'll only stay here, I'll have him come to you, and I'd be willing, when I'm not at home, I'll let you . . . you . . . go with him and— *(He can speak no more.)*

HUA *(sullenly)*:   What?

HSING: For . . . for your sake, I . . . I'd be willing!

HUA *(exploding)*:   Bull!

HSING: What?

HUA *(hateful to the extreme)*:   You think I'm a pig. You're a bastard!

HSING: What?

HUA: You cuckold!

(Hsing slaps her on the face.)

HSING: You! *(Looking at Hua, his eyes filled with tears. He closes his eyes; tears flow down. He hates himself.)* I love you so very much. But you're really not worth it. *(Opening his eyes)* All right, Chin-tzu, you want to go with him? Go.

HUA *(with unchanged expression)*:   Then?

HSING: I'll kill him!

HUA: You wouldn't dare.

HSING: If I can't do it, the posse'll take care of him.

HUA: What, you told the posse?

HSING: That's right. *(Intently determined)* I told 'em.

HUA *(hatefully)*:   But we can still get away from here.

HSING: Maybe, but there's only one way.

HUA: What?

HSING: You'll have to kill me first!

(Chiao enters by the left door.)

CHIAO: What are you jabbering about there?

HUA *(amazed that Chiao has emerged by the left door)*:   Oh, weren't you staying in your room?

CHIAO: Who said I wasn't? My room doesn't have another door, where would I go out?

HUA: You didn't see Doggie go in looking for you?

CHIAO: Doggie, oh!

HUA: Yes?

CHIAO: What about Hu-tzu?

HUA: He just went out.

CHIAO: Who told him to go out? Who let him get away?

(Ch'ou Hu enters by the left door; Hua and Hsing are startled.)

CH'OU *(cunningly)*:   I didn't go out, Kan-ma, I'm still here in the room.

CHIAO ⎫
HUA ⎬ *(simultaneously)*:   What?
      ⎭

CH'OU: I was just coming back from outside, when I saw Kan-ma climbing in through the window of her room. I thought, well, if an old woman didn't mind a little trouble, what trouble would it be for a young guy like me? So, I climbed in through the window, too.

CHIAO: Ah, then, *(not naturally)* very well, I'll let you stay in my room, I'll sleep outside. Chin-tzu, did you fix the bedding?

HUA: Yes.

CHIAO: Then you two go inside and sleep.

(Pai Sha-tzu hurries in by the center door.)

PAI: Ta-ma, Ta-ma.

CHIAO: What?

PAI: Ch'ang Wu, Ch'ang Wu.

CHIAO: Shut up.

PAI *(anxiously)*: He— he's lookin' for you again.

CH'OU *(half understanding)*: Ch'ang Wu?

(Again the baby bawls out from his dreaming.)

CHIAO: Go on! Go on! Sleep! Sleep! You've scared the baby into waking up again.

(Hua and Chiao Ta-hsing enter the room on the right; Ch'ou Hu enters the room on the left.)

CHIAO *(to Doggie)*: Get out! You fool!

(The light gradually dims and the stage becomes completely dark. After ten seconds the stage again lightens. An hour has already passed; it is midnight and the Chiao house is all asleep. From the left room comes the sound of Ch'ou Hu's snoring. Ta-hsing has fallen asleep in the room on the right, and because of his nightmares, he is groaning deeply and ceaselessly. The oil lamp on the square table on stage has been turned down, so that the room is darker; the lamp in front of the idol puts out a gloomy, dim light. Chiao sits on a bench in the black shadows, stroking the baby. To the side a narrow plank bed has been put up, covered over with bedding. Chiao is concerned about something; she had been lying down just then, but she has risen again. Outside there is a "cuckoo" quietly singing, crisply and happily; but it sings for only a moment and then stops. There is a fearful whistling sound in the air from the slight vibration of the distant telegraph lines.)

CHIAO *(listening attentively to the snoring from the left as she pats the baby)*: Oo! —Oo, baby sleep. Oo—oo—oo. *(Lowering her voice)* Sleep—sleep, oo—oo—oo. *(She stands up, and hearkens alertly to the left; she walks a couple of steps, still mumbling—)* Oo—oo—oo.

(Someone knocks softly on the center door outside.)

CHIAO *(feeling her way to the door)*: Who is it?

VOICE OUTSIDE: It's me—Ch'ang Wu.

CHIAO: Come in.

(Ch'ang Wu enters; he has thrown on a black garment and carries a red lantern.)

CHIAO *(in a low voice)*: Quiet now.

CH'ANG *(anxiously; pointing to the left)*: What, is Hu— Hu-tzu asleep?

CHIAO: Listen!

CH'ANG *(hearing how steady his snoring is; gladly)*: He's fast asleep.

CHIAO *(the red lamp reflecting against her stern face)*: Now?

CH'ANG *(turning his head to look)*: I've already reported him to the posse.

CHIAO: Did you really go this time?

CH'ANG: Of course, they—they said they'd come right away.

CHIAO: Right away?

CH'ANG *(ingratiatingly)*: Right away! *(Suddenly with covetousness)* But the reward—the reward, that hundred and fifty dollars?

CHIAO: You'll get it.

CH'ANG *(surprised)*: You, you don't want it?

CHIAO: No, *(sullenly)* I only want to get rid of this sore in my heart as soon as I can. *(Suddenly)* How come, how come we haven't seen anybody from the posse yet?

CH'ANG: Soon—soon. They said they haven't got a lot of men, they can't handle him. They said it'd be better if he were dead. Save 'em a lot of trouble.

CHIAO *(suddenly an idea flashes through her mind)*: What? They want him dead, too?

CH'ANG: The posse said, "dead or alive, it's all the same", but, *(niggardly)* for a dead guy it'll only be a— a hundred dollars.

CHIAO *(gnashing her teeth)*: Yeah, "dead or alive, its all the same."

CH'ANG *(not understanding)*: What?

CHIAO: Ch'ang Wu, go out with me now.

CH'ANG: Go out?

CHIAO: To see if anybody's come yet.

(Ch'ang Wu and Chiao exit by the center door. Hua enters by the door on the right, holding a candle. She wears blood-red, close-fitting garments; her hair is in disarray and her eyes flash a frightening light. She puts the cloth bundle in her hand on the stand, and then slowly walks to the door on the left. Suddenly she shivers and turns her head to glance toward the center door. Just then Ch'ou Hu comes out through the door on the right; he is bare to the waist, his chest-hair black and thick, his muscles tautly bulging. A pistol, half-wrapped in a red cloth, is stuck obliquely into his broad leather belt; holding a blue coat in one hand, he pats Hua lightly on the shoulder.)

CH'OU *(in a low voice)*: Uh!

HUA *(so scared she nearly cries out; turning around)*: Oh! It's you, you could've scared me to death.

CH'OU *(urgently)*: Blow out the candle.

HUA: Why? The blind one can't see.

CH'OU: There are others who have eyes to see.

HUA: Oh, Ch'ang Wu! *(She blows out the candle immediately.)*

CH'OU *(gravely)*: It's so dark! *(The two of them stand together holding their breaths.)*

HUA *(in the darkness; hurriedly)*: Things have gotten worse.

CH'OU *(severely)*: I know. They reported me to the posse.

HUA: Oh, *(hatefully)* then what Ta-hsing said was true.

CH'OU: So, Ta-hsing's in this, too.

HUA: That's what he said.

CH'OU: If that's the way it is, then he's done for, too.

HUA: I'm afraid we can't get away; he said he'd die before he'd let us go.

CH'OU *(mindfully)*: Then the time's come.

HUA *(pulling Ch'ou's hand; expectantly)*: Do you mean we should go now?

CH'OU: No, *(his eyes flashing a frightening light)* now we must make our move.

HUA *(terrified)*: Hu-tzu, must you really—

CH'OU *(nodding)*: How many times in your life can one afford to play a game like this? *(Pointing to the cradle)* Take the baby into the other room.

HUA *(walking to the cradle; looking at Ch'ou)*: Wh—why?

CH'OU: He makes so much noise. If he should wake up, his crying'll make trouble.

HUA *(picking up the baby)*: But Hu-tzu—

CH'OU *(waving her away)*: Take him into the other room now.

(Hua takes the baby and exits by the door on the left; Ch'ou Hu starts searching about him for something, without success. As he is looking, Hua enters by the left door.)

HUA: What are you doing?

CH'OU *(looking at Hua, he suddenly is aware of something; pointing in front of him)*: Did you see it?

HUA: What?

CH'OU *(with dignity)*: My father was here.

HUA *(in a low voice; hurriedly)*: Hu-tzu.

CH'OU *(as though he is looking at something)*: He told me to look for it; he told me there was a knife in this room.

HUA *(pretending ignorance)*: A knife?

CH'OU *(looking at Hua)*: He said it was right herebe fore my eyes.

HUA *(involuntarily pulling out the dagger from her bosom)*: Hu-tzu, I—

CH'OU *(extending his hand)*: Give it to me.

HUA *(unwilling at first, she looks at Ch'ou's face; suddenly with violence)*: All right, take it. Finish him off quick!

CH'OU *(in a low voice)*: Has he fallen asleep?

HUA *(bowing her head; softly)*: I—I coaxed him to sleep.

CH'OU: Keep watch outside for me. *(Treading toward the left door; quietly)* Ta-hsing! *(There seems to be a groaning within, as if someone were talking in his sleep; to Hua)* Listen!

VOICE FROM WITHIN *(muffled and hurriedly)*: . . . Quick . . . quick! Chin-tzu, *(weakly)* my knife, my knife. *(Painfully)* Chin-tzu! *(Becoming indistinct)* Chin-tzu! . . .

HUA *(whispering)*: He's—he's moaning in his dreams.

CH'OU: Such scary dream words. *(Looking closely at the doorway on the left; in a low voice)* Ta-hsing.

VOICE FROM WITHIN *(with a long gloomy sigh)*: So dark! So dark! *(Groaning fearfully)* So dark is the world! *(He sighs another long painful sigh, and then he is quiet.)*

HUA *(trembling; in a low voice)*: He—he seems to be talking to us.

CH'OU: Ta-hsing! *(There is no response within.)* Ta-hsing! *(Still there is no response; suddenly he turns toward the front of the stage, into space.)* Father, you must help me! *(Quickly he enters the left door.)*

(Hua waits outside; apprehensively but attentively she listens to the sounds inside; she is anxious.)

(Far away outside, wild dogs bark wildly, like a pack of hungry wolves. Hua looks out unquietly. Inside she suddenly hears someone gasp from suffocation, and then fall to the ground as though choked.)

HUA: God!

(Ch'ou limps in from the left room, his eyes wide open, appearing to be possessed by demons.)

CH'OU *(the dagger in his hand is daubed with blood; his voice is nearly inaudible)*:   It's finished, even he is finished.

HUA *(unable to gasp, she points to Hu-tzu's bloody hand)*: Oh, your hand, your hand.

CH'OU *(lifting up his shaking hands; remorsefully)*:   My hands, my hands! I've killed, I've killed many men, but this is the first time my hands have trembled like this. *(Letting out a sighing sound from within his chest)* Living doesn't mean a thing, but when you're dead, then it becomes real. *(Fearfully)* I grabbed him and suddenly he woke up—the way he looked at me. He wasn't afraid, he was drunk, but he looked at me as though he wanted to say something; he stared right at me. *(Nodding slowly; sympathetically)* I know he was sad in his heart, so sad he couldn't tell anybody. *(Suddenly with force)* I raised the knife, and then he knew he had only a moment left; he was suddenly very afraid. He looked at me, *(lowering his head; slowly)* but he was laughing in his throat, laughing so queer-like; he pointed at his heart, and then he nodded to me— *(Shaking his head suddenly; harshly)* And then I stabbed him! *(Suddenly his voice is nearly inaudible.)* He didn't make any cry; he just closed his eyes. *(Throwing the dagger to the floor)* A man's really just a worthless thing, a handful of dirt, a hunk of meat, a heap of bleeding flesh; you get knocked off sooner or later, and then it's over, it's over.

HUA: Wash off your hands quick.

CH'OU: There's no use washing. You can't wash off the blood.

HUA: Then let's go.

CH'OU *(lifting up his head)*: Go? *(Looking at Hua)* Yes, let's go! *(He walks a couple of steps.)*

HUA *(stopping suddenly)*: Listen!

CH'OU: What?

HUA: Somebody's out there! *(Running to the window; Ch'ou Hu follows behind.)* It's a red lantern, a red lantern, they—they've come.

CH'OU *(at the window)*: No, no, it's the blind one; it looks like Doggie beside her; he's carrying the lantern.

HUA *(nodding)*: Oh! Oh, yes! *(Suddenly)* The blind one—she's . . . she's coming.

CH'OU: Yes, she's looking for me.

HUA *(fearfully)*: She's singing something to herself, isn't she?

CH'OU *(hatefully; in a low voice)*: I know! *(Slowly)* "Dead or alive, it's all the same."

HUA: Don't talk.

(Chiao enters by the center door. Ch'ou and Hua stand still, holding their breaths at the window, and watch her step majestically to the incense table and lift up the heavy iron staff. As she walks to the right door, Hua nearly shouts out in fright. Chiao listens for a moment and then locks the right door; her face suddenly shows an abnormal ferocity. Holding the iron staff lightly, she walks to the door on the left, as Ch'ou and Hua's eyes follow her. Ceremoniously Chiao enters the left door.)

(There is no sound in the room; only far off one can hear wild dogs howling like ghosts or wolves. Hua looks at Ch'ou Hu; Ch'ou Hu stares at the left door.)

HUA *(in a low voice)*: That's strange, what'd she go into that room for?

CH'OU *(pressing her hand)*: She wants to kill me.

HUA *(whispering)*: With—with what?

CH'OU *(hurriedly)*:   Didn't you see that iron staff she was holding?

HUA: How?

CH'OU *(demonstrating a downward striking motion)*:   Like that!

HUA *(suddenly realizing, her whole body quakes; in a low voice, hurriedly)*:   The—the baby's on your bed.

CH'OU *(scared)*:   What, the baby—?

HUA *(in wild anxiety)*:   The baby's on that—that bed—
(Suddenly one can hear inside a muffled but heavy pounding on the bed; a small animal seems to make a light cry, and then there is silence.)

CH'OU ⎫
       ⎬ *(at the same time)*:   Oh, God!
HUA   ⎭

(Chiao suddenly makes a sharp cry from the left room.)

CHIAO *(extremely fearful)*:   Oh—baby, my baby!   *(It is quiet again.)*

CH'OU *(afraid)*:   It's too late!

HUA *(abruptly)*:   Let's go! Let's go, quick!

CH'OU *(also frightened)*:   The baby's dead.

HUA: Put on some clothes fast, there must be somebody out there. If you go out that way, they'll see you.
(She puts a shirt on Ch'ou Hu and then hurries to pick up the cloth bundle and the dagger; Ch'ou Hu buttons his clothing less than half-way. Chiao walks out by the left door. With her two hands she holds the little baby, covered over with a black cloth shirt. Her face is like a tragic mask, her eyebrows gnarled in pain, the corners of her mouth drooping into two deep ditches. She neither weeps nor cries, but standing at the door she resembles a horrible spirit of death. Ch'ou and Hua unconsciously back off in fear; they press closely together in a corner.)

CHIAO *(with an inhuman voice)*:   Hu-tzu!   *(Stopping a moment, but perceiving no response)* Hu-tzu!   *(Still no answer; gravely)* I   know   you're   here.   *(Suddenly bursting out)* You're too vicious, Hu-tzu; Heaven won't take you! It's true, the Chiao family has wronged you, but your revenge is too savage. *(Her pain increases to near madness.)* You were right, look! I killed the baby with my own hands. But if I take him to the shaman and she can't save him, Hu-tzu, *(cruelly)* I'm going to be after you wherever you go, I'll be after you. *(Severely)* Hu-tzu, I'm leaving you now. *(Speaking toward the center door)* If you want to kill me, then kill me! But I'm telling you, *(having just arrived at the door)* the posse's already outside with their guns ready, and they're going to come in and kill you.

(Holding the baby, Chiao exits by the center door. The two of them stand motionless. Outside they hear Chiao calling out in a low voice, "Doggie!" and then they hear a strange coarse voice singing: ". . . On the first and fifteenth the temple gate opens, . . . the ox- and horse-headed demon-messengers align on either side. . . ." The two of them turn around and listen carefully.)

HUA *(apprehensively)*: Who is it? Who's that singing now?

CH'OU *(restrains himself with great effort)*: It's Dog— Doggie.

VOICE OUTSIDE *(becoming more grievous)*: ". . . His Highness Yen-wang sits in the center; a gust of chilly wind. . . ."

HUA *(looking up; suddenly in a loud voice; pointing)*: Yen-wang's eyes are moving again, they moved.

CH'OU *(alarmed)*: What?

HUA *(very much afraid)*: He wants to talk!

(Ch'ou Hu draws his pistol and fires four shots toward Yen-wang's portrait on the wall; immediately the painting falls to the floor.)

HUA: Hu-tzu!

(Outside they think Ch'ou Hu is trying to fight his way out; they fire their guns into the room.)

CH'OU: They've really come.

(In the midst of the shooting outside Ch'ang Wu is yelling: "Don't shoot back there! Don't shoot, I'm up here." *He stumbles witlessly in through the center door.)*

CH'ANG *(seeing Ch'ou Hu, he freezes where he is)*: God! *(He wants to turn around and go out again.)*

CH'OU *(grabbing onto Ch'ang Wu)*: So good of you to come! *(Pointing the gun at him)* So good of you to come. *(Calling toward the center door)* Don't shoot, you guys! *(There is still shooting outside; turning to Ch'ang Wu)* Talk to them, tell them not to shoot.

CH'ANG *(leaning toward the window; shouting rapidly)*: Captain Liu! Don't shoot, it's me, Ch'ang Wu, Ch'ang Wu.

(The gunshots stop suddenly.)

CH'OU: Tell them you're in my hands now, tell them not to fire, I'm coming out.

CH'ANG *(at a loss for words)*: Captain Liu! I, I've been captured by Ch'ou Hu. I'm in his hands, Captain Liu, he's holding me, and he's coming out, don't fire, d'you hear?

CH'OU *(in a loud voice)*: You guys, there's nothing between us; I came here to pay back the hate of two generations; let's be friends, you guys, let me have a way out. If you don't give me a break, I'm going to kill your spy, Ch'ang Wu, right now.

CH'ANG: Captain Liu! Captain Liu!

CH'OU: Well, is it yes or no? You won't say, huh? If your answer is no, fire one shot, if it's yes, fire two shots. What d'you say?

(It is quiet outside.)

CH'OU: So, you won't answer, huh! I'm going to count to ten. If you don't answer after I get to ten, *(to Ch'ang Wu)* you'll have to forgive me.

CH'ANG: Captain Liu! Captain Liu!

CH'OU *(starting to count)*: One, two, three, four, . . .

CH'ANG *(shouting nearly at the same time)*: Captain Liu! Captain Liu! There's a whole lot of us in the Ch'ang Wu family. If I die, they're going to be after you for their revenge, Captain Liu!

(It is quiet all about.)

CH'OU: Eight, nine,—

CH'ANG: Liu—

(Outside a single shot is fired.)

CH'OU: One shot.

CH'ANG: Captain Liu! Liu—

(Outside there is another shot)

CH'OU: Two shots!

CH'ANG *(sighing)*: Phew!

CH'OU *(poking the gun against Ch'ang Wu's back)*: Move! *(To Hua)* Let's go.

(Hua takes the cloth bundle and follows the two men out through the center door.)

(There is no one in the room; it is quiet. After a pause, one suddenly hears two gunshots far away; then the gunshots become successively closer together. As the curtain slowly descends and is about to close, the gunshots become more rapid.)

(CURTAIN)

ACT THREE

Scene I

*The same day, past one o'clock at night; Ch'ou Hu and Hua are
fleeing through the Dark Forest.*

*At forked paths in the wood—it is a gloomy and dense forest.
Twenty feet beyond, a drizzling mist can be seen rising from the
wilderness, a dim veil that shrouds the black timber in a primeval
animosity. The forest is mysterious; in its midst, hidden deeply
among a thicket of trees, is a black swamp, where the light of a clear
rushing stream of water penetrates the overgrowth, queerly like a
woman's pale face in the night. The forest is brimming with
primitive life that thrusts itself toward the sky, the huge branches and
leaves obscuring the stars. Dismal light rays reflect off the swamp
water, and in the foreground one can vaguely make out through the
dull fog the long-time remains of a mill—the small circular ground
overgrown with artemisia to the height of half a man, and the bulky
millstone sleeping away, eroding in its thicket of vegetation. Among
the weeds a small dirt mound rises abruptly; beneath it, perhaps, lie
the bones of the former landowner. Life here is menaced by fear, by
the incoherence of primitive man's imagination. For indeed, anxiety
squats amid the forest, its countless short and stout dense trees
seeming to hide in wait among the foliage, like so many headless
ghosts of war; and when the wind comes by, they sway back and
forth like balls of flesh amassed heap upon heap. On the right,
beneath the tree roots, is buried a dry well filled with crushed stones.
Creeping plants have climbed snugly over its banks, their contorted
forked branches concealed in the grey fog. If one looks up, the open
sky cannot be seen, for the thick, enveloping white poplars spread their*

*enormous dragon-scale-like leaves; and when the wind blows, the
heavens sound a mournful, somber, awesome noise. The light from
the sky will seep through the cracks between the leaves, flashing on the
trunks and lighting up the white bark; one seems to be surrounded
by numerous white-garmented phantoms. From the right a forest
trail draws in and circuits to the left, and in the center there is a
wider abandoned path that reaches into deeper darkness. At the front
of the stage a strange irregular stone tablet rises up, impeding the
way; from the top of it hangs a hideous forked bough, which somewhat resembles a great beast opening his blood-smelly jaws.*

*As the curtain opens, the wind blows through, and the heavens
sound out the groaning of the white poplar leaves; everywhere black
shadows dodge about the forest. The mist gradually scatters now;
and when the wind has ceased, the dim fog disappears, sinking into
the distant vista.*

*The noise of the wind lessens, as far away intermittent gunshots
are heard, and close by a few animals scurry across, panting softly.*

*Hua walks out tiredly by the path on the right; she shoulders a
small white cloth bundle. The light rays leaking down between the
foliage flash upon her oily-bright face; her forehead is dripping with
sweat. Her blood-red jacket clings closely to her body and the buttons
on her right lapel have come off. She gasps with agitation like an
injured leopard; her clothing has been rent by thorns at one place, and
the barbs still cling to her. She stands at center, looking about
anxiously, not knowing the road that will bring them out of the
forest, and takes out a large, colored handkerchief to wipe the beads
of sweat from her eyes.*

HUA *(panting; letting out a long sigh)*:   Oh! It's so dark!
(Timorously) What is this place? *(Suddenly she sees a long,
frightful, white-clothed object flash out in the black shadows; in
a low, urgent voice)* Hu-tzu, Hu-tzu! *(She waits for a reply,
but there is none. Distantly there is a gunshot; a bullet pierces
through space with a hissing sound. She does not dare shout again
but backs off, running into a white tree trunk; she turns about
hastily to see what it is. A gust of wind sweeps through, and the
heavens sound that mournful, fearful, wretched noise; surrounded*

by white-clothed trunks she looks above her. Light rays burst forth, and everywhere the shadows of forest vegetation shake chaotically; shouting in fright) Hu-tzu! Hu—tzu! Hu—tzu! *(The gust passes by and the trees suddenly quiet down; again, in a low but urgent voice)* Hu-tzu! Hu-tzu!
(Silence.)

VOICE FROM THE RIGHT *(a fatigued sigh)*:   Uh! What is it?

HUA *(walking forward a step)*:   Hu-tzu! Where are you?

VOICE FROM THE RIGHT *(hoarsely)*:   Here. Chin-tzu, come back now.

HUA *(calming herself)*:   I can't see the road, there isn't any light ahead. *(Still she walks toward the right.)*

VOICE FROM THE RIGHT *(hearing the footsteps; warning)*: Stand still, don't move.

HUA *(in a low voice)*:   What is it?

VOICE FROM THE RIGHT *(in a low voice)*:   I think somebody's following us.

HUA: Somebody? *(Scared)* Somebody's following us?

VOICE FROM THE RIGHT *(lowly)*:   Look! A light! A red light!

HUA *(toward the right)*:   A red light?
(Suddenly a man yells out from the right.)

VOICE FROM THE RIGHT *(hitting the yelling man's mouth)*: Shoutin', shoutin', huh?
(Suddenly there is a deathly quiet.)

HUA *(urgently)*:   What? What is it?

VOICE FROM THE RIGHT *(calmly)*:   Nothing! It's Ch'ang Wu. Chang Wu wants to die! *(Suddenly to Ch'ang Wu; in a low voice; snarlingly)* Ch'ang Wu, you shout one more time, damn it, *(striking him again)* you just do that once more and you're dead!

HUA: What, haven't you let him go yet?

VOICE FROM THE RIGHT: Soon as we get out of the forest I'll let him go. *(To Ch'ang Wu)* Move! Move!

(Ch'ou Hu enters from the right with his back to the audience; he holds a pistol in his right hand, and with his left he feels occasionally to his rear for the dagger under his belt; he glances backward from time to time. As Ch'ou Hu enters the wood, all at once he becomes strangely in harmony with his surroundings. There is a rip in the back of his clothing, which exposes a very dark flesh; his long sleeves are so torn they have become scattered shreds, and cloth strips bind his injured wrist. His hulky arms resemble iron pillars, and his monstrous back is humped slightly so that the back of his neck makes an abrupt right angle like that of an ape; from the rear he looks like a column of black smoke curled up by the wind. But just then he turns about and at last one can see the store of alarm and apprehension in his eyes. When, momentarily, his spirit is gripped by fear, he suddenly comes to resemble his ancestor, the primitive ape-man, trembling against the barbarity of midnight. There is an extreme disquiet in his expression; hope, pensiveness, fear, and exasperation pelt steadily upon his imagination, causing in him a sudden marked rise in his hallucinations. Amid this black wilderness we can discern in him not a thread of "bruteness"; instead, we begin to discover in him something beautiful, something that is worthy of man's precious sympathy. He represents a genuine man, heavily persecuted, whose injustices are being reenacted in this forest. His wiliness in the prologue, the deceiving character, is slowly disappearing, just as Hua has reacted to this nocturnal trial by sublimating the carnal lust she has for Ch'ou Hu into a spiritual love.)

(Ch'ang Wu, following Ch'ou Hu, emerges on the right. His black robe has already been torn; his manner is very troubled. He holds his hands and looks dumbly at Ch'ou Hu; he enters, limping.)

HUA: Hu-tzu! Hu-tzu! Where are you? I can't see you.

CH'OU *(walking in, turning his head)*: Here.

HUA *(running to Ch'ou Hu, grabbing at him)*: Hu-tzu, I'm so afraid.

CH'OU *(his face covered with perspiration)*:   Chin-tzu, I think someone's following us.

HUA: Who could it be?

CH'OU *(in a low voice)*:   Wherever we go that red light's there, too.

HUA: God, that couldn't be—

CH'OU *(opening wide his eyes)*:   You mean—

(Far away there is a gunshot.)

CH'OU *(suddenly restraining Hua with a hand)*:   Chin-tzu.

HUA: Let's go! Let's go! They're coming after us again.

(Ch'ang Wu's spirits rise; he listens.)

CH'OU: No! No! Listen again.

(Far away there is another gunshot.)

HUA: They're right behind us! *(Pulling Ch'ou Hu)* Let's go, quick.

CH'ANG *(apprehensively)*:   Mrs. Ta-hsing, we've been running nearly seven miles without a rest, I . . . I just can't go on.

CH'OU: You old devil, listen! *(He listens carefully.)*

(In the distance there is another shot, but the sound is further off.)

CH'OU *(relieved)*:   It doesn't matter, those dogs are getting farther and farther away; they're chasing us toward the west.

HUA *(worriedly)*:   Hu-tzu, when are we getting out?

CH'OU: Soon! I think a mile more and we'll be almost there. Sit down! *(He sits upon the millstone and holds up his head with both hands in deep thought.)*

CH'ANG: Ch'ou . . . Ch'ou, sir, where . . . where are you two taking me?

CH'OU *(raising his head)*:   We're taking you to the Western Heaven.

CH'ANG: Mrs. Ta-hsing . . . Mrs. Ta-hsing, this—you, you have to say something for me, Mrs. Ta-hsing.

CH'OU *(exploding)*:   You old fool! I told you not to mention that name! D'you hear me?

CH'ANG *(looking at Hua)*:   But Mrs. Ta-hsing!—

CH'OU *(standing up abruptly and raising his pistol toward Ch'ang Wu)*:   You old fool! What are you yelling about Ta-hsing for?

CH'ANG: Oh, you don't want me to talk about Ta-hsing? Oh! Then, sure, I won't talk, I won't talk about him! But you said you wanted me to go to the Western Heaven, the Western Heaven. *(To Hua)* Say something, *(unconsciously)* Mrs. Ta-hsing.

CH'OU *(unable to bear anymore he fires a shot over Ch'ang Wu's head)*:   You!

CH'ANG *(feeling himself)*:   My—my head.

HUA: Hu-tzu, what's the matter with you? Why are you shooting again?

CH'OU: I—I don't know what happened. When he mentioned him—him—I, *(sitting down)* I'm mixed up, mixed—

HUA *(changing the subject)*:   Hu-tzu, please let Uncle Ch'ang Wu go back.

CH'OU: Yeah, *(lowering his head)* I had that in mind.

CH'ANG: Really?

CH'OU: Eh . . .

CH'ANG: Now?

CH'OU: Eh . . .

HUA: But Uncle Ch'ang Wu, it's so dark, you—

CH'ANG *(at once)*:   No problem, I can stay at the temple. *(To Hua)* So, see you later! I—I'll be going. *(He starts to walk toward the right.)*

CH'OU *(suddenly)*:   Wait! What'd you say? Where're you going to stay?

CH'ANG: I said the temple, I'm going to stay at the temple, yes?

HUA *(to Ch'ang Wu)*:   Go—go on!

CH'OU *(in a low voice)*:   The temple?

CH'ANG *(dumbly)*:   It's the temple that the blind one goes to every day.

CH'OU *(suddenly smiling in an odd manner)*:   Chin-tzu, we were right after all about going through the forest.

HUA: Why?

CH'OU *(gravely)*:   The blind one must be in the forest, too.

HUA: Yes, I know.

CH'OU *(as though he has seen something)*:   I keep getting the feeling that she and the baby are following us every step of the way. *(Shuddering suddenly)* Maybe that, that red light is her!

HUA *(looking at him and lowering her head again)*:   I—I already knew that!

CH'OU: How come you didn't tell me?

HUA: I was afraid to tell you.

CH'OU: Afraid! Afraid! *(Restraining himself with force)* Afraid of what?

HUA *(in a low voice; fearfully)*:   She said, if the child couldn't be saved, she'd follow us wherever we go.

CH'OU *(to Ch'ang Wu, rapidly)*:   Where's the temple?

CH'ANG: Not far, it's—it's very near.

CH'OU *(quickly)*:   Did you see the blind old woman come out holding the baby?

CH'ANG *(retreating)*:   I—I saw her.

CH'OU *(pulling his arm)*:   Which way?

CH'ANG *(pointing)*:   West.

CH'OU: Which way is west?

CH'ANG *(sputtering)*:   I saw Doggie carrying the lantern, leading her into—into the forest.

CH'OU: Into the forest?

CH'ANG: Yes.

CH'OU *(releasing his hand; turning his head and looking into the deeper woods)*:   Good! Good! *(He walks to the rim of the well.)*

HUA: Uncle Ch'ang Wu, you, you go on!
(Ch'ang Wu walks toward the right.)

CH'ANG *(questioning Hua in a low voice)*:   What happened, is the—the baby dead?

HUA *(in a low voice)*:   The—the baby—

CH'OU *(jumping up; in a wild state)*:   What'd you say, what'd you say? I didn't kill the baby, I didn't kill the baby. *(Jumping up on the rim of the well and raising his hands)* God! I only killed the baby's father to avenge the hate of two generations! I didn't kill the baby, I didn't make the baby die that way! I didn't! God! *(Jumping down; entreatingly)* The cruelty of the baby's death—it was her gramma who did it, don't blame me, don't blame me for this! *(He sits on the rim of the well and lowers his head.)*

HUA *(perceiving that Ch'ang Wu is in a state of alarm)*:   Uncle Ch'ang Wu, go, quickly, be careful he—

CH'ANG *(hurriedly)*:   Yes, yes, I'm going.

CH'OU: What'd you say?

CH'ANG *(startled)*:   I—I didn't say anything.

CH'OU *(rising suddenly)*:   Get out of here! Quick, get out of here!
(Ch'ang Wu runs off on the right and Ch'ou sits on the rim of the well once more.)

HUA: What's the matter?

CH'OU: I'm so thirsty, *(rubbing his head)* so thirsty! *(Ripping off some of his torn clothing)* Where can I get some water, some cool water? *(He rubs off the sweat on his face with the clothing he has ripped off.)*

HUA *(warningly)*:   Hu-tzu, don't wipe it! Don't wipe it!

CH'OU *(looking at her)*:   Why?

HUA: Be careful the blood on your hand doesn't get on your face.

CH'OU: What are you afraid of? It doesn't matter what the blood gets onto, people will see it just the same. I can wash the blood away, but my heart—who can wash it clean? Ah, the forest's so dark! No moon, no stars.
(He sighs.)

SMALL VOICE AT CH'OU HU'S EAR *(as at the end of the second act, when Ta-hsing was in the other room talking in his dreams; sighing a long sigh as if in response; gloomily)*:   Dark! So dark!

CH'OU *(apprehensive)*:   Listen!

HUA: Listen to what?

CH'OU: You . . . you didn't hear it?—"Dark—so dark!"

SMALL VOICE AT CH'OU HU'S EAR *(more gloomily)*:   "So dark! So dark is the world!"

CH'OU *(like a lullaby; mumbling)*:   Uh, "So dark is the world!" *(Fearfully)* God!

HUA *(curiously)*:   Hu-tzu! What, what are you saying? These—these are Ta—Ta-hsing's words?

CH'OU: Why? Didn't—didn't you hear it?

HUA: Hu-tzu, don't be ridiculous! What did you hear?

CH'OU: Nothing. I don't know why, I'm just so scared. It's like I—I—

HUA: Hu-tzu, what is it? Why all of a sudden did you start telling Ch'ang Wu about all that?

CH'OU: I, I don't know. I'm thirsty, my head went black.

HUA: Why'd you start talking about Ta-hsing again; you said you kill—killed Ta—Ta-hsing!

CH'OU *(dizzily)*:   I . . . I killed Ta—Ta-hsing?

SMALL VOICE AT CH'OU HU'S EAR *(dreamlike; with a muffled, asthmatic breath)*: " . . . Quick . . . Quick! . . . My knife! My knife . . ."

CH'OU *(murmuring)*: . . . My knife! My knife!

HUA *(speaking nearly simultaneously)*: You talked about the—the baby to him, too.

CH'OU *(in a low and slow voice)*: The baby?

SMALL VOICE AT CH'OU HU'S EAR: "Oh—, so dark!" *(It sighs a long painful sigh.)*

CH'OU *(jumping up suddenly; toward the black wood)*: Ta-hsing, I didn't kill him, I didn't kill the baby. Ta-hsing, you mustn't follow me! Ta-hsing! We've been good friends a long time; I've hurt you now, but I'm not bad, it was your father, Yen-wang's evil doing, your father; the cruelty of the baby's death—your mother did it, I'm not ashamed to look at you; you can't follow me, you can't— *(Unmindfully he draws out his pistol.)*

HUA *(backing up in fear; gasping)*: Hu-tzu, what—what are you doing? What are you thinking? You didn't kill the baby, Heaven knows that, and Earth knows it! Why do you keep thinking this? We still have to run. My life's in your hands, Hu-tzu, don't scare yourself, don't keep stalling; if it gets light and they see us we're done for.

CH'OU *(looking into the darkness)*: I know, I know! But *(contritely)* the baby—

HUA: Hu-tzu, move! Don't think!

CH'OU: Let's go! Let's go! This isn't a good place, we must get away from here, quick.

HUA *(changing the subject)*: When it's light we can get to the station.

CH'OU: We can get there even before dawn.

HUA *(forcing enthusiasm)*: We'll fly wherever we want to fly.

CH'OU *(trying to equal her enthusiasm)*:   Yes, fly wherever we want to fly.

HUA *(suddenly; pointing toward the distance)*:   Listen!

CH'OU: What?

(Gradually they discern a far-off train racing rapidly beyond the forest.)

HUA: The train, the train.

CH'OU *(listening carefully; nodding)*:   Yes, the train! *(Sighing)* But it's still a long way from us, isn't it?

HUA: So, let's move on, let's get out of this forest.

CH'OU: Uh, let's move on! There's a road to life there when we're out of the forest.

(A gust of wild wind rushes through the wood; everywhere resounds the mournful, fearful soughing of the leaves, as skylight leaks from above like raindrops, and black shadows quiver everywhere.)

HUA: God! *(She clutches Ch'ou Hu's wrist tightly.)*

CH'OU: It's the wind! You afraid?

HUA *(straightening her head)*:   No, let's make use of these dots of light, hurry! *(Hand in hand the two of them go a couple steps, but Hua pulls at Ch'ou Hu, shouting fearfully.)* Stop! Hu-tzu! *(Retreating a step)* Hu-tzu, *(in a low voice)* look, what's up ahead?

CH'OU *(concentrating)*:   Leaves, grass!

HUA *(pointing)*:   No, those heaps.

CH'OU: What?

HUA *(fearfully)*:   Those heaps of black heads.

CH'OU *(firmly)*:   Those are stones.

HUA *(pointing at the low and plump shrubbery shaking in the wind; gasping)*:   Look, what are those? Heaps of round black balls of flesh, moving back and forth, rolling— rolling towards us.

CH'OU: Nonsense, those are bushes! Let's go! *(The two of them walk lightly a step, but Ch'ou Hu stops suddenly again. From the right comes mysteriously the sound of drumbeats, so very tedious; initially they are somewhat weak, but gradually they grow in intensity; they continue through the remainder of the scene.)* Don't move!

HUA: Why?

CH'OU: Listen, what's that?

(The drumbeats resound monotonously within the forest.)

HUA *(fearfully)*: The drum!

CH'OU *(a little frightened; in a low voice)*: The drum!

HUA *(weakly)*: The temple drum!

CH'OU *(turning his head to look at Hua)*: In the middle of the night, what for?

HUA *(alarmed)*: The blind one has gone into the temple.

(The sounds of drumbeats increase gradually.)

CH'OU: The drum is scary, isn't it?

HUA: It's strange! The drum gets louder and louder.

CH'OU *(in deep thought)*: Will the drum make the baby live?

HUA: Who knows? It's the way the shaman performs for the blind one.

CH'OU: What's she doing?

HUA *(whispering)*: Chanting the sutras, beating the drum, praying to the Dipper God, calling the spirits; in a while she'll come out to chant.

CH'OU *(hopefully)*: Can his soul be called back?

HUA: Even if he can't be called back, what's the harm?

CH'OU *(listening carefully; unconsciously)*: The drum! The drum!

HUA *(looking at him strangely)*: What are you listening to? We must hurry! Are your legs rooted to the ground?

CH'OU: There's something peculiar about this place! We must go! We must—

A MOURNFUL VOICE OFFSTAGE *(distantly)*: Come back! Baby, come back!

HUA *(in a low voice)*: God, she, she's coming out now!

VOICE OFFSTAGE *(extendedly)*: Baby! Come back! My baby, come back!

CH'OU *(frightenedly)*: She, she's not far away.

VOICE OFFSTAGE *(nearly roaring)*: Baby! My baby! Come back!

HUA *(looking suddenly to the right)*: The light! The red light!

CH'OU *(looking toward the right)*: Yes. It's her, that light!

HUA *(speaking as she looks)*: Someone's in front of her holding the lantern! *(To Ch'ou)* They're getting closer and closer. *(To Ch'ou)* Who's that one ahead of her?

CH'OU: Dog—Doggie!

VOICE OFFSTAGE *(closer)*: Come back, baby! You must come back! Baby!

CH'OU *(trembling)*: She—she's coming!

HUA *(grabbing Ch'ou Hu)*: Here! Behind the tree! Quick! *(The two of them hide behind the tree.)*

(Holding the red lantern, Doggie guides Chiao out from the right. Chiao's hair is in disarray and her clothing has been torn by wild thorns. She has put one hand upon Doggie's shoulder, and has let the other drag down; her eyes gaze forward with teardrops suspending from them. When the wind blows, the light of the sky leaks down from the trees intermittently, illuminating the blind one and Doggie walking side by side. Chiao has painfully knit eyebrows, like a tragic mask. Doggie still has his dawdling way about him, his eyes looking stealthily at Chiao and his mouth muttering incoherently.)

CHIAO (*yelling out in a quavering, piercing, ghostly wail*): Come back, baby, my dear, come back! Come back! My dear, come back now! (*Calling out as she walks*) Come back, my little grandson! My little grandson, (*all but weeping and crying*) you must come back!

(*Doggie leads her off toward the left.*)

CH'OU (*exposing his head through the cracks between the trees; afraid*): Ah, this is just like being in Hell.

HUA (*also emerging*): Let's go!

CH'OU (*afraid*): Go? But—listen!

DOGGIE'S VOICE OFFSTAGE: The road ahead's not too good, let's go back to the temple, back to the temple.

(*Again Doggie leads Chiao on from the left.*)

PAI: Listen, the drum, the drum! Don't—don't go further, can't come back.

CHIAO (*still crying out*): Come back! My little grandson! Gramma didn't kill you! Come back, my little grandson, it was that bad-hearted Hu-tzu—he's the one who killed you. Come back, my baby! Gramma's waiting for you, my grandson, come back!

(*Doggie leads Chiao off on the right.*)

HUA (*walking out from the clump of trees; in a low voice*): Hu-tzu! She's gone! Come on out!

(*Ch'ou walks out from the clump of trees. Anxiety, remorse, and primitive fear pounce successively upon his heart. In a fraction of time his manner has undergone a near complete transformation; his hallucinations more distinct, he seems to have become a statue standing mutely in place.*)

HUA: Let's go!

CH'OU: Let's go! (*Still he does not move.*)

HUA (*urgently*): Move!

CH'OU (*raising his head*): Listen, what's that?

HUA: The drum!

CH'OU: Oh, yes, the drum! The drum! *(Imitating the drumbeats in a mumble)* "Tung! Tung! . . ."

HUA: Why aren't you going?

CH'OU *(looking toward the left)*:   Look, someone's coming there.

HUA *(curiously)*:   What?

CH'OU: He's carrying a red lantern, too.

HUA: No, it's too dark. Where's a lantern coming?

CH'OU *(obstinately)*:   There is! There is! That's funny, he carries an umbrella, too.

HUA: Umbrella? *(Unbelievingly)* What's he doing with an umbrella under a clear sky?

CH'OU: Yes, he's holding an umbrella and a lantern, and he's coming toward us, coming this way. *(He looks fixedly.)*

HUA: Hu-tzu, don't—don't do this, you—

CH'OU: It's true, he—he's coming! *(He looks more strangely.)*

HUA *(apprehensively)*:   Hu-tzu!

CH'OU: Look!

(At that moment, a figure moves gently onstage. Just as Ch'ou Hu describes him, he holds an umbrella and carries a lantern; the umbrella covers the top half of his body so no one can see, and only on the lower half is there exposed a pair of blue-cloth trousers. The figure halts.)

CH'OU: Oh, pardon me! Brother! How do you get out of this forest?

HUA: Hu-tzu, don't scare me, who—who are you talking to?

CH'OU: Don't you see the man right there before your eyes?

HUA: N—no.

CH'OU (*pointing to the figure holding the umbrella*): That's funny, isn't that him?

HUA: Where?

CH'OU (*pointing again*): Here! (*To the figure*) Hey, brother, why don't you say something?

HUA (*begging*): Oh, Hu-tzu, really, who are you talking to, don't—don't scare me, will you?

CH'OU: Why, don't you see? He's right before our eyes!

HUA: Right before our eyes?

CH'OU: Hey, brother, don't hide your face, tell us! How do you get out of the forest?

HUA: Hu-tzu!

(*The figure walks up next to Ch'ou Hu.*)

CH'OU: Look, (*turning his head toward Hua*) he's come up to us. (*As he turns his head, already the figure has walked up in front of Ch'ou Hu. With the umbrella hiding his face, the audience is unable to see him; he stops. When Ch'ou Hu turns back his head, he faces the man directly. He still cannot see him clearly; he only gasps and retreats a step.*) Hey, bro—ther! (*The figure lifts the red lantern to his face, lighting it up so that Ch'ou Hu sees him properly. Hu-tzu lets out a sudden strange and piercing cry, desolate and frightful, that resounds through the woods.*) Ah—ah—ah—ah!

(*At his crying out the figure holding the umbrella and red lantern disappears suddenly. Just then a gale wind blows briskly, and the forest hisses a mournful noise—*)

HUA (*backing away, fearful*): Hu-tzu!

CH'OU (*with wide, frightened eyes*): Let's go! Go quick!

HUA (*amid the gale*): What'd you see?

CH'OU (*disturbed*): Let's go! I can't say! Let's go! Go!

(*The whole forest shakes with heavy black shadows; they flash upon Ch'ou Hu as he pulls Hua in wild flight down the center abandoned path.*)

(*The drumbeats resound monotonously from afar.*)

Scene II

In the Dark Forest—two-thirty at night.

An area of marshland in the forest—moss grows on the earth, smooth and soft. At center stands a deep concentrated mass of timber, dark and gloomy, that extends to the left and right and encircles the central low ground. One can see a stretch of eroded embankment before the forest, with wild creepers and climbing plants crawling and coiling upon it. The land is high on the right, where stands an old tree killed by lightning, its jointed forked branches sticking into space, its body burned into only a shell. The trunk has been made into a cavern by the incessant pecking of woodpeckers; it is full of eyes now, and looks more grotesque. Amid the profuse vegetation and poisonous flowers under the trees there are autumnal insects droning lowly. Where the ground dips on the left, a telegraph pole stands lonesomely upright, long unrepaired and somewhat bent over. The interconnected wooden pillars are drawn toward center and far away, passing beyond the embankment in the middle and into the inscrutable wood. Beside the telegraph poles have been placed large stones, strung askew upon the marsh. Standing in the marsh, one can see the pitch-black sky. The awesome moon, half-hidden by black clouds, is obliquely inlaid among the trees, and the white light of a dim halo is cast upon the center marsh, transforming it into an uncanny region, like a residence for departed spirits. The dark clouds of the Heavens in unbroken crow-black mountain-peaks and the despondent forest on the earth become fused into the mystery of the wilderness.

When the wind blows, the telegraph wires give off slight whistling sounds; far off the monstrous drumbeats are so weak one's heart must be silent to hear them clearly.

Ch'ou Hu staggers out from the right, gasping continually; he has already lost one shoe and his upper clothing has been nearly covered with brambles, which have ripped it into shreds; sweat streams down his face. From time to time he feels for the pistol and ammo packet stuck at his waist. His countenance is agitated, his two anxious eyes looking around everywhere.

CH'OU: Oh, Ma! *(Wiping off the perspiration on his forehead with the back of his hand)* Where have I gotten to? *(He looks about him.)*

HUA *(offstage)*:   Hu-tzu, do you know the road?

CH'OU *(turning his head)*:   I—I can't see too clear. Chin-tzu, come here now! The moon's come out, maybe we can find the road. *(Fatigued, he leans against the decayed trunk of the dead tree.)* Ah! Thirsty! So thirsty! *(He gulps on some saliva.)*

(Hua enters from the right, head down, supported by a rough tree branch. Walking in and raising her head, she looks fearfully all about and at the dim, sad face of the moon in the sky. Her hair has rolled down in disorder, and although she constantly flicks it back, as she walks a couple steps it falls obstinately upon her forehead again. Sweat has also covered her body; her clothing sticks closely to her front and rear, and at a few places rips have become holes. There is fear and then hope in her eyes. She still holds the small cloth bundle, and looks worriedly at Ch'ou Hu.)

HUA *(sighing; hopefully)*:   Will we get out of the forest soon?

CH'OU *(still leaning against the tree; looking at the sky)*:   Who knows, maybe soon!

HUA *(hope burning)*:   Soon?

CH'OU *(nodding; mechanically)*:   Soon!

(Suddenly a bird in the tree starts a sustained pecking, a hollow "po-po" sound.)

CH'OU *(suddenly jumping up from beside the tree)*:   Ah? *(He looks up.)*

HUA: What! What!

CH'OU: Listen! *(The hollow "po-po" sound issues once more from the tree.)*

HUA: What?

CH'OU: A bird! A woodpecker!

HUA: Oh, this forest will scare us to death.

CH'OU: No, no, we must get out. Look, we've already walked another three miles or so.

HUA: Then shouldn't we be out soon?

CH'OU: Yes, but—but *(suddenly exasperated)* we've lost the way.

HUA *(sighing repeatedly)*: We've lost the way and we don't know the road.

CH'OU: We've lost the way! We've lost the way! *(His heart on fire)* Where shall we go? *(Whirling about)* East? West? South? North? Oh, Ma! Where shall we go? This big black sky, we can't see the road, we can't find anybody to ask. I can't find any landmarks that were here when I walked this road before; we've gone more than three miles and we're still in the forest! We've gone almost seven miles and we're still in the forest! We've been running all night, ten miles it's been, but still we're in the forest. If we don't get out of the forest, we won't see the railroad; and if we can't see the railroad, we can't find our road to life; and if we can't find our road to life . . . *(Suddenly)* Ah! Ah! Ah! *(Once, twice, thrice he rips off parts of clothing, exposing the black and luxuriant hair on his chest; he seizes his pistol; in despair)* All right, come on. If it's just one of you, I'll kill just the one of you; if it's two of you, I'll kill the both of you. I've had enough of your bullying, your false accusations, your cheating ways since I was born. I suffer from a bad fate, but still I must die for a worthy cause! Chin-tzu, if we hear any more gunshots, let's charge out even if it means death.

HUA: Hu-tzu! *(Consolingly)* Don't worry yourself! You're thirsty, I know you don't feel right. Hu-tzu, we mustn't die, we mustn't die; we aren't bad people. Hu-tzu, weren't you forced to do what you did? And wasn't I forced, too? Who made you kill a man, wasn't it Yen-wang? Who made me follow you, wasn't it Yen-wang, too? I didn't want to marry into the Chiao family, and you didn't want to hurt the Chiao family either. We're a couple of pitiful worms who can't be their own masters. Even if we've both done wrong, Heaven must take pity on us, for we shouldn't be responsible for what we've done.

CH'OU: Huh, Heaven is partial to those in power, not to people like us.

HUA: Then, is Heaven blind?

CH'OU: Who said it isn't. *(Mechanically)* Let's go!

HUA: Go! Where will we go?

CH'OU *(in a whisper)*: Where will we go?

HUA: We've lost the way.

CH'OU *(hopelessly)*: We've lost the way?

HUA *(suddenly; fearfully)*: Hu-tzu, listen!

CH'OU *(lifting his head)*: What is it?

HUA *(to the right)*: Listen, far off.

CH'OU *(still unclear)*: Wh—at?

HUA *(in a low voice)*: You didn't hear it? The drum! The drum in the temple.

CH'OU: The drum?

(The monotonous sound of the drum gradually increases.)

CH'OU *(angrily)*: Yes, it's the drum! It's the drum!

HUA *(in a low voice)*: We haven't even left the temple.

CH'OU: Why, we're still going round and round the temple, we're still here! We're still here!

HUA *(unable to stand it)*: Oh, my God! What's happened to us? *(Embracing Ch'ou Hu, shaking him)* What's happened to us?

(The woodpecker in the tree continues his "po-po" sounds, so resonant and strange. They break their embrace suddenly and look up to the top of the tree. Just then from somewhere deep in the wilderness comes a piercing voice calling. They turn their heads anxiously; but, as if hypnotized, they become gradually subdued by the sound.)

A FARAWAY VOICE CALLING *(heart-breaking; drawn-out)*:
Come back, my little grandson! Come back to the
living now. Come back, Gramma's waiting for you!
(In an unhuman voice) Come—back—ba—by! Come—
back—now!

CH'OU *(transfixed; in a whisper)*:   Baby! Baby!

HUA: God, *(in a low voice)* she . . . she's really following us.

CH'OU *(whispering)*:   Baby! Baby!

HUA: What you say?

CH'OU: She—she's coming again.

HUA *(looking at Ch'ou Hu; apprehensively)*:   Who?

CH'OU: She! She! *(Suddenly toward the left)* Look! She!
She's coming.

*(Chiao's figure walks softly on from the left, her two hands
holding the baby, her eyes closed. She goes to the right, walks up
to Ch'ou Hu's face, and stands there.)*

CH'OU *(afraid; in a low voice)*:   Look, she's come to get
me again.

HUA: Hu-tzu, what's wrong with you, what do you see?

(Chiao's figure opens her eyes and stares at Hua and Ch'ou Hu.)

CH'OU *(shaking his head)*:   W—we—didn't—we didn't—

HUA: Who'd you say? Hu-tzu!

CH'OU *(in a low, dumb voice)*:   The blind one and—and
the baby are right before your eyes.

HUA *(crying out and running to the telegraph pole)*:   Hu-tzu,
you—you're taken by devils again.

(Chiao's figure gazes directly at Ch'ou Hu.)

CH'OU *(to Chiao's figure; beseechingly)*:   It wasn't me!
Not—not me! I didn't mean to kill your baby, I killed—
killed Ta-hsing. But I— *(gasping)* I've had enough
already, don't look at me that way, don't look at me
that way! I didn't kill your grandson, I tell you, I didn't!
I didn't! I didn't! I didn't! I didn't . . . *(His words
become weaker and weaker; the figure's eyes look unswervingly*

at him; again she walks quietly off on the right. Hu-tzu watches her depart and wipes the sweat from his eyes.) Ah, God!

HUA *(walking slowly forward)*:   What is it?

CH'OU: She's gone.

HUA *(suddenly in doubt, clutching Ch'ou Hu)*:   Hu-tzu, tell me, how did the baby really die?

CH'OU *(mechanically)*:   His gramma beat him to death.

HUA: I know. But why did you make me take the baby to that other room?

CH'OU *(lowly)*:   I wanted to catch them all and not leave a single one.

HUA: Why?

CH'OU: The way the Chiao family hurt me was worse than this.

HUA: Then you put the baby in the other room on purpose?

CH'OU *(painfully)*:   Yes, on purpose!

HUA: You already knew that the blind one would go to your room with that stick.

CH'OU: I knew.

HUA: You did want to kill the baby.

CH'OU: Yes!

HUA: You thought she'd take that iron staff on the baby and beat—

CH'OU *(exploding)*:   No, no, I didn't, I didn't. I didn't think of that; I only hated the blind one at first! I only thought of destroying with my own hands the person she loved the most, and then I'd go away. But after Ta-hsing was dead I wasn't a sane man anymore; for a moment I lost my mind. I forgot the baby was in the other room; and when I saw her walk in there, damn it! *(Rapping upon his head)* I forgot about the baby, 'til you reminded me, but then he was already crushed— *(Painfully)* Look, how can I be blamed for this?

HUA: Then, why do you always keep thinking about it?

CH'OU *(depressively)*. I don't want to think about it, it's the blind one, it's the baby, it's Ta-hsing, it's all of them going before my eyes. Listen, that drum, that soul-calling drum! It's not calling for the baby's soul, it's calling for my life.

HUA *(wanting to change his mind; in a loud voice)*: Hu-tzu, have you forgotten your father?

CH'OU: No, of course, I haven't!

HUA: Hu-tzu, do you still remember your little sister?

CH'OU: Sure, I do, of course, I do! They died wrongly, *(mumbling)* I know, I know, I know! Yen-wang buried my old father, and he sold my fifteen-year-old little sister, yes! He sold her to die in that—

(The woodpecker makes his hollow pecking sound again.)

HUA: Listen! What's that?

CH'OU *(disregarding her)*: He sold her to die in that brothel, yes! I suffered in prison, and my woman was swindled from me, and our land was taken, and my leg was crippled, yes, yes! I'm a good citizen, and a bitter man who's come up against so much deceit, and injustice, and evil, I know! I know! I know! What does it mean that I've killed one of his Chiao family? Or that I've killed two? And what if I killed the whole family? Yes! Yes! Ta-hsing's dead, why should I care? Right! His son's dead, why should I care! Right! Why am I so mixed up? I'm always thinking about the Chiao family, about those three generations, those three ghosts, I know it! I know it! My very own old father, his hair all white, *(suddenly he sees something emerge from the darkness on the right; slowing down unconsciously)* and he could hardly walk!

(Amid the darkness on the right a firefly with a blue-green light floats by imperceptibly, gliding toward the dirt embankment.)

HUA *(still wanting to change his mind)*: Hu-tzu, look, a firefly, a firefly!

CH'OU (*with gazing eyes and an open mouth, he looks beyond the firefly to see a group of people; slowly*): He could hardly walk, but they still sold him to the bandits! Yes . . .

(*The firefly reels toward the earth embankment, followed by a multitude of silent people who also walk softly toward the dirt slope. In front are three fierce men in short costume, carrying iron spades and wooden sticks and taking long strides. Pressing from the rear is Hung Lao, a coarsely short and stout man with a round, vat-like body; he whips a plantain-leaf fan against his sweat-streaming face, wiping and gasping as though he were on a long journey. Amidst them a white-haired farmer is being pushed along—Ch'ou Jung—a thin, small man, humped over from the hardships of his later years. He follows the men's footsteps anxiously, turning his head from time to time to look at Hung Lao; his eyes show an earnest, imploring expression. The monotonous drumbeats increase more and more in intensity; the group of figures accompany them like puppets moving woodenly in a thin mist. The dull light of a darkened moon illumines the embankment, and the sky is filled with black clouds; the earth is half in shadow. Suddenly from a high place on the embankment there appears gradually a fierce-looking figure with his back to the audience; he is wrapped in a black cape, and underneath it he is wearing what seems to be yellow military trousers, but one cannot see clearly. The man is pushed up to the bank; Hung Lao, after a reverent word with the turned figure, faces the audience directly. The white-haired farmer nods his head and stands silently to one side.*)

HUA: Hu-tzu, what are you looking at?

CH'OU (*in a low voice*):   Isn't—isn't that Hung Lao? What, what's he come here for?

HUA (*looking at Hu-tzu*):   Where?

CH'OU: The bank—on the bank. (*He looks dumbly at the group of people.*)

(*The turned figure seems to be giving Hung Lao several orders; Hung Lao nods continually. He then turns about and raises his hands menacingly toward the downcast old man. Two men surround the old man, and seem to press in upon him. One man among them is scooping out a pit, while they search for things from the old man's bosom. Hung Lao offers them to the turned figure, but the man shakes his head and throws them down.)*

HUA: Hu-tzu!

CH'OU *(inhaling a quick breath)*:   Isn't this old man my father? But he's dead. God, how could this be?

(As Hung Lao continues to search him, two strong-men make him turn away his face; they seem to torture him. At first the old man only droops his head in silence, but finally he shouts out as if in pain. A fifteen-year-old maiden runs out suddenly from the left, panic-stricken; she seems to cry out wildly. In her hands she holds a deed; she gives it to the turned figure and begs him to release the old man.)

CH'OU: Oh, my God! Is this my little sister? My little . . . sister!

HUA *(pulling Ch'ou Hu)*:   Hu-tzu, what's wrong! Get a hold of yourself! Get a hold of yourself!

(Hung Lao sees the deed, and he is pleased. The little maiden walks to the old man and kneels before him, but the old man scolds her for coming out. The turned figure orders Hung Lao to pull them apart and tells his two henchmen to start burying the man. The little maiden begins to cry when she hears this, and the old man, spinning around and looking up at the sky, starts to wail out; he looks straight at Ch'ou Hu.)

CH'OU *(abruptly awakened from his hypnotic state, he regains his consciousness; shouting wildly)*:   Father! Father! My father!

HUA: Hu-tzu, *(pulling at him)* are you taken by spirits? Who are you calling to?

CH'OU: Father! Father! Hu-tzu's here! Hu-tzu's here! *(Turning his head toward Hua)* Let go of me! *(With one hand he throws off Hua, and pulling out his pistol, he rushes to the embankment; to the turned figure, violently)* You bandit, you— *(Suddenly the turned figure whirls about; he is like the very model of Chiao Yen-wang's portrait. He wears the uniform and regalia of a captain; appallingly he stands there. The sad moon shoots dimly upon his face, and the fearful black eyes beneath his thick eyebrows emit a frighteningly malevolent light. Ch'ou Hu stops short; maliciously)* Yen-wang!

HUA *(below him; greatly afraid)*:   Yen-wang?

CH'OU *(like a wild beast)*:   I meet you at last! *(He fires three shots at Yen-wang. The figures disappear instantly.)*

HUA: Hu-tzu! Hu-tzu!

(The black clouds cover the moon and the earth below darkens suddenly.)

CH'OU: Chin-tzu! Chin-tzu! Where are you?

HUA: Here!

CH'OU *(hurrying down)*:   Did you see them?

HUA *(fearful)*:   No!

CH'OU: Let's go now! There's no more light on the ground.

(Ch'ou Hu pulls Hua and races off left. The drumbeats still come monotonously out of the forest.)

SCENE III

In the Dark Forest—three o'clock at night.

A pond in the forest. Behind it are still the dark woods; the surface of the water is broad, and one can see the floating reflections of a nebulous sky. The black clouds do not scatter, and yet the moon is not hidden. The half lunar-disc drifts heavily in space, while a light mist enshrouds the earth; the fog is still peculiar and abstrusely tranquil. Among the growing reeds and in the shallow water frogs croak lowly and endlessly. Leaning against the right bank is an old, decayed tree branch that had been used for washing clothes and cleaning rice. But if anyone were to walk on it now it would shake as if about to break. An ancient willow bends low across the left shore, its branches dipping to brush against the water. Before the pond is a plot of grass and to the left stands a rank of ragged balustrades with a cock-eyed gate. Wild artemisia, the height of a man, has sprouted on the right side, and next to it is a small tree and a few rocks.

From afar come mystically the weak monotonous drumbeats; not until the wind blows can one hear them somewhat distinctly; slowly they become once more inaudible.

In a moment, from the wild artemisia on the right, comes a confused bustle and a painful gasping; the frogs stop their croaking suddenly, as from the right Ch'ou Hu and Hua bore their way out of the wild artemisia, nearly dead from fatigue. Ch'ou Hu's legs are covered with cuts; blood streams down profusely. He bears a small cloth bundle on his shoulder and holds a stick in his hand. His appearance is more that of a wild man; his hair is covered with thorns, and beads of sweat drip down; his feet are bare, and his toes, crushed by rocks, are bandaged with strips of cloth. The thick black hair on his chest has been greased by clods of mud; he is like a frightened, pent-up beast, his breast violently rising and falling. Hua follows Ch'ou Hu's footsteps watchfully. Her sleeves have been rent by the wild artemisia, ripped into shreds, so that the two gold bracelets on her wrist show clearly; they copy her sharp shaking movements. The running has made her so dizzy she wants to fall over. Her hair, drenched by perspiration, sticks together in spots, and her face is completely wet. Two or three buttons have broken open at her neck so that her breasts are barely concealed; her pant legs are rolled up as if she had crossed a shallow river.

Ch'ou Hu pulls out Hua with one hand; throwing the stick to one side and leaning against the trunk of the small tree, he sighs and looks up at the sky. Their line of sight being obstructed by the artemisia, they cannot see the pond.

Ch'ou: Oh, God! *(He uses his hand to rub the sweat from his face.)*

Hua *(near collapse; standing next to Ch'ou Hu)*: Ah, finally we get out.

Ch'ou *(shaking his head painfully and closing his eyes)*: Yes, we've got out of the wormwood, but we're still in the forest!

HUA *(grievously)*: We're still in the forest! Oh! *(She slips and falls, plopping down on the rocks.)*

CH'OU *(hurrying to help her; worriedly)*: Chin-tzu! Chin-tzu! What's the matter?

HUA *(pushing him away)*: Nothing, I just can't go on!

CH'OU: You can't go on?

HUA: I'm dizzy, I want water, a drink of water!

CH'OU *(hopelessly)*: Water! Water!

HUA *(sighing)*: Where's the water, just a sip of water, *(in a low voice)* just a sip of water!

CH'OU *(drooping upon a higher rock, his hands propping up his jaw; dumbly)*: Where's the water! Where's the water! *(Painfully rubbing his gullet and swallowing some spittle)* Ah, I'd give a bucket of gold for a pail of water. But— *(sighing)* where's the water?

HUA *(gritting her teeth)*: Oh, my foot!

CH'OU: What is it?

HUA: My foot's all blistered, it hurts so the pain drills into my heart.

CH'OU *(somberly)*: Chin-tzu!

HUA: What?

CH'OU: Running away with me has only made you suffer.

HUA: But my—my heart is happy.

CH'OU: They think I'm a thief.

HUA *(forthrightly)*: Then I'm the thief's woman.

CH'OU: They'd kill me if they caught me.

HUA: Then I'll give you a son to avenge your hate.

CH'OU: But why— *(looking at her movingly; suddenly)* why do you want to follow me?

HUA *(staunchly)*: I'm going with you to that gold-covered land.

CH'OU *(lowering his head; looking at his own ugliness)*:   But why me?

HUA *(definitely)*:   You're the only one worthy enough to go there, and me— *(lowering her head)* I'm worthy, too.

CH'OU: But there's no such city in the world where gold covers the ground.

HUA: There is, there is, You don't know. I've dreamed about it. *(Suddenly)* Listen!

(Far away there seems to be the sound of an onrushing train.)

CH'OU: What?

HUA: We're almost out of the forest!

CH'OU: What is it?

HUA *(the shadow of a smile materializing)*:   It's the train, isn't it? "Tu—tu—tu—tu! Tu—tu—tu—tu!" Don't you hear it?

CH'OU *(looking at her strangely)*:   Where? You're dreaming.

HUA: Who s dreaming? Listen! *(The sound of the train seems to gradually diminish as it rushes farther and farther away.)* "Tu—tu—tu—tu, tu—tu—tu—tu!" Listen, slowly it disappears, *(looking at Ch'ou Hu suddenly)* now it's gone.

CH'OU *(knowing these sounds are all her hallucinations; sighing sympathetically)*:   Chin-tzu, maybe I have been to that wonderful place where gold covers the ground. But *(enraged)* I only think about the suffering I went through there, day and night, every month, year after year, the toil, the dirt clods I carried, the whippings I got, 'til my leg got lame; and then I got sick, and they put me off to the side; and after that I ran away. My brothers there suffered the same as me: some died, some got sick. There's gold there all right, but it's not for us. One by one, we all got thin like ghosts, *(his voice decreasing)* like ghosts in misery—misery—misery. . . .

(A frog calls out from the pond suddenly.)

HUA: Listen! Isn't that a frog?

CH'OU *(listening carefully)*: Yes, it's a frog! Then, *(ecstatically)* there's water!

HUA *(shouting)*: Water! *(Suddenly in the area hidden by wild artemisia she can see a pond; shakingly)* Oh, Hu-tzu! Water! *(Ch'ou also runs out; Hua hastens to the side of the pond and kneels down to get some water, but she is hampered by the reeds; she cannot get her hands down into it.)*

CH'OU *(tremblingly)*: Water! Water! Chin-tzu, there's a board! *(Pointing to the plank beside the pond)* If you go up there you can crawl out and drink; when you've had your fill then I'll drink.

(Chin-tzu hurries to the rickety board and crawls out on it to drink the water; Ch'ou Hu waits anxiously beside the reeds on the bank of the pond. From the left there arises gradually an indeterminate noise like groaning, or like the sound that many people make as they work together; it can be heard by the audience. It is tedious and mournful, and in the moonlight it is strange to the ear, inhuman. It is like the droning of many rueful souls, who otherwise would not dare to make any sound at all. Ch'ou Hu's ears prick up; he turns around and listens with rapt attention.)

HUA *(on the board)*: Hu-tzu! Hu-tzu! Come, over here, I've scooped up some water, you drink.

CH'OU *(his eyes looking unavertedly to the left; mechanically)*: Eh . . .

(Pairs of figures pace slowly out from the left; apparently they are all prisoners, with grey clothing, bare feet, and sweat streaming down their bodies. Some wear straw hats, others are bare-headed; still others hold sweat rags. Some have their waists girded by chains while others have manacles fastened to their ankles; several are as thin as dry brushwood; they are linked in twos. A couple of the men hold up a large open basket of dirt clods. There are about ten of them, each with drooping head, and each groaning slowly—"heng" in the front, "ai" in the rear. They walk by in pairs about five feet from Ch'ou Hu.)

CH'OU *(open-mouthed)*: God! It couldn't be them!

HUA *(coming off the wooden plank)*: Hu-tzu! Hu-tzu! Why don't you drink?

CH'OU *(perturbed)*: Don't talk, listen!

(Another pair of prisoners walks out from the left, carrying a water bucket with a ladle floating in it. The men in front hold iron shovels, while those in the rear drag along iron hoes. "Heng-ah"! "Yo-ah"! "Heng-ah"! "Yo-ah"!)

HUA: Listen to what?

CH'OU *(still staring at them)*: Don't you hear them? Like this! Like this! "Heng-ah"! "Yo-ah"!

HUA *(realizing he is having hallucinations again)*: Oh, Hu-tzu!

(A gigantic man, with a bald head and a warden's yellow uniform hanging over his forearm, walks out from the left; he holds a hat in one hand and a leather whip in the other, and wears only an undershirt over his sweating torso. His bare, watermelon head is oily bright. He looks back and forth with cruel eyes, and from time to time feels for the pistol on his body. He turns his head and looks toward the left, where behind him there are still several prisoners in the gloom, intoning heavy exasperated "Heng-ah"- "Yo-ah"s as they work without stop. Just then the forward inmate puts down the dirt basket so that everyone can wipe off his perspiration; he uses his hat to fan himself.)

CH'OU: Ah, *(looking at the prison warden and trembling)*: it's him! He's still alive!

HUA: Hu-tzu, let's go! Let's go! What are you seeing again?

CH'OU *(shaking his hand)*: No, no.

(Among the resting prisoners on the right some are sitting, some are squatting, and some are leaning against the dirt basket; some stand talking stealthily with their companions, others lower their heads in silence, and still others quietly wipe away their tears. Just then a sturdy, long-legged man in the middle with a face full of scars notices Ch'ou Hu, pointing at him as though he were talking about him. The scarred man seems to beckon Ch'ou Hu

then, as if to say: "Hu-tzu, why, why don't you come on over, all your brothers are here." *)*

CH'OU *(suddenly noticing him)*:   Isn't that "Train Engine"? *(Pleasantly surprised)* "Train Engine", "Train Engine". *(Scarred "Train Engine" continues to beckon him in reply, and even tells the other prisoners.)* I'm Hu-tzu—Little Hu-tzu!

HUA *(pulling Ch'ou Hu)*:   Hu-tzu—don't be this way!

CH'OU *(ignoring her; he sees the group of prisoners look at him one by one; they show pleasant surprise, but with sorry countenances; some wave him on, while others call to him not to come. Ch'ou Hu raises his hands toward them. There is a slender, thin one among them, with a big nose and a comical manner, who claps his hands and makes faces, telling him to hurry on over)*:   That isn't "Old Pumpkin", is it? "Old Pumpkin", how are you all? *(Several men shake their heads melancholically. "Old Pumpkin" is beckoning him again, and a short pock-marked man admonishes him.)* Don't worry, "Pa Pock", I'm not going, I've escaped. *(Suddenly to the thin, weak prisoner who is wiping away his tears)* Hey, "Little Widow", how come you're still crying? *("Little Widow" lifts his head and looks at him, then nods and weeps again. Suddenly a dark-skinned man, bearded and moustached, grabs up a flat stick; apparently he wants to run toward Ch'ou Hu. He strikes toward him, but a prisoner beside him with a big mouth and small eyes restrains him.)* "Chang Fei Rival"*, does he still have a grudge and want to hit me? "Wild Ass", you don't need to pull at him, he can't hit me, I've escaped! *(Happily)* I've run away. *(The prisoners seem to get more and more excited and ferocious; the warden turns his head suddenly and, raising his leather whip, lashes toward the prisoners. One man among them pulls at the warden and points to Ch'ou Hu, claiming that this time he was the one responsible for the fighting. Hearing this, the warden turns and looks at Ch'ou Hu; Ch'ou is very apprehensive;*

---

* Chang Fei was a noted and feared general in Shu-Han during the Three Kingdoms period (Minor Han dynasty, established in Szechwan, A.D. 221–263).

he turns about as if he wants to flee, but the warden appears to yell at him and Hu-tzu stands transfixed. The gaoler points the whip at him and again at the prisoners on the right; he orders him to come quickly back to his work, seeming to shout: "Get back here! Ch'ou Hu!" *Hu-tzu trembles at one side of the stage; he lowers his head.)* I'm coming! I'm coming! I'm coming!

HUA *(greatly disturbed)*: Hu-tzu, don't go! Don't go! *(But seeing Ch'ou Hu's fearful eyes, she can only let go her hands and stand there dumbly.)*

(Ch'ou Hu enters the group of prisoners; the warden commands them to put manacles on his feet, and he has a prisoner hold the whip to urge them on. Ch'ou Hu picks up the dirt basket and follows behind, but for a moment he falters and the warden yells out for him to be beaten; the prisoner holding the whip strikes him savagely.)

CH'OU *(involuntarily rubbing his spine with every blow, shouting out)*:   Ah! Ah! Ah!

HUA *(painfully)*:   Ah! Hu-tzu! What are you yelling?

CH'OU *(in a low voice to the neighboring prisoners)*:   He's crippled one of my legs, and he wants to cripple the other.

(The prisoners passing in front walk off right; one prisoner drops his load of dirt and goes to the water bucket for a drink, then another is drinking, and another . . . and another. Ch'ou Hu stands to one side, envious; he simply cannot endure his deep thirst. He runs to the water bucket and picks up the ladle to get some water. But suddenly the warden, as if roaring, walks up; knocking down the ladle, he grabs his whip and lashes it toward Ch'ou Hu. Ch'ou Hu stiffens without a word, and as the warden is catching his breath, he seizes his whip suddenly and starts to beat the gaoler down.)

CH'OU: I don't care, I'll beat you dead! Beat you dead! Beat you dead!

(The warden suddenly draws out his pistol and shoots it at Ch'ou Hu, but there is no report; the gun will not fire.)

CH'OU *(laughing wildly)*: You, too, have your day! So your gun doesn't work, eh? But still you want to persecute us! Now you'll see what I can do! *(He draws out his own pistol from under his belt; all the prisoners back away, shrinking into a clump. The warden, greatly afraid, runs in panic. Ch'ou Hu fires two shots at him; the figures suddenly disappear. Ch'ou gazes around apprehensively and glances at the moon; he bends down to look at his feet, but they show no traces of the manacles.)* Oh, God!

HUA *(she has been completely confused by Ch'ou Hu's solitary wailing; but now that he has awakened, she scoops up a mouthful of water and walks slowly to him)*: Hu-tzu, drink some water.

CH'OU *(mechanically)*: Drink some water? *(Just then he wants to dip his head and drink—)*

(Suddenly a gust of wind blows past; very distinct drumbeats strike one by one upon the eardrums, awesome and frightful.)

CH'OU *(to Hua)*: The drum! The drum! The drum! *(Suddenly)* What, are we still here, are we still here? *(Shouting)* We've been possessed by spirits! *(He pushes away Hua's water-cupped hands and, pulling Hua, they run off left.)*

(The drumbeats resound monotonously.)

SCENE IV

In the Dark Forest—four-thirty in the morning.

Near the small unkempt temple in the forest. Everywhere one is surrounded by black oppressive woods; looking into the center—into a deep and endless terror—one can see an undulating path draw out from the cave-like forest. In the foreground is a rough grassy area; beneath the short wild grass hide autumn crickets giving vent to a low humming sound. Along the path have been constructed telegraph poles of uneven texture; those to the outside are still clear, while those to the inside appear much like long teeth in the mouth of a black cave. Towards the right side and back stands a broken-down dirt hovel of half a man's height; at one time it had been used for holy sacrifice, but now it is in ruins. In front of the small temple is an earthen platform about a foot high pierced by incense; the beating of rain and the blowing of wind over many years have gradually levelled it. The small temple's dirt roof has already become canted, so that from a distance the temple looks like a chair, and the earthen platform before it like a small table; there are a few rocks standing beside the tree. To the left and front is a rigid white poplar, whose upper leaves make a bleak noise. An elongated stone is set horizontally in front of the trees, covered over with green moss; probably in some forgotten year of prosperity a stonemason had chiseled it level for a devout parishioner to rest upon. The leaves of the forest are so close together that only in direct center does there remain a view of the sky. Indeed the sky is once more hidden by black clouds and the moon is invisible; it is pitch-black here, gloomy and frightening. When the wind blows, the leaves and telegraph lines vibrate in concert as if a wild animal were passing through the wood.

Ch'ou Hu, supporting Hua, drags himself in step by step along the deep trail at center. They both are covered with mud; all that remains on Ch'ou Hu is a pair of trousers, ripped along the sides into short strips like dogs' teeth. Hua's shoes have also been lost in the water; her clothing drips with moisture and her pants have been rolled up higher. She holds the cloth bundle. Ch'ou Hu carries the pistol and ammo packet with one hand and supports Hua with the other. Though his dishevelled body is soaked through, defiance burns suddenly in his eyes. He turns his head to look mutely into the deeper darkness and shivers.

They enter hurriedly.

CH'OU: Ah! It's so dark. *(Once again becoming unconsciously afraid)* How do we keep going into such a dark place as this? Chin-tzu, *(feeling Hua slipping down)* Chin-tzu! Chin-tzu!

HUA *(lifting her head and flipping away the hair in front of her eyes)*: I—I just can't go on.

CH'OU *(pointing to a stone before them)*: Then, sit down. *(He helps Hua to sit down.)*

HUA *(shivering)*: It's so cold! *(Hopefully)* Maybe if we cross this steam we'll be out of the woods soon.

CH'OU *(sitting down)*: Maybe, when we've crossed the river; it looks like it's a little more open.

HUA *(turning her head to look)*: It looks as if we've been walking a great road.

CH'OU *(signing)*: At least the drum's gone.

HUA: Yes, the drum's gone; *(aroused)* then, we'll soon be out of the woods.

CH'OU *(suddenly rising in excitement)*: Yes, we'll soon be out of the woods, out of the woods! When we do get out of the woods and catch the train may—maybe it'll still be dark. *(Looking up at the sky suddenly)* Funny, there's no moon in the sky anymore.

HUA *(insensibly, also looking up)*: Oh, it was there just now, how come in a moment there isn't even one star?

CH'OU *(suddenly frightened; losing his voice)*: Chin-tzu!

HUA: What is it?

CH'OU: It's true, there isn't even one star.

HUA: We still have the box of matches, don't we?

CH'OU: There're only two—two matches left.

HUA: Then how can we go on?

CH'OU *(hopelessly)*: How can we go on? *(Sitting on the rock)* It's dark, dark, it's so dark there isn't light from a single star. How can we go on? How can we go on?

HUA *(mumbling)*: How can we go on? *(Suddenly walking beneath the white poplar and kneeling down)* Oh, God, have pity on us, give us a little light, spare us just a little bit of light! *(Beseechingly)* Oh, just a little while, a little while; God, have pity on us, we've nowhere to go—

CH'OU *(exploding)*: Chin-tzu, who are you begging to, who are you begging to? God, God, God, what God? *(Waving his hands in exasperation)* There isn't any, there isn't any, there isn't any! I hate this God, I hate this God. Don't beg to Him, don't beg to Him!

HUA *(feeling a drop of rain sprinkle upon her)*:   Hu-tzu!

CH'OU: What?

HUA *(slowly)*:   It's raining.

CH'OU: You mean you felt it sprinkle a little?

HUA: It's on my face, too.

CH'OU: It's my blood, it dropped from my arm.

HUA *(apprehensively)*:   You're bleeding again?

CH'OU: Yes! *(Somberly)* This is what God is like! So what's the use of begging to Him?

HUA *(shaking her head)*:   Poor Hu-tzu. *(Sitting down on the long rock in front of the poplar)* What's happened in a single night has made you insane.

CH'OU *(enraged)*:   Insane? Huh, I am insane. I've gone through a whole lifetime today; I was born to be a moral man, and I shall die to be an honorable ghost. If I die today and see the King of Hell I will ask him plainly why I was born to be cheated and put down like this. Even if it means going all the way to the King of Hell's palace, I must settle my accounts with the House of Chiao.

HUA *(fearing he is talking nonsense again)*:   Hu-tzu, listen, there's something in the bushes!

(An autumn insect hums among the vegetation.)

CH'OU: What?

HUA: A cricket!

CH'OU: Oh.

(Far away comes the cry of a "cuckoo".)

HUA *(suddenly happy)*:   "Ku-ku, ku-ku", "ku-ku, ku-ku".

CH'OU *(listening a moment; suddenly sighing)*:   Finished! We're finished!

HUA (*understanding his meaning; however—*):   Why?

(*Before she can finish speaking a breeze blows by; the telegraph lines cry out and the white poplar leaves roar chaotically amid the soughing of the wind.*)

HUA (*shivering*):   Oh, Hu-tzu!

CH'OU: Don't be afraid.

HUA (*concealing her feelings; shivering*):   No, but it's so cold. (*Pointing to the ruins on the right*) What—what's that?

CH'OU: Some broken-down temple.

HUA: Hu-tzu, let's go now.

(*The wind blows through; from afar a grievous voice calls out, long and dismally, at once distant and nigh.*)

THE VOICE (*somewhat muddled by the distance; severely*): Come back, my grandson, come back now, my little grandson.

CH'OU (*changing his voice suddenly, harshly*):   Listen! What's this? What's this?

THE VOICE (*more piercingly, closer*):   Come back! My little grandson! Come back!

HUA (*frightened*):   She!—She!—She!

CH'OU: She's following us again.

THE VOICE (*strangely harsh; inhuman, gradually receding*): Soul, come back now, my baby! Soul, come back now, my dear grandson.

HUA (*suddenly embracing Ch'ou Hu*):   Oh, God!

CH'OU (*shaking*):   Let's go—go, quick.

HUA: Uh, (*walking a couple of steps, she steps on something soft but thorny; shouting loudly*) Oh! Hu-tzu, my foot!

CH'OU: What?

HUA: Under my foot, something soft, and thorny! Thorny! It's moving!

CH'OU (*taking a match out of his ammo packet and striking it; they look down*):   Where?

HUA: Here! Here!

CH'OU *(the two of them surround the thing; the match light reflects upon their frightened faces)*:   A porcupine!

HUA *(relieved)*:   A porcupine.

(Just then from far away in the center there is a strange singing: "On the first and fifteenth the temple gate opens." *Ch'ou Hu turns his head suddenly.)*

CH'OU: What's that?

HUA: It sounds like—like Doggie.

(Suddenly from everywhere a group of deep forbidding voices sing: "On the first and fifteenth the temple gate opens," *like so many oppressed and persecuted spirits of the dead.)*

CH'OU: Chin-tzu, listen, that bunch of people singing.

HUA: Now?

CH'OU: Yes!

HUA *(shaking her head)*:   There's—there's no one singing.

(Immediately, from far into the center there is again a harsh, fearful singing: "The Ox- and Horse-Headed-Demon-Messengers align on either side.")

CH'OU: Who—who's singing again?

HUA *(listening carefully)*:   It's—it's Doggie.

(Following this, many low voices sing around them, repeating grievously, "The Ox- and Horse-Headed-Demon-Messengers align on either side!" *This time Ch'ou suddenly sees Ox- and Horse-Headed-Demon-Messengers rise imperceptibly in the darkness to the right before the broken-down temple; they stand facing him like a pair of clay puppets.)*

CH'OU *(apprehensive, in a low voice)*:   What—is—this?

HUA *(not understanding)*:   What?

CH'OU *(in a still lower voice)*:   Didn't you hear them?

(Far into the center they sing again: "The Judge of Hades before the temple officiates the registers of the living and the dead.")

CH'OU: Did you hear it?

HUA: Yeah, I heard it, it must be Doggie imitating you.

(Immediately there is all around them that deep mournful singing: "The Judge of Hades before the temple officiates the registers of the living and the dead." *Once again Ch'ou Hu has hallucinations of a Judge of Hades in a cloak of thin, blue-green silk and a black cap stuck with black feathers beside the earthen platform in front of the temple; like a clay statue he stands there quietly.)*

CH'OU *(gasping)*:   How—could—this—be?

HUA: Hu-tzu!

CH'OU: Oh, my God!

(Uninterruptedly they sing again from far into the center: "The blue-green-faced ghostling holds warrants for the seizure of spirits.")*

HUA *(pulling Ch'ou Hu)*:   Let's go! Hu-tzu!

(Ch'ou Hu doesn't move.)

(Immediately from all about: "The blue-green-faced ghostling holds warrants for the seizure of spirits." *Ch'ou Hu sees a Blue-Green-Faced Ghostling clutching a tablet appear gradually in the darkness, standing by the earthen platform, very like a clay statue.)*

CH'OU: Ah! *(He wipes away the sweat on his head.)*

(From far into the center there is more singing, but this time it is overpowering: "His Highness Yen-wang sits in the center.")*

(Suddenly, as though from every direction comes that heavy, severe phrase, like so many underground voices in unison, shouting out in low tones, painfully and frightfully: "His Highness Yen-wang sits in the center." *They appear to be waiting for the final judgment. In the obscure and dreary mist Ch'ou sees a dark-faced King of Hell slowly appear, with a flat crown on his head and a ritual tablet in his hands; he sits erect upon the earthen temple with the earthen platform before him as his*

judicial bench. The King of Hell looks just like statues seen in temples—completely motionless.)

CH'OU *(his eyes wide open; his mouth agape)*:   Ah!

HUA *(in a lower voice; Ch'ou Hu's awesome state makes her afraid to draw in breath)*:   Hu-tzu, what—is—it—you see?

CH'OU: I, I can't say.

(From far into the center there is a lonely, afflicted singing: "A gust of chilly wind wafts in a female spirit!"*)*

(Just then, seemingly from everywhere, in scattered tones blows a sorrowful wind, and all about a sustained, gloomy, grievous chorus, this time mostly low female voices: "A gust of chilly wind wafts in a female spirit!" *Along with the pervading sounds of wind and wailing, a thin, small maiden wearing a garment of moon-white pongee appears quietly out of the darkness. The maiden's manner is not different from what was seen in the second scene, only more timid and pale; mint ointment has been applied to her temples,* and in her hands she holds a hemp rope. She moves by delicately, like a breeze, undefiled, to the judicial bench, before which she kneels.)*

CH'OU *(apprehensively)*:   Ah, my tortured little sister.

(Hua makes no sound; seeing Ch'ou Hu's extreme fright, she does not know how best to approach him.)

(The King of Hell commences the trial, with puppet-like movements, as the Judge of Hades at one side examines the court record in his hands. All around there seem to be many hapless spirits, sobbing and moaning, and in the rear several obscure moving figures. The maiden in pongee appears to be relating pitifully the sorrows and misfortunes of her past life; her eyes full of tears, she tells how her father died, and how her elder brother was put into prison, and how she herself was sold into a brothel and forced to hanging herself by the daily beatings of the brothel master and his customers. As she finishes, she kowtows deeply in supplication for the King of Hell's just verdict.)

---

* Refers to a cosmetic decoration in fashion during the 1920s and 1930s.

Ch'ou (*restraining his tears he listens to her petition; he weeps involuntarily, wiping his eyes again and again; in a low voice*): Oh, my little sister! My pitiful little sister, you died so tragically! So wrongly!

(*The King of Hell appears to have a brief conference with the Judge of Hades; and then they order that Ch'ou Jung be brought forward for judgment. The Blue-Green-Faced Ghostling before the bench takes the register of souls, and as he carries it inside, he seems to be shouting something; from everywhere come the low mournful responses of several departed spirits. Another Blue-Green-Faced Ghostling with long projecting teeth walks out from the darkness, bringing a white-haired, senile old farmer; they walk up to the bench. The old man, bound in leg-irons, looks at his daughter; they both hold their heads and cry—silently. The Judge of Hades seems to yell out something and the two people kneel down together. The old one kowtows repeatedly and, in a pitiful appeal, relates the full story of how Yen-wang persecuted him to death.*)

Ch'ou (*seething*):   Oh, Father, my tortured father! If we don't get justice today, then there's simply no justice in the world!

(*The King of Hell beats his gavel and calls out something to Ch'ou Hu; Ch'ou Hu raises his head. The Judge of Hades, the Ghostlings, the Ox- and Horse-Headed-Demon-Messengers, and the King of Hell—all stare forbodingly at him; he is almost too frightened to turn around. The surrounding voices shout deeply, as the Blue-Green-Faced Ghostling takes his register of spirits and raises it toward Ch'ou Hu; Ch'ou Hu walks toward them involuntarily.*)

Hua: Hu-tzu! Hu-tzu! Where are you going? (*She cannot pull him back, so she lets him go.*)

(*Ch'ou Hu sees his father and his little sister and he tries to restrain the tears; he nods his head and kneels before the bench. The King of Hell begins his deliberations; all about, there are many in low, whispered discussion.*)

CH'OU *(lowering his head, in a strange voice)* : A humble man, such as I am, has been in a sea of injustice for two generations. My elderly father and my weak little sister of my past life—both of them were murdered by that wicked Captain Chiao; they died unnatural deaths. My old father and my weak little sister—they've been put into the house of the Judge of Hades now; what they just now said is true, none of it's false. When I was in the upper world, the greedy officials and their grabby underlings—they were duped by this ruthless Captain Chiao, too; he betrayed me and he tortured me to confess. So I went to prison for eight years and was beaten into a cripple. He killed my father and my weak little sister; he broke my leg and he took my property; it's all because of that scheming animal Captain Chiao. What I have given in appeal is true, there's nothing false. If indeed there's anything untrue, then I shall be willing to go up the hill of knives and go down into the cauldron of oil; I rely only on the fair decision of the Judge of Hades, and I shan't complain. But having been in such a sea of injustice for two generations, I have only your Highness to look to for justice. *(He kowtows deeply.)*

(The King of Hell suddenly calls for Captain Chiao. As the Ghostling shouts out the name, the departed spirits growl in chorus, and Captain Chiao walks out from the darkness. His expression haughty, he wears, as before, a captain's uniform with a sword hanging by him and riding boots; very martially he walks up to the King's bench, but he does not kneel.)

(Ch'ou Hu sees Captain Chiao and wants to stand and fight him, but he is quieted by the Judge of Hades, and he kneels once more.)

(The King of Hell seems to ask Captain Chiao about Ch'ou Hu's testimony; Captain Chiao denies everything, and even increases the charges.)

CH'OU *(kowtowing)*:   I must tell your Highness that what he says is only clever talk, a one-sided story.

(Captain Chiao wants to make another statement.)

CH'OU *(kowtowing immediately)*:   I've spoken nothing but the truth.

(Captain Chiao again wants to dispute him.)

CH'OU *(kowtowing again)*:   Please, your Highness, find this man guilty, now. Don't listen to him anymore.

(The King of Hell beats his gavel, ordering him not to speak. Captain Chiao goes forward and makes further criticism; the King of Hell nods repeatedly, expressing his acquiescence.)

CH'OU *(peeping up at him, shouting)*:   Your Highness, don't believe him, don't believe him, don't believe him; in the upper world he was Yen-wang himself.

(The King of Hell becomes suddenly enraged; he orders the Judge of Hades to announce his judgment to Ch'ou Hu's father and little sister; they cry at its reading, and are dragged off by the Ghostlings.)

CH'OU *(greatly agitated)*:   What? My father must still go up the hill of knives? My little sister must still go down into Hell? You're— *(The Ox-Headed-Demon-Messenger pokes his back with a fork; he falls to the ground mutely.)*

(The King of Hell orders the Judge of Hades to announce a further judgment. Captain Chiao gloats at his success, while Ch'ou Hu is so enraged his body contorts and trembles.)

CH'OU *(jumping up)*:   What! You still want to pull out my tongue, and let him, *(pointing at Chiao Yen-wang)* and let him go up to Heaven? If he goes up to Heaven, *(yelling hysterically)* what kind of law is this? What kind of law is this?

(With a plunge of his fork the Horse-Headed-Demon-Messenger forces him suddenly to the ground. Captain Chiao cries out audibly—in a strange laugh—and every "ghost", even the King of Hell, guffaws wildly with satisfaction; their voices shake

Heaven and Earth. Ch'ou Hu lifts his head from the ground; as he looks at the Ox-Headed-Demon-Messenger, the Demon-Messenger stops laughing, and his face changes into Chiao Yen-wang's hateful countenance. He turns around toward the Judge of Hades; the Judge of Hades also stops laughing, and his face, too, changes into Chiao Yen-wang's hateful countenance. He looks directly at the King of Hell, and the King of Hell stops laughing as well; indeed, the King of Hell is Chiao Yen-wang's hateful self. The stage is silent; Ch'ou looks about at the Chiao Yen-wang faces around him and steps back.)

CH'OU *(gnashing his teeth; in a low voice)*:   All right, all right, Yen-wang! Yen-wang! It was you from the beginning, it was all of you; while we lived we suffered all your punishment, and now that we're dead, you still want to come here and make fools of us. *(Towards the uniformed Yen-wang; cruelly)* You've put on this show to make fools of us!

(Suddenly from everywhere comes hatefully once more the loud, satisfied sound of Chiao Yen-wang's voice; the noise is like a roll of thunder.)

CH'OU *(pulling out his pistol abruptly; aiming it at them and firing three shots)*:   You bunch of liars! Robbers! Laugh! Laugh! Laugh!

(The scenery is buried in darkness.)

HUA *(painfully)*:   Hu-tzu, what's this fuss you're making? Let's go!

CH'OU: I . . . I . . . *(He feels his head.)*

(A cock crows far away.)

HUA *(startled)*:   It'll be light soon!

CH'OU: Light soon.—

(A gunshot suddenly spurts out from the right, and a bullet whistles in flight.)

HUA: A shot!

(Another shot comes toward them from center.)

CH'OU *(listening carefully)*:   Damn it! The posse must've found us again.

(Suddenly gunshots sound out haphazardly from right center.)

HUA *(pulling at Hu-tzu)*:   They want to surround us.

CH'OU *(pulling Hua)*:   Let's go get 'em! Damn it all! Let's fight 'em! *(He fires a shot to his front; all around them the shooting becomes more rapid.)*

(They run off left.)

SCENE V

As in the prologue, near the railroad bed in the wilderness—about six o'clock.

The sky shows a pale light; as before, the earth is a mass of blue indistinctness. A wild fire seems to be set upon the horizon, for along the distant skyline a red sunstreak burns gently. Sunlight pierces through the black clouds, transforming them into an illusionary, grey, inky sea, like a fire dragon rising from the ocean bottom; the edges of the cloudy sea are washed gradually with an exquisite golden red. The floating clouds drift apart, and in the cracks appear spots of clear, deep blue. In the left half of the sky is suspended a morning moon, like a thin piece of paper. A slight wind blows perpetually across the wilderness.

The earth breathes lightly, and the giant tree retains its awesomeness. It stands maliciously upright at center, still a defiant spirit. Everywhere the blades of grass sparkle, and the crow-black railroad flashes. Far away wild birds and cuckoos prattle cheerfully.

Behind the stone marker beside the railroad bed snores Pai Sha-tzu. He leans sideways against the marker, while next to him is an extinguished paper lantern, lying askew on the ground. Sha-tzu's clothing has also been torn open by brambles, and his face has been smeared with much dirt; his feet are bare and his worn-out shoes have been tossed to one side. For many years Sha-tzu has dreamed a sweet dream; on his face is a calm and happy smile.

Far away a cock calls out gayly.

PAI *(in his dream; muffled)*:   "Tu—tu—tu—tu—, tu—tu— tu—tu. . . ."

(The sound of the train whistle far off.)

PAI *(in deep slumber; muddled)*:   "Chi—cha—ka—cha, chi—cha—ka—cha—"

(Far away there is a sudden gunshot; bullets pierce the air, whistling.)

PAI *(scared awake, he stands up, rubs his eyes, and looks about him curiously; he sees the lantern on the ground and picks it up; suddenly he recalls that he was leading Chiao through the forest in the middle of the night, that he left Chiao behind and could not find her after that. Anxiously)*:   Ah, damn! *(Picking up the lantern and running toward the east)* Chiao Ta-ma! Chiao Ta-ma! Doggie is here. *(Realizing that he has turned in the wrong direction, he runs toward the west.)* Chiao Ta-ma! *(There is no response; he stops short and walks slowly back to the center of the railroad; he rubs his head in thought; suddenly he turns around and yells toward the horizon, toward the wild pond.)* Chiao Ta-ma! Chiao Ta-ma! *(Lifting the lantern, speaking)* Lantern here! *(Patting himself)* Doggie here, too! *(Still there is no response; suddenly)* Oh, hell! *(In the spirit of his words he throws the lantern heedlessly into the pond.)* She may be dead! *(Just then he sees his own lantern in the pond, floating on the surface; startled)* Ay ya! Water! Lantern! Her lantern! Water! Water! *(Hurriedly he jumps down off the railroad bed, and scampers to the side of the pond; one can hear the splashing sounds Doggie makes there.)*

(Ch'ang Wu walks nervously on from the left. His collar is not bound well and he looks as though he has just gotten out of bed.)

CH'ANG *(shouting)*:   Chiao Ta-ma! Chiao Ta-ma! Chiao Ta-ma! *(Wiping away the sweat; chattering to himself)* Damn! I said before the shaman was a cheat; the little one wouldn't come back to life in that temple. The old woman's been out calling his soul all night, and now she's disappeared! Chant curses! Beat the drum! Chant curses! Beat the Drum! Chant the damn curses!

(Shouting) Chiao Ta-ma, chant curses! Beat the drum! Beat the damn drum! *(Shouting in every direction)* Chiao Ta-ma! Chaio Ta-ma! *(No response, puzzled)* Funny, where'd Doggie lead her off to? *(Yelling)* Doggie!

PAI *(suddenly leaping out by the railroad bed; the lower half of his body drips with water; in his right hand he holds a soaked lantern, and in his left the iron chain Ch'ou Hu threw into the pond ten days before; chuckling)*:   What?

CH'ANG *(frightened; as though he is both calling and scolding him)*:   Doggie! Why didn't you answer me before?

PAI *(whimpering)*:   You, you didn't call, call me.

CH'ANG: I didn't call you, but you just— *(suddenly changes his wording)* what about Chiao Ta-ma?

PAI *(lifts up the dripping lantern)*:   Oh! Here!

CH'ANG: What's this for?

PAI: This, this is her lantern.

CH'ANG *(impatiently)*:   I know that! You dumb fool bastard! I asked you, where's Chiao Ta-ma? Where'd you lead her off to so late at night?

PAI: Oh, oh! Last night! *(With wide eyes)* She . . . she call the little baby, uh, she call the little baby. And I hold the lantern. I, I was in the front, she—she was in the back, she walk, and I—I walk, too, I walk, and she walk after me . . .

CH'ANG *(sick of his prattling)*:   I know! I know!

PAI *(gesticulating)*:   First, first I hold her; then she—she hold me. She, the more she call the more happy she get, then she, she didn't hold me anymore. First I walk ahead, and she always follow me. Then later, I, I—

CH'ANG *(unable to be patient anymore)*:   Then, you ran?

PAI *(shaking his head)*:   No, no. I still walk ahead, but when I turn my head—

CH'ANG: What happened to her?

PAI: She didn't follow me. She was gone, she was gone.

CH'ANG: And you didn't look for her after that?

PAI: Who says I didn't? I look, I look, I look blind in the dark, in the wilderness; and I find this place, and then I— *(embarrassedly)* and then I fall asleep.

CH'ANG: You dumb fool bastard, get out o'here!

PAI: Get out o'here?

CH'ANG: Go on! There're soldiers everywhere now; they're armed and they're looking for Ch'ou Hu. Run, quick! One shot'll kill you!

PAI *(apprehensively)*:   To the temple again?

CH'ANG: To the temple? The shaman in the temple's been taken away.

PAI: What?

CH'ANG: The old guy in the temple's a slave peddler, a kidnapper. Some official from the county seat took him away. Let's go, what's the use of talking to you, you wouldn't understand.

PAI: Go where?

CH'ANG: To look for Chiao Ta-ma! *(Pointing to the iron chain in Pai's hand)* Hey, where'd you find that?

PAI: You mean this bracelet; I got this out of the pond, *(raising it)* you want it?

CH'ANG: You bastard! Put it down! *(Pai throws it onto the railroad bed.)*

CH'ANG: Move! *(He walks toward the left)*
(Suddenly from the left comes a gunshot, and then another. Then abruptly it is quiet.)

PAI: What?

CH'ANG *(rising up on his toes to see; frightened, in a low voice)*: It's Hu-tzu, Hu-tzu!

PAI *(not understanding)*:   Tiger?

CH'ANG *(pulling Pai)*:   Let's go, quick!

(Ch'ang and Pai turn and go off right.)

(More shots are fired; bullets whistle in flight. Hua, bent over, enters running from the left. Ch'ou Hu, looking back as he supports her, walks forward. Ch'ou Hu's back is humped, his face sweaty; he seems to be shouldering a thousand catties. The muscles of his arms jut out agitatedly and his eyes bulge; in one hand he holds the pistol, while the dagger stuck at his waist flashes. He is more like a wild man now, fighting for his life with his enemies all about him. He sees the giant tree, and between his eyebrows there is great determination; he looks ahead fixedly. Holding the cloth bundle, Hua paces painfully along with difficult steps; but the night's suffering has made her brave, and she looks nervously but alertly about her.)

CH'OU *(turning his head hatefully)*:   Pack of mongrels! They've surrounded us.

HUA *(gasping)*:   Hu-tzu, let's go! Let's keep going!

CH'OU: There's no use going anymore, there's a sentry post ahead! Didn't you just hear them firing all around?

HUA *(pulling him)*:   But they don't know we're here.

CH'OU: They'll come looking for us in a while.

HUA *(pleading)*:   Then, we have to go, quickly!

CH'OU *(shaking his head)*:   No, I'm not going. To go a couple of steps more, it's all the same— *(suddenly)* I've run far enough!

HUA: Hu-tzu, what are you afraid of, we still have a gun.

CH'OU: We have a gun, but we can't—use it anymore.

HUA *(apprehensively)*:   You mean the bullets are already—

CH'OU: Only two left.

HUA: Two?

CH'OU: You only have to fire one shot and they'll be here.

HUA: Hu-tzu, do you mean we've come—come to the end?

Ch'ou: No! No! We can't be finished. When I'm finished there's still my brother comrade; and when my brother comrade's finished, there'll be another brother comrade. We can't suffer this injustice generation after generation. Have you forgotten what I just told you?

Hua: You mean—no, Hu-tzu, I can't, I won't go, I won't go without you.

Ch'ou: Chin-tzu, go! You can get out by yourself, they're not after you. Me, they all know me! You go now, there's some money in the cloth bundle.

Hua: Hu-tzu, you want me to go away!

Ch'ou *(hard-heartedly)*: Yes.

Hua *(her tears flowing)*: But Hu-tzu, where do you want me to go?

Ch'ou *(firmly)*: I just told you.

Hua: Your——your friends, can they be trusted?

Ch'ou: They're all good brothers of mine, men of all talents. Tell them that Ch'ou Hu wasn't weak, and tell them that right to the end, Ch'ou, Ch'ou Hu never begged from anybody. Tell them that Ch'ou Hu doesn't believe in Heaven now; he only believes that if his brothers unite and struggle together, they'll survive. But if they separate, they'll lose. Tell them not to be afraid of authority, and not to be afraid of difficulty; tell them that if we take up the struggle now, then someday our sons and grandson will rise up.

Hua: Hu-tzu, what are you saying? I'm not going.

Ch'ou: Chin-tzu! *(Pulling at Hua)* Have you forgotten what you said to me?

Hua *(not understanding)*: What'd I say?

Ch'ou: You said, these last few days, that you and I, that maybe you—

Hua: Oh, that!

CH'OU: Maybe, maybe it's true. *(Suddenly more urgently)* Chin-tzu, I really believe it could be. But if you're not in luck, then even—even the baby won't—won't—

HUA: But, Hu-tzu—

CH'OU *(suddenly seeing something at his feet)*: Chin-tzu! What's this?

HUA *(scared)*: An iron chain!

CH'OU *(picking it up and looking at it)*: Uh, my old friend! *(Bitterly)* My old friend comes back. Chin-tzu, do you know *(holding the iron chain until the end of the play)* why it comes back to me?

HUA *(pretending she doesn't know)*: Why?

CH'OU: Because this time it wants to be with me for a lifetime.

HUA *(suddenly embracing Ch'ou Hu)*: No, Hu-tzu, you can't go.

CH'OU *(looking strangely at Hua)*: Me! I'm not going.

HUA: You're not going?

(The frogs on the bank of the pond croak suddenly.)

CH'OU: No, I'm not going. *(Looking suddenly at the giant tree, and the wild pond)* It's funny, do you still remember this place?

HUA: I remember.

CH'OU: We've come here again now.

HUA *(distressed)*: Ten days—like the wink of an eye.

CH'OU: Yes, the wink of an eye. I took this thing off that day, *(pointing at the iron chain)* today I have to put it back on. Chin-tzu, are you sorry?

HUA: Sorry? In all my life it's only with you these ten days that I've really lived. Huh, sorry!

CH'OU: But, now—

(From nearby comes the merry singing of a cuckoo.)

HUA: Listen!

CH'OU *(with a thread of a smile)*:   "Ku—ku—ku—ku"!

HUA: Hu-tzu, listen to that, don't you want to go there?

CH'OU: Go where?

HUA: That gold-covered land?

CH'OU *(sadly)*:   Now only you are worthy of going to that gold-covered land.

HUA *(startled)*:   What'd you say?

CH'OU *(suddenly lifting up Chin-tzu's cloth bundle; |determined)*:   Chin-tzu, I want you to go!

HUA *(taking the cloth bundle)*:   Hu-tzu!

CH'OU: Go!

HUA: I won't.

CH'OU: If you don't go, *(using his last resort to make her leave)* I'll shoot.
(He raises the pistol toward the sky.)

HUA: What for!

CH'OU: To make them come.

HUA: No, Hu-tzu.

CH'OU *(yelling out painfully)*:   Go! *(He fires two shots toward the sky, and then throws his pistol into the pond; immediately a gunshot is returned.)* Ah! Chin-tzu! *(There comes directly the sound of many bullets.)* Run, fast! Chin-tzu!

HUA *(shouting)*:   Oh, my Hu-tzu.

CH'OU *(holding his dagger with one hand and stamping his foot)*:   Chin-tzu, if you don't go, I'll never forgive you.

HUA *(knowing there is no other way; tears well up suddenly; stretching out her hands and looking at Ch'ou Hu as she backs away)*:   I'm going, I'm going.
(The gunshots are more rapid.)

CH'OU *(looking at Hua, his eyes are filled with tears)*:   Remember, Chin-tzu! When the baby's born, tell him that his father didn't let this pack of dogs get him. Tell my brothers that Ch'ou Hu wouldn't *(lifting up the iron chain)* wear this, that he was willing to— *(suddenly stabbing himself in the heart)* die this way! *(He leans against the giant tree, stiffening, unwilling to fall.)*

HUA *(screaming and running back; embracing Ch'ou Hu)*: Hu-tzu! My Hu-tzu!

CH'OU *(exuding large, yellow drops of perspiration; biting his lip)*:   Run! Chin-tzu, tell my brothers what I said.

HUA *(weeping so she cannot look up; she lies prostrate at his feet)*:   Ah, you, you! *(The gunshots are nearer.)*

CH'OU *(gasping)*:   Run, fast, the guns are near, I must see you go. *(Suddenly a bullet flies, whistling by Hua's head, hitting her left arm; Hua turns her head; Ch'ou Hu yells.)* You're still not— *(kicking Hua down upon the railroad bed with one foot)* going!
(Hua rolls down, then lifts her head and looks at Ch'ou Hu. But Ch'ou Hu doesn't turn around to her. Covering her eyes with her hands, she runs off left; she cannot bear to look at him again.)

CH'OU *(waiting until she is gone, then quickly turning to look after her, to see her run away safely. The gunshots are everywhere more rapid, closer; suddenly raising the iron chain to his eyes and smiling hatefully, and yet happily—)*:   Ha! *(He turns himself around, and with force flings it onto the distant railroad, with a clank; Ch'ou Hu's body collapses heavily.)*

(CURTAIN)